REFLECTIVE PRACTICE

WRITING AND PROFESSIONAL DEVELOPMENT

Third Edition

GILLIE BOLTON

Los Angeles | London | New Delhi
Singapore | Washington DC

© Gillie Bolton 2010

First edition published 2001
Reprinted 2003, 2004
Second edition published 2005
Reprinted 2006, 2008 and 2009
This edition published 2010
Reprinted 2010

SAGE Publications Ltd
1 Oliver's Yard
55 City Road
London EC1Y 1SP

SAGE Publications Inc.
2455 Teller Road
Thousand Oaks, California 91320

SAGE Publications India Pvt Ltd
B 1/I 1 Mohan Cooperative Industrial Area
Mathura Road
New Delhi 110 044

SAGE Publications Asia-Pacific Pte Ltd
33 Pekin Street #02-01
Far East Square
Singapore 048763

Library of Congress Control Number: 2009931510

British Library Cataloguing in Publication data

A catalogue record for this book is available from the British Library

ISBN 978-1-84860-211-3
ISBN 978-1-84860-212-0 (pbk)

Typeset by C&M Digitals (P) Ltd, Chennai, India
Printed and bound in Great Britain by
CPI Antony Rowe, Chippenham, Wiltshire
Printed on paper from sustainable resources

MIX
Paper from
responsible sources
FSC® C013604

Dedicated to all who heal, care, and educate

Knowledge is limited. Imagination encircles the world. (Einstein [1929] 2002)

Try to love the *questions themselves* like locked rooms and like books that are written in a very foreign tongue. Do not now seek the answers, which cannot be given to you. *Live* the questions now. (Rainer Maria Rilke [1934] 1993)

CONTENTS

FOREWORD

Narrative competence – that is, the mastery of several kinds of narrative skills – has increasingly been seen as desirable for professionals, and especially for those in medicine. One way to foster such narrative skills is the practice of reflective writing that Gillie Bolton describes in her book. This process of writing depends upon the intuitive, linguistic and imaginative capacities rather than the rational and quantitative modes of thought that dominate much of professional training and practice.

Although the process may sound simple, if practised well, such writing requires honesty and courage and can lead to unexpected insights and new ways of knowing. The results may improve practice as well as revitalise the practitioner.

As one who has had the privilege of participating in a reflective-writing workshop led by Gillie Bolton, I can affirm the validity of testimonials to its power. I can also affirm this book's opening reminder that the best way of undertaking reflective practice is to do it rather than to read about it. But for those who have not yet had that opportunity, this book offers the next best thing. Read it as a prelude to, rather than a substitute for, engaging in the reflective practice it encourages.

Anne Hudson Jones
Institute for the Medical Humanities
The University of Texas Medical Branch at Galveston

ACKNOWLEDGEMENTS

Many practitioners and colleagues have enabled *Reflective Practice*, generously giving time, enthusiasm and insight into your experience, knowledge and feelings, and – perhaps most vitally – warmth. Heartfelt thanks is all I can offer for our adventures, your sensitivity, and permission to be quoted. I thank Sheffield University Institute of General Practice Master in Medical Science and Master in Education graduates, Institute of Public Health in Ireland Leadership Programme graduates, Nottingham Community Health nurses, participants in medical, nursing, social work counselling/therapy, education, and management development programmes.

There are some without whom I could not even have laced my boots. Rosie Field dances hand in hand with me along the most rocky and precipitous paths; Kate Billingham laughingly points out contours I had missed, and Amanda Howe lakes; Julian Pratt, Alan Bleakley, Faith McLellan, Anne Hudson Jones, Trisha Greenhalgh, Tom Heller, John Goodwin, Lindsay Buckell illuminate our track; Leslie Boydell and Angela Mohtashemi have led me off my map; Nigel Mathers, Sir Kenneth Calman, David Hannay, Steve Dearden, Pat Lane, Craig Newnes, Tony Warnes, Sonya Yates, David Greaves, Ken Martin, Andrew Eastaugh, Jeannie Wright, Paul Schatzberger, Jonathan Knight, Lucy Henshall give support, advice and insight. Marianne Lagrange is a fearsomely able editorial guide in velvet gloves, and Matthew Waters supportive; Cecil Helman offers flasks opportunely. I can't sufficiently value Moira Brimacombe, Jo Cannon, Helen Drucquer, David Gelipter, Charles Heatley, Martin McShane, Bob Purdy, Caroline Walton, Jane Searle, Helen Starkey, Rosie Welch, Shirley Brierley, Clare Connolly, Naomi Dixon, Maggie Eisner, Seth Jenkinson, Sheena McMain, Mark Purvis, Becky Ship, Bev Hargreaves, Di Moss, Janet Hargreaves and Gail Young. Marilyn Lidster, whom I miss, endlessly picked up bits of me from the cliff-foot. Dan Rowland says 'Oh Gillie!' but helps me again to click, and discusses everything important and unimportant. Alice Rowland advises on colours and coats, and how not to slip on mud.

Stephen Rowland has travelled this and many other roads with me so closely I am no longer sure if it is his journey or mine. This third edition is another milestone in our shared adventure. He not only makes sure I have warm jerseys, compass, whistle, the right map, and right words, but fills my rucksack with goodies.

PREFACE: MIND THE GAP

> In the end I found that the reflective process itself was where the bounties lay, and no amount of reading about reflecting could help me. (Reflective practitioner)
>
> This writing allows you to touch things you otherwise couldn't. (Reflective practitioner)
>
> This is an opportunity to inhabit the unknown. (Reflective practitioner)

If the first speaker above is right you should shut this book now. So why do I want you to read it? Reflective practice is only effectively undertaken and understood by becoming immersed in doing it rather than reading about it or following instructions. An initial guide can save time; this one will, I hope, enable you, my reader, to engage in the process as dynamically as he did.

This updated, revised, extended authoritative third edition sets reflective practice within a broad web of disciplines, drawing upon a wide range of authorities. It is appropriate to medical and healthcare professionals, social workers, therapists, counsellors, teachers, lecturers, tutors, clinical psychologists, lawyers, police, clergy, leadership developers, and in management and business consultancy.

Bank Underground Station, London, is built on a curve, leaving a potentially dangerous gap between platform and carriage to trap the unwary. The loudspeaker voice instructs passengers to 'Mind the gap': the boundary between train and platform. Gap can be used as image for other boundaries, such as between professional me and parent me. We spend our lives minding gaps to protect ourselves from being hit by trains, eaten by bears (Milne [1924]) or falling into uncomfortable situations where we do not know the answers.

Awareness of such gaps can lead to thorough self-questioning. At such moments of openness and uncertainty understandings can flash 'And [when I write] sometimes, sometimes I have a ahh, ahh now I understand' (student, in Wright 2005, p. 512). Cunliffe (2002, 2004) draws upon Wittgenstein who said we're suddenly *struck* and 'understand something which is already in plain view' but we'd never noticed before (Wittgenstein 1953, p. 89). Epiphanies happen of allowing myself to stop thinking, stop carefully being myself, and allow other possibilities to present themselves. At these times and places we are open to querying, or potentially querying, situations, knowledge, feelings and understandings. Such deeply reflective questions are bridges which cross troubled moral gulfs:

> Bridges are sort of the opposite of boundaries, and boundaries are where wars start. (Levi 1988, p. 104)

Borders and *frontiers* are sensitive politically. We use them to tell us who we are, and how to relate to others (Friend or family? Stranger or fellowcountryperson? Colleague or client?). We take on varied roles – lover, parent, chauffeur, academic, supervisor, counsellor, friend – all with uncertain boundaries; we strive for clarification. We also strive to know the answers relevant to our roles: doctors assume patients want answers; parents want to give children correct answers. Yet, saying 'I don't know', at least to oneself, can be positively life changing.

In striving for certainty in an uncertain world, for clarity of boundaries in professions where ambiguities abound, we forget to ask personally and professionally developing reflective questions about gaps, and issues found there. Philip Pullman explored strict frontiers being breached, in his award-winning *His Dark Materials* (1995): enormous fatal energy forces gaps between worlds, dangerous disturbing elements cross illicit frontiers, inter-world war ensues. *Reflective Practice* deals with positive dynamic exploring of boundary gaps (licit and illicit).

Writing exploratively and expressively can take practitioners up to and beyond their habitual boundaries, overcoming previously perceived barriers to perception and understanding. Practitioners can begin to leave at the border professional assumptions, such as clinical detachment or the inadvisability of sharing significant doubts and disasters with colleagues. Such critical enquiry is at the heart of professional development.

> How difficult it is for professionals in such anxiety-producing work to remain open and responsive (rather than reactive); routinised responses and procedures (though an essential framework for action) can also lead to a rigidity which is inimical to the uniquely personal response needed in the caring professions.
>
> Effective learning is therefore dependent, at least in part, on access to that world of feeling and phantasy, which allows structures of meaning to be recognised, and to be open to change, in a way which facilitates a different (and perhaps more constructive) professional response. (Yelloly and Henkel 1995, p. 9)

Reflective practice: aesthetic and artistic

Reflective practice can enable a mindfulness of the gap, an awareness of and willingness to tackle border issues: excitingly, if carefully. Winter et al. (1999) maintain reflective practice is one way of redressing the 'devaluation, deskilling and alienation' now suffered by the caring and teaching professions:

> The late 1980s saw professional staff beginning to sense their autonomy being reduced, decision-making mechanized, expertise fragmented, and their 'artistry' abolished . . .
>
> The reflective paradigm assembles its theoretical resources in order to defend professional values, creativity, and autonomy in a context where they are generally felt to be under attack from political and economic forces which threatened to transform the professional from an artist into an operative. (Winter et al. 1999, p. 193)

Working reflectively with our whole selves entails harnessing the artistic alongside other talents. If practice itself is an art, then reflection upon it is also artistic (Bleakley 1999; Winter et al. 1999). Expressive and explorative writing relies on our habitual communicating medium, words, gives validity, form and coherence over time and space, and aesthetic illumination.

Here is a senior practitioner's response to my initial writing exercise (see Chapter 6):

Mind the Gap
Blank. Blank. Blank.
No thinking, just writing
On a white, blank page.
How fun!

It's the emptiness that allows
Everything to exist,
To flow, to manifest.

Meditation is reflection?
No. It is the space
That provides reflection to happen.
It is the gap.
The gap of mindfulness.
So, mind the gap. (M. Alejandro Chaoul)

ABOUT THIS BOOK

This book offers an authoritative introduction to effective reflective practice using writing, based on teaching and research experience with a wide range of professions. Practitioners write stories, poetry or drama about their work, or their research data, then submit these to discussion with a facilitated group, supervisor, mentor or peer-mentor; they then write further developmental pieces.

The processes of writing develop and clarify writers' understanding of data or experience; discussions draw out issues and locate gaps and queries, extending the learning process for writer as well as group (mentor). Writers become readers and co-critics, listeners co-authors. A closely observed event, however small, written about, reflected upon, discussed critically, and re-explored through further writings stands metonymically for the whole of that reflective writer's practice (metonym = part standing for whole, the pen is mightier than the sword: pen and sword stand graphically and metonymically for huge social, political and cultural areas: literature and war).

This critical research also encompasses the reading of a wide range of appropriate texts, embedding the reflective process consciously in the practitioner's wide political, cultural and social/professional context. Boundaries, categorisations and assumptions are questioned and dissolved, and new appropriate, clearly understood ones created.

This book gives why, what and how, as well as where, who, when. Background information is clear, as is detailed careful guidance and advice on exactly how to go about it, with plenty of illuminative examples from practitioners and students. It assumes nothing, and explains clearly, approachably and engagingly. Knots are unmuddled, and the complexity of reflective practice clarified.

The first section describes and illuminates firm pedagogical principles and theoretical background. Underpinning ethical values and models are explained. The vital difference and relationship between reflection and reflexivity is clarified, with examples from many authorities.

The second section tells you *how* in detail. Practitioners and students can go away and do it; tutors and facilitators find out how to enable, elucidate and enthuse. This 'how' includes: starting and developing reflective and reflexive writing and learning journals; assessment and evaluation; facilitating reflective practice writing; using reflective writing for team development; and how to approach other methods of reflective practice.

The final section demystifies the foundations of *through-the-mirror* writing. Narrative, metaphor, and other writing forms (such as poetry and genre) are explained, exemplified and elucidated in detail.

There is also a companion website to the book, which contains additional free materials to the book. The full contents list for the website is: www.uk.sagepub.com/bolton.

'"What is the use of a book," thought Alice, "without pictures or conversation?"' (Carroll [1865] 1954, p. 1). Wise Alice knew texts have to capture heart, imagination and spirit, as well as mind, to communicate. This text is fully illustrated and exemplified throughout with original writings from colleagues, students and publications. These are first-hand accounts of practice, discussions about writings, reflections upon the usefulness of the reflection and reflexivity, and a range of descriptions of methods and their effectiveness. Reflective and reflexive processes are as old as thinking people: ancient wise texts offer simple windows on understanding.

A suggested criterion for my Master's students' final assessment was *evidence of enjoyment* (as well as *evidence of substantive reading*, and so on). My involvement in marking was increased when students' enjoyment oozed off the page. We only learn effectively when doing what we want to do. Stefano's research conclusions at the Neurosciences Research Institute, New York State University, include: 'pleasure is our brain's way of subconsciously and continuously ranking what is most important to us: pleasure leads to pure rationality' (2004). This book concerns critical, enjoyable, always challenging reflexivity and reflective practice.

The aha moment

Rowing is a precise art. You must have confidence in your boat and oars, but also confidence in your ability to let go and trust your natural instincts.

I will let you into a secret. The best way of introducing this feeling is to take away for a moment the crew's vision. To get them to shut their eyes. This lifts outside interference and pushes back those constraints of *how it ought to be* to *how it is*.

Shutting your eyes and letting those natural instincts take over can be daunting but liberating.

SEE HOW IT CAN BE DONE IF YOU JUST LET GO . . . (Jo Turner)

Oars are 'wings that make ships fly', according to Odysseus (Homer 1996, p. 464). If we continue Jo's metaphor of rowing for reflective practice, I hope *Reflective Practice* will enable you, reflective practitioner reader, to fly, and to find 'goodness there':

Just halfway through this journey of our life
I reawoke to find myself inside
A dark wood, way off course, the right road lost.
How difficult a task it is to tell
What this wild, harsh, forbidding wood was like
The merest thought of which brings back my fear;
For only death exceeds its bitterness.
But I found goodness there. (Dante, 1988, Canto 1, ll 1–8)

KEY TERMS

Reflective Practice uses key terms, explained below. They are sometimes used inaccurately and superficially in professional development; some are from other disciplines and can seem foreign. These explanations are accompanied by a brief description of *through-the-mirror* reflective writing, at the heart of this book's method.

Reflective practice: **Reflective practice** is paying critical attention to the practical values and theories which inform everyday actions, by examining practice reflectively and reflexively. This leads to developmental insight.

Reflection: **Reflection** is an in-depth consideration of events or situations: the people involved, what they experienced, and how they felt about it. This involves reviewing or reliving the experience to bring it into focus, and replaying from diverse points of view. Seemingly innocent details might prove to be key; seemingly vital details may be irrelevant.

Reflexivity: To be **reflexive** is to find a way of standing outside the self to examine, for example, how seemingly unwittingly we are involved in creating social or professional structures counter to our espoused values. It enables becoming aware of the limits of our knowledge, of how our own behaviour is complicit in forming organisational practices which, for example, marginalise groups or exclude individuals. Reflexivity uses such strategies as internal dialogue to make aspects of the self strange. It requires being able to stay with personal uncertainty, critically informed curiosity, and flexibility to find ways of changing deeply held ways of being: a complex, highly responsible social and political activity.

Values: **Values** are manifest in practice: we *are what we do*; *actions speak louder than words*. Professional integrity can be defined as working according to consonant values coherently integrated within daily action: **values in practice. Espoused values** are stated and might therefore be at variance with values in practice. One of the major aims of reflective practice is enabling people to make their values and practice consonant.

Models: **A model,** within the context of *Reflective Practice*, is a coherent structure of theoretical principles which fit together into a practical whole. They are idealisations helping us to understand; they are not descriptions and do not tell us how to act. *Through-the-mirror* reflective writing is a model. **Muddles in the models** happen, for example, when a way of working is chosen as if off a shelf, and combined with another with different theoretical principles. Education or practice, based on such muddled models, is likely at best to fail, at worst to cause significant damage.

Authority and responsibility: A *through-the-mirror* reflective practitioner has **authority** over and **responsibility** for their own learning and practice. A facilitator or mentor's role includes the creation of safe-enough educational environments with clear boundaries. In such spaces, practitioners can be brave enough to stay with uncertainty and self-doubt, thereby gaining confidence in and authority over their own thoughts, feelings and actions. Enquirers begin to realise and wield the full extent of their responsibility through reflection and critical reflexivity, leading to significant development and change.

Some models, often expressed in terms of *stages*, *levels*, *cycles* or *styles* of learning or development, have been used to constrain reflective practice. While seeming to create sufficient security for reflection, such methods can strip responsibility and authority from practitioners over their own education and development, and therefore will not be critically reflexive.

Narrative and story: People think about their lives in terms of **narrative**. Situations can be narrated as **story**, with beginning, middle and end; characters demonstrate intentions and interact over a specified time period; events occur in specific places. Life as lived is not story, mostly because it is all middle with no real beginnings and endings, it goes on and on: and then, and then, and then… .

Metaphor: **Metaphor**, a major way of making sense of the world (along with narrative), is a frame through which we perceive, understand and feel. A form of cultural interpretation, it is a foundation of communication, values, ethical beliefs and practices, shaping our perceptions and prescribing our understanding. Attitudes are formed, certain elements foregrounded, others ignored by the metaphors we use. Each metaphor, consciously used or created, gives authority, and extends and vivifies that which it describes. Metaphors used unwittingly restrict perception and understanding.

A metaphor is something otherwise unrelated or logically inconsistent standing in place of another: 'my work is the baby thrown out with the bathwater'. Metaphor makes abstract concrete. Feelings, spiritual experience, abstractions such as the mind cannot be touched, heard, smelt or seen. Metaphors give vital yet difficult-to-grasp everyday areas of our lives tangible concrete form, such as perceiving the mind as a computer. Critical insight into metaphor can enhance reflective practitioners' authority.

Perspective: Experience is always perceived from a **perspective**, a point of view. Assumptions that clients, patients, students, members of the public share practitioners' viewpoints, for example, are likely to be dangerously wrong, yet such assumptions are made every day. In reflective practice, one attempts to perceive from others' perspective.

Description: A carefully observed **description** of an event, place or person is reflective and analytic. Something observed acutely and critically is something understood, because observers grasp relationships between separate parts of a whole, and/or elements in a sequence of events. Close and accurate description is therefore a significant aspect of reflective practice.

***Through-the-mirror* writing for personal and professional development:** This model is so called because writers are taken right through the mirror's glass and silvering to a reflective and reflexive world where nothing can be taken for granted: everyday actions, events and assumptions about other people take on radically different significance. The perspectival nature of experience is explored via narrative, metaphor and description. Greater authority over personal principles and values can be gained, and greater responsibility over professional assumptions. Other methods of reflection help practitioners to look in the mirror and see an image of themselves reversed, but otherwise just the same.

The writing process *is* the *through-the-mirror* reflective process.

Through-the-mirror writing can develop professional and personal understanding and insight, each writer responding to their own concerns, wants, needs and interests. Writers can discover more about themselves, and clarify their values, professional identity and boundaries. They learn about diversity of perspective, and recognise and challenge assumptions about political, social and cultural norms.

An experience narrated in writing can be powerfully illuminative. Practitioner writers retain full authority and control: writings are theirs to store unread, read privately deciding whether they should be shared developmentally with others, or possibly destroyed. Confidential discussions with trusted carefully facilitated boundaried groups or mentors, following the reading of reflective writing, can focus quickly and deeply, and enable dynamic understanding leading to significant development and change.

Through-the-mirror writing shares some processes with the initial explorative expressive stage of literary or creative writing. The story form (narrative) is used because it is the human natural communicating medium. This writing also harnesses powers of metaphor, observation and description, and imaginative exploration of perspective. Fiction and other literary modes can develop perception of, for example, alternative points of view (for instance, client). The examination of metaphor clusters used habitually at work can help reveal social and cultural forms creating professional and personal constructs (for example, hospital as marketplace; human body as machine). Insight can be developed by exploring personal metaphorical analogies for professional issues (for example, my work is an elephant/Christmas tree). This conscious examination of point of view and metaphorical base can deepen awareness of the perspectival and socially constructed nature of experience, helping professionals towards a deeper perception and more responsible grasp of relationships, events, consequences and possible courses of action. Greater authority is gained over role and practice.

Some reflective writers craft writing beyond the explorative expressive stage, redrafting sometimes for professional publication. Critical redrafting can offer personally developmental insight, by focusing on significant expression of vital material in a form which communicates to a wider readership. Processes borrowed from poetry, fiction, drama, auto/biography or journalism refine texts. They become interesting and comprehensible to unknown readers, and less emotionally disclosive or cathartic for the writer. Published literature is read for content, not personal interest concerning the writer. Some autobiographical published accounts (my cancer journey/how I lived with having killed a pedestrian) appear disclosive, but are carefully crafted. Few reflective practice writers redraft to create a product for wide publication, though some craft or rewrite dynamically and some for professional publication (for example, the *British Medical Journal* and *The Lancet* regularly publish such informative and personal pieces).

Writers and readers of *through-the-mirror* writing are significantly concerned with their own and each other's professional and personal development. They write for the power of the process to inspire critical insight.

SECTION 1

REFLECTION AND REFLEXIVITY: WHAT AND WHY

CHAPTER 1

REFLECTIVE PRACTICE: AN INTRODUCTION

Chapter 1 introduces and describes reflective practice, outlining its political and social responsibility. Reflection and reflexivity are defined and explained. The particular nature of *through-the-mirror* writing is introduced, its relationship to mindfulness, and the way it can tell the truth while accepting the impossibility of objectivity.

> We do not 'store' experience as data, like a computer: we 'story' it. (Winter 1988, p. 235)

> You understand how to act from knowledge, but you have not yet seen how to act from not-knowing. (Chuang Tsu 1974, p. 68)

> I'm no longer uncertain about being uncertain: uncertainty is now my mantra. (Reflective practice student)

Reflection is a state of mind, an ongoing constituent of practice, not a technique, or curriculum element. *Reflective Practice* can enable practitioners to learn from experience about themselves, their work, and the way they relate to home and work, significant others and wider society and culture. It gives strategies to bring things out into the open, and frame appropriate and searching questions never asked before. It can provide relatively safe and confidential ways to explore and express experiences otherwise difficult to communicate. It challenges assumptions, ideological illusions, damaging social and cultural biases, inequalities, and questions personal behaviours which perhaps silence the voices of others or otherwise marginalise them. *Reflective Practice* can enable enquiry into:

- what you know but do not know you know
- what you do not know and want to know
- what you think, feel, believe, value, understand about your role and boundaries
- how your actions match up with what you believe
- how to value and take into account personal feelings.

This form of reflection seems to enable practitioners to explore and experiment with areas of experience difficult otherwise to approach, such as:

- what you can change in your context; how to work with what you cannot
- how to value the perspective of others, however different they are to you
- how others perceive you, and their feelings and thoughts about events
- why you become stressed, and its impact on life and practice
- how to counteract seemingly *given* social, cultural and political structures.

Through-the-mirror writing is intuitive spontaneous, similar to initial drafting. Writings then inform discussion in trusted confidential forums. Reflective practitioners write for self-illumination and exploration, not to create a product.

We know a great deal more than we are aware, absorbing information unwittingly, and data we do not use and think we have forgotten, and challenging material shoved into boxes mentally labelled *do not open*. *Through-the-mirror* writing can give confidential and relatively safe access, using narrative and close and accurate observation. It enables the vital skill to use knowledge thus gained (for perceptive diagnosis for example). Constraining structures and metaphors can become clear, offering power to take more responsibility for actions.

All action is founded upon personal ethical values. We are what we do, rather than what we say we are. Yet it is hard to gain clarity about ethical values expressed in practice, far easier to *say* what we believe (espoused values). *Through-the-mirror* writing enables discovery of who and what we are in practice, and why we act as we do (for an exercise, see Bolton, 2009). This process can be unsettling (Pollner 1991) or even uneasy, leading to the uncertainty of genuine questioning, the foundation of all education. Education is about perceiving and developing our own searching questions, rather than being given answers. The search for solutions leads to yet more pertinent questions and more learning. In learning and und   ing about human rights, for example, law students need to learn   tice of law. Rather it means the practice of people, their lives and   , beliefs that people hold and wish to protect, or promote, or   2002; Williams 2002, p. 134).
           rror writing can help practitioners towards perceiving and   ibility. It is never good enough to say: 'I don't have time to   cause my senior instructed me to/it was in the protocol',

'I thought everyone did Y', 'Oh I've never thought about why I do that, or if I should!' There is much in life we are genuinely not in control of, such as birth, death, illness, accidents, and others' impingements upon ourselves (for example, a bureaucratic rule-bound manager with no interest in developing staff). We may not be in control of responsive feelings and thoughts, but we are surely responsible for our actions.

Reflection and reflexivity are essential for responsible and ethical practice, yet there have been arguments against it. One is lack of time (Copeland et al. 1993) and packed curricula taught by demotivated and over-stretched tutors (Davis 2003). Current expectations of constant activity and busyness make reflection a luxury; this, paradoxically makes it more important to point out the value of reflection (Hedberg 2009). Reflection and reflexivity can be seen as threats to position or status in organisations, where such practices are often impeded by prescriptive meetings with a low level of engagement, high role-based demarcated and political dimension, high degree of threat and task orientation (Heel et al. 2006).

Reflective practice leading to change and development only happens in learning organisations (Gould 2004), with supportive mechanisms of coach, mentor or facilitator (Gray 2007), and not when top-down, organisational visions are imposed leading to compliance (Senge 1992). Effectively facilitated reflective and reflexive professional development is amply repaid however, as practitioners take decisions more accurately and quickly by drawing upon effective trustworthy intuition (Cartwright 2004). And organisations gain from workplace reflection because critically reflective practitioners have increased morale, commitment to clients, openness to multiple perspectives and creative innovative non-dichotomous solutions, and clearer boundaries (Fook 2002). Reflection on the part of professional evaluators is also crucial, given the inherently politicised and value-based nature of evaluation, and the need for critical monitoring of bias (Clark/Keefe 2007).

Reflective practice which genuinely affects practitioners' lives, and those around them, needs confident experienced teaching and facilitating. Students or employees required to write journals and accounts of practice without being inducted and facilitated well are likely to experience feelings of helplessness, frustration and eventual burnout (Gray 2007), be resistant (Bulpitt and Martin 2005), negative (Hobbs 2007), or even 'angry, challenged, threatened, demoralized, shocked, and put off by the *leap into the unknown*' (Trelfa 2005, p. 206), and they might focus merely on technical skills (Truscott and Walker 1998), or write safely and hypothetically about themes rather than specific experiences (Clarke 1998). Leadership development students in business environments often block reflection due to negative 'mindsets' (Smith 2001) if appropriate educational environments are not created, and tuition offered. There are no half measures: if organisations want reflective reflexive practitioners they need to pay in time and facilitation.

Creating this environment can be complex and perplexing, and managerialism will always be a significant block to practitioner critical reflection (Heel et al. 2006; Redmond 2006). The most effective education has never been easy, as any reader of Socrates (Plato)'s dialogues knows. Good facilitation can lead to: '83% of the professionals with whom I had worked within the reflective teaching model considered that, over two years after the end of the course, they were significantly more confident of being able to introduce change within their organisation' (Redmond 2006, p. xii).

Change and development take time, energy and commitment. Instructional how-to and information-giving can seem to give instant 'results' making reflective practice seem 'soft and unquantifiable' (Regan 2008, p. 219), 'self-indulgent' (Bulman and Schutz 2008).

Instruction resulting in neatly ticked competencies is tidier, less demanding than challenging students and practitioners to question the very roots of their practice, themselves as practitioners, and significantly critique their organisations. According to Groom and Maunonen-Eskelinen, narrative exploration and reflective practice are more used and valued in teacher education in Finland than in the UK, where development of competencies is valued more highly. European teacher training is less inhibited in promoting reflective practice as liberating force than in the UK (Groom and Maunonen-Eskelinen 2006).

Write to learn

This third edition not only clearly and thoroughly explains *what* reflective practice and reflexivity are and *why* they are essential, it also clearly and straightforwardly demonstrates *how* to start and develop, *with whom*, *when* and *where*. In this book you will discover how to *write to learn* as well as *learn to write*. *Reflective Practice* offers practical and theorised methods for understanding and grasping authority over actions, thoughts, feelings, beliefs, values and professional identity in professional, cultural and political contexts. It suggests processes for critical reflection upon the forms, values and ethics of institutional organisations and structures in which professionals work. This critique can result in radical movements for change. Most training and post-experience courses include elements of reflective practice and reflexivity. Danger lies in it being a separated curriculum element, however: it is a foundational attitude to life and work, not a set of exercises.

A paradox is that systems require reflective practice as curricula or professional development element. Since its nature is essentially personally, politically and socially unsettling, it lays open to question anything taken for granted. Enquiry-based education, 'education for creativity, innovativeness, adaptability, ease with difference and comfortableness with change ... [is] education for instabililty' (Reid and O'Donohue 2004, p. 561).

Smooth-running social, political and professional systems run on the well-oiled cogs of stories we construct, and connive at being constructed around us. Welcoming of diversity can be mere window dressing. Effective reflective practice and reflexivity are transgressive of stable and controlling orders; they lead cogs to decide to change shape, change place, even reconfigure whole systems.

The structures in which our professional and personal roles, values and everyday lives are embedded are complex and volatile. Power is subtle and slippery; its location is often different from how it appears. Reflection and reflexivity for development involve:

- recognizing *authority* over and *responsibility* for personal and professional identity, values, action, feelings
- *contestation* of lack of diversity, imbalance of power, the blocking capability of managerialism, and so on
- willingness to stay with *uncertainty*, unpredictability, doubt, questioning.

The route is through spirited enquiry leading to constructive developmental change and personal and professional integrity based on deep understandings. It is *creative, illuminative, dynamic, self-affirming*. Academic study has lost its suppressive attitude to artistry (Glaze 2002). 'Any dinosaurian beliefs that "creative" and "analytical" are contradictory and incompatible modes are standing in the path of a meteor; they are doomed for extinction' (Richardson and St Pierre 2005, p. 962). People only learn and develop when happy and benefiting personally. The route is not through angry confrontation: such revolution leads to destructive cycles of action and reaction. Yet it is not a thornless rose bed, as any dynamic process.

Einstein ([1929] 2002) was successful partly because he doggedly and constantly asked questions with seemingly obvious answers. Childlike, he asked why? how? what?, rather than accepting givens or taken for granteds. He 'love[d] the *questions themselves* like locked rooms', and certainly '*live[ed]* the questions' (Rilke [1934] 1993, p. 35). Stories make sense of ourselves and our world. This world and our lives within it are complex and chaotic: seemingly governed by forces not only beyond our control, but beyond our understanding. We tell and retell episodes both minor and major to colleagues, loved ones, therapists and priests, strangers on the train, a wedding guest (Coleridge [1834] 1978). A dynamic way of grasping understanding, it prevents us being pawns in events seemingly beyond our control. The danger is that story making can merely be tucking ourselves securely under a quilt patchworked out of safe and self-affirming accounts: our stories can only too easily be essentially uncritical. Or, even worse, they are censoring tools: 'cover stories' (Sharkey 2004). This self-protectiveness can ensure our stories do not explore sensitive issues, but are expressions of what we feel comfortable with, or would like to be.

Knowing what to reflect upon out of the whole of one's professional experience is not a clear process. The more it is focused upon, the more the truly important issues become elusive. It can become like looking for Piglet: 'It was still snowing as [Pooh Bear] stumped over the white forest track, and he expected to find Piglet warming his toes in front of the fire, but to his surprise he found that the door was open, and the more he looked inside the more Piglet wasn't there' (Milne [1928] 1958, p. 163). Milne's Winnie-the-Pooh stories are celebrated because they express natural philosophy. Here Milne says in simple terms how the more we look for something important the more it is not there. Only with the courage to stop *looking* and trust the reflective and reflexive processes, will we begin to perceive the areas we need to tackle. Discovering what needs to be reflected upon, and how, can be an exhilarating journey. Insights gained and inevitable changes seem obvious afterwards. Although reflective practice has become a standard in initial and continuing professional education and development, it is often elusive to curriculum planners. *Through-the-mirror* writing is an educational approach which makes the difference between 20 years of experience and one year of experience repeated 20 times.

Through-the-mirror writing uses an intuitive spontaneous form, the way a novelist or journalist writes their first draft. The writings then inform discussion in trusted confidential forums. Reflective practitioners write in order to learn: a self-illuminatory and exploratory process, rather than one focused upon creating a product.

Writings often focus on *non*-critical incidents, or perhaps *non*-'critical' aspects of such events. Insight is gained by allowing reflective and reflexive processes to light upon and enlighten that which most needs examination. These areas might be simple daily habitual actions, rather than 'critical'. Or actions hitherto unnoticed because focusing upon them is more problematic, often for unexamined reasons. 'Critical' incidents, described by Brookfield (1990, p. 84) as 'vividly remembered events', such as giving the wrong vaccine because they had been stored higgledly-piggledly in the fridge, will inevitably be examined. The events we 'forget' most need reflection, and give rise to the deepest reflexivity: 'we need to attend to the untold' (Sharkey 2004). Jonathan Miller said 'it is a passionate, almost religious belief of mine that it is in the negligible that the considerable is to be found … The unconsidered is deeply considerable' (Miller 2009, p.12). A human resource development exercise is writing what you *do not* remember (Goldberg 1991; Joy-Matthews et al. 2004). Plato, who said 'the life without examination is no life' (Plato 2000, p. 315), reckoned education is finding pathways to what we do not know we know.

This is probably a return to the original meaning of *critical incident*: critical processes are brought to bear upon what might have been a routine or typical event, rather than the event itself being critical. A problem has arisen with the term, leading many reflective practitioner students to think they must focus upon the dramatic, disturbing or otherwise seemingly significant. We need to be critical *about* incidents.

Reflective practice and reflexivity are states of mind, an ongoing constituent of practice, not a technique, or curriculum element, but a pedagogical approach which should 'pervade the curriculum' (Fanghanel 2004, p. 576): the pearl grit in the oyster of practice and education. To be effective they need dynamic methods. The method of travel affects what happens along the way and the destination. A medical student commented: 'we spend so much time studying medicine we never have time to study sick people'. Reid and O'Donohue (2004) argue that enquiry-based learning (a form of reflective practice) should become the organising logic of entire teacher education programmes, with students learning *through* enquiry rather than being prepared *for* enquiry. Curricula need shaking up, and more enquiry-based methods introduced. *Curriculum* is Latin for race course (Rome's oval Piazza Navona was one): perhaps we need to progress from chasing each other and ourselves round a set track.

A story is an attempt to create order and security out of a chaotic world; strong stories have unique power to make sense of issues (Weick 1995). Stories penetrate human understanding more deeply than the intellect: they engage feelings. All learning involves emotion as well as cognitive engagement. 'Reflection without passion is meaningless' (Gully 2004, p. 314). But for our experiences to develop us – socially, psychologically, spiritually – our world must be made to appear strange. We, and our students, must be encouraged to examine our story-making processes critically: to create and re-create fresh accounts of our lives from different perspectives, different points of view.

We must rewrite our stories to question assumptions about our own actions, intentions and values, and every taken for granted about others, particularly those with less power (patients, students, less dominant colleagues), and every unthought-through acceptance of the status quo, even that seemingly written in stone. And we must elicit and listen to the responses of peers. Listening critically to the stories of those peers also enables developmental learning from their experience. It is the exploration of experience, knowledge, values, identity that matters, rather than any attempt to arrive at a 'true' account (Doyle 2004).

> Important knowledge about reality always comes out of [writing] ... through a ... transformation of reality by imagination and the use of words ... When you succeed in creating something different out of ... experience, you also achieve the possibility of communicating something that was not evident before ... But you cannot plan this transmission of knowledge. (Llosa 1991, p. 79)

Postulating what other actors might have thought and felt, empathising with them and the situation, as well as imaginatively reconstructing the situation in fresh ways, offers understandings and insights as no other process can. For example, a practitioner can retell a story from the point of view of students or clients, reconstruct it with the genders of the actors reversed, or create a satisfactory ending in place of a horrible one.

Effective reflective practice and reflexivity meet the paradoxical need both to tell and retell our stories in order for us to feel secure enough, and yet critically examine our actions, and those of others, in order to increase our understanding of ourselves and our practice, and *develop dynamically*.

What's in a name?

The term *reflective practice* is not a terribly useful one. The metaphor it embodies is limited: a mirror reflection is merely the image of an object directly in front of it, faithfully reproduced back to front. What is the reflection of shit? Shit.

Through-the-mirror, however, is a creative adventure right through the glass to the other side of the silvering. Such reflective practice can take us out of our own narrow range of experience and help us to perceive experiences from a range of viewpoints and potential scenarios. It can do this by harnessing a vital human drive – to create stories about our lives, and communicate them.

The mirror image model of reflection suggests a *me out there* practising in the big world, and a reflected *me in here* in my head thinking about it. This model is located in unhelpful modernist duality: *this* as opposed to *that*, *in* and *out*, *here* and *there*. An ancient Zen Buddhist text tells us:

> You must first forsake the dualities of: self and others, interior and exterior, small and large, good and bad, delusion and enlightenment, life and death, being and nothingness. (Tsai Chi Chung 1994, p. 95)

The word *reflection* has static connotations, meaning 'the action of turning [back] or fixing the thoughts on some subject' *(Oxford English Dictionary)*, with the associated definition of the reversed reproduction of an image. *Reflective practice* is purposeful, not the musing one slips into while driving home, which can be as dynamic as *rumination*, a sheep chewing smelly cud. I have a cartoon of a sheep nose to nose with the reflection of herself and the surrounding meadow. She's saying: 'I'm sure the grass is greener in the mirror, but whenever I try to reach it, this ugly ewe bars the way and butts me on the nose.' The 'ugly ewe' is of course herself reflected. We need intensive explorative and expressive methods in order not just to be confronted by our own 'ugly ewe' reflection. We need to get beyond a notion that to reflect is self-indulgently (or painfully critically) thinking about ourselves. Isolating the pawn of myself to reflect upon away from the chess game is not helpful. It *is* helpful to reflect in order to locate the white pawn which is me, clearly, boldly and *critically* within the four-dimensional chess game of my life and work.

The *through-the-mirror* reflective practice writing model involves wide potential interactions, opens up developmental reflexive and reflective space. 'Reflection is the central dynamic in intentional learning, problem-solving and validity testing through rational discourse' (Mezirow 1981, p. 4). Yes, true, but there is an awful lot more than just the 'rational' for us to explore.

Professionals can be enabled to think and discourse *way beyond the rational* using the methods outlined in the following chapters. They can explore the wide and rather perplexing other side of reflection, questioning everything, turning their world inside out, outside in and back to front.

Reflective practice: a political and social responsibility

Practitioners need to take responsibility for all their own actions and values, and their share of responsibility for the political, social and cultural situations within which they live and work. Reflective practice can fall into the trap of becoming only confession. Confession can be a conforming mechanism, despite sounding liberating, freeing from a burden of doubt, guilt and anxiety (Bleakley 2000b). Confession has a seductive quality because it passes responsibility to others.

The desire to hold an audience with a 'glittering eye' (Coleridge [1834] 1978) is strong. Jennifer Nias, a researcher into the experience of women teachers (Nias and Aspinwall 1992), noted with surprise that all her potential interviewees were keen to tell their autobiographies at length. People always are, but they do not want their stories questioned: *this* is the role of reflective practice.

Reflective practice is more than an examination of personal experience; it is located in the political and social structures which are increasingly hemming professionals in (Goodson 2004). Their right to make moral and professional judgements is being eroded; they are being reduced to technicians, their skills to mere technical competencies. Practitioners are increasingly under pressure to perform, to have 'strong and stable personalities and to be able to tolerate complexity', are pushed destructively and distortingly by obsessive goals and targets in a masculine culture of assertiveness and competitiveness (Garvey et al. 2009, pp. 97, 153, 217). A supported process which allows, encourages even, doubt and uncertainty paradoxically gives them strength in the face of such attempts to control. In order to retain political and social awareness and activity, professional development work needs to be rooted in the public and the political as well as the private and the personal.

To this end, examinations of practice need to be undertaken alongside open discussions with peers on pertinent issues, an examination of texts from the larger field of work and politics, and discussions with colleagues from outside practitioners' own milieu. Reflective practice work can then become politically, socially as well as psychologically useful, rather than a mere *quietist* navel-gazing exercise. It supports, demands even, practitioners thinking about values. Stephen Pattison et al.'s experience is similar: if we had asked people to talk about their values in abstract terms, we would have received generalised responses. By asking them to tell [write] stories about important experiences, we were able to see something of how values reveal themselves in a complex, varied and shifting way in practice (1999b, p. 6).

Values in practice are rarely analysed or questioned. Espoused values (those readily stated as being foundational to practice) are recognised and routinely stated both by organisations and individuals. Through reflexive practice professionals realise dissonance between their own values in practice and their espoused values, or those of their organisation, leading them to make dynamic change. This might not be easy, particularly if they realise an action, or an aspect of their organisation has been (or is) against their own ethical code, or that they are in an untenable but unalterable situation (Rowland 2000). Examining such fundamental areas requires a supportive, confidential, carefully facilitated environment.

Goodson creates a distinction between *life stories* and *life history*. The latter is the former plus appropriate and challenging data from a wide range of sources, and evidence of vital discussion with colleagues. 'The life history pushes the question of whether private issues are also public matters. The life story individualises and personalises; the life history contextualises and politicises' (1998, p. 11). In a similar process (*currere*, coined by Pinar 1975; Grumet 1981) education postgraduate students *play* with the method (Gough 1998).

Gomez et al. (2000, p. 744) found how education students' reflection was unchallenging and non-risk-taking, because they only wrote personal narratives of their classroom teaching, from their own point of view: 'The nature of personal stories as ones that people actually lived limited the ways in which they could be interrogated. Questioning the viewpoint resulting from an event in someone's life was tantamount to challenging her overall integrity.' Future student narratives will be written from multiple perspectives, enabling challenge and insight. Medical students write from the point of view of patients (Engel et al. 2008).

Cartoons in another study offered a 'playfully ironic dimension for intensifying the process of critical reflexivity' (Cavallaro-Johnson 2004, p. 423). Visual images, which allow subtexts to appear unwittingly, enabled the autobiographical stories to be critical, examining values in practice for example, preventing them from being merely confessional. I would argue that a range of different forms of text, such as from different points of view, can similarly offer layers of unwitting subtext for critical review.

Trainee cognitive therapists reported a 'deeper sense of knowing' of cognitive therapy (CT) as a result of reflective practice writing (Bennett-Levy et al. 2003, p. 145). 'The written reflections are, in my view, crucial to the process, enabling trainees to look in depth at the implications for themselves, for their clients, and for cognitive theory' (ibid. p. 205).

School students are encouraged to write reflectively too. Science students 'write to learn ... to help acquire a personal ownership of ideas conveyed in lectures and textbooks ... [which] promotes the production of new knowledge by creating a unique reflective environment for learners engaged in scientific investigation' (Keys 1999, pp. 117, 119). Phye (1997) reports school students similarly writing reflective portfolios. Kim (1999) reports a highly supported model: nurses write and share descriptive narratives in interview with a researcher, developing depth of description and reflexive and reflective critique.

Reflection and reflexivity: demystification

Through-the-mirror writing enables both reflection and reflexivity. There is a clear distinction between the two.

Reflection is learning and developing through examining what we think happened on any occasion, and how we think others perceived the event and us, opening our practice to scrutiny by others, and studying data and texts from the wider sphere.

Reflection is an in-depth consideration of events or situations outside of oneself: solitarily, or with critical support. The reflector attempts to work out what happened, what they thought or felt about it, why, who was involved and when, and what these others might have experienced and thought and felt about it. It is looking at whole scenarios from as many angles as possible: people, relationships, situation, place, timing, chronology, causality, connections, and so on, to make situations and people more comprehensible. This involves reviewing or reliving the experience to bring it into focus. Seemingly innocent details might prove to be key; seemingly vital details may be irrelevant.

Reflection involves reliving and rerendering: who said and did what, how, when, where, and why. Reflection might lead to insight about something not noticed in time, pinpointing perhaps when the detail was missed.

Reflexivity is finding strategies to question our own attitudes, thought processes, values, assumptions, prejudices and habitual actions, to strive to understand our complex roles in relation to others. To be reflexive is to examine, for example, how we – seemingly unwittingly – are involved in creating social or professional structures counter to our own values (destructive of diversity, and institutionalising power imbalance for example). It is becoming aware of the limits of our knowledge, of how our own behaviour plays into organisational practices and why such practices might marginalise groups or exclude individuals. And it is understanding how we relate with others, and between us shape organisational realities' shared practices and ways of talking. Thus, we recognise we are active in shaping our surroundings, and begin critically to take circumstances and relationships into consideration rather than merely reacting to them, and help review and revise ethical ways of being and relating (Cunliffe 2009b).

To be reflexive involves thinking from within experiences, or as the *Oxford English Dictionary* puts it 'turned or reflected back upon the mind itself'. This feels like a pretty difficult contortion: hence the need for innovative illuminative methods, like the *through-the-mirror* model recommended in these pages. A reflexive-minded practitioner will ask themselves, why did this pass me by: where was my attention directed at that time? Reflexivity is: 'What are the mental, emotional and value structures which allowed me to lose attention and make that error?' This deep questioning is missed out if the practitioner merely undertakes reflection as practical problem-solving: what happened, why, what did I think and feel about it, how can I do it better next time?

Reflexivity is making aspects of the self strange: focusing close attention upon *one's own* actions, thoughts, feelings, values, identity, and their effect upon others, situations, and professional and social structures. The reflexive thinker has to stand back from belief and value systems, habitual ways of thinking and relating to others, structures of understanding themselves and their relationship to the world, and their assumptions about the way that the world impinges upon them. This can only be done by somehow becoming separate in order to look at it as if from the outside: not part of habitual experience processing, and not easy. Strategies are required such as internal dialogue, and the support of others. This critical focus upon beliefs, values, professional identities, and how they affect and are affected by the surrounding cultural structures, is a highly responsible social and political activity.

Reflexivity involves coming as close as possible to an awareness of the way I am experienced and perceived by others. It is being able to stay with personal uncertainty, critically informed curiosity as to how others perceive things as well as how I do, and flexibility to consider changing deeply held ways of being. The role of a trusted other, such as a supervisor or peer-reader of an account, is vital.

> Reflexivity is a *stance* of being able to locate oneself in the picture, to appreciate how one's own self influences [actions]. Reflexivity is potentially more complex than being reflective, in that the potential for understanding the myriad

ways in which one's own presence and perspective influence the knowledge and actions which are created is potentially more problematic than the simple searching for implicit theory. (Fook 2002, p. 43)

A definition of reflective practice is that it 'is designed to facilitate identification, examination, and modification of the theories-in-use that shape behaviour'. It is a process of professional development which 'requires change in deeply held action theories' (Osterman and Kottkamp 2004, pp. 13–14). In order to create a clear and straightforward method, readily adapted to classrooms and individual portfolios, this book does not differentiate between reflection and reflexivity. The *through-the-mirror* method enables a reflexive and reflective journey without analysing which is taking place at any one time (though this could readily be done if required).

Mindfulness

An invaluable approach, mindfulness, a conscious exclusion of other elements of life, apart from that which is being attended to (Johns 2004), is achieved when senses and awareness are tuned into present action: the opposite of multi-tasking (Epstein 1999). Being mindfully aware develops accurate observation, communication, ability to use implicit knowledge in association with explicit knowledge, and insight into others' perceptions. Frank speaks of *practical wisdom*, from Aristotle: '*Phronesis* is the opposite of acting on the basis of scripts and protocols; those are for beginners, and continuing reliance on them can doom actors to remain beginners' (2004, p. 221).

The observation skills and awareness required of a reflective writer develop mindfulness, and are developed by it. Both require an acute focus upon what is happening at any time. Being fully conscious of actions can also enable awareness of their likely or possible outcomes, and therefore the appropriateness of the intended action. Mindfulness resembles reflection-before-action, which Wilson (2008) considers has immense value: for example it might have prevented the abuse and death of Victoria Climbié (Knott and Scragg 2007). Doctor-writer Verghese exhorts: 'We should be ministers for healing [and educating], storytellers, storymakers, and players in the greatest drama of all: the story of our patients' [students' or clients'] lives as well as our own' (2001, p. 1016).

Ours is an age of anxiety, tension, hyperactivity (multi-tasking, hot-desking, hitting the ground running), an era of inflated public emotion (a sea of flowers for a dead princess, road rage, televised war-torn victims). There is little reflective, reflexive, or simply mentally absent space allowed: 'A poor life this if, full of care, / We have no time to stand and stare (William Henry Davies). We have lost even more than Davies's everyday consciousness of 'squirrels' and 'streams full of stars, like skies at night'. It is loss of professional agency and responsibility, because we are unaware of things of which we so need to be aware.

An example: Sam, a midwife, brought a furious account of an angry mother she had attended as a National Health Service (NHS) midwife: 'stupid, hostile upper-middle-class bitch who felt she had the right to boss me around, tell me what to do'. The birth had been exhausting and disastrous for both mother and midwife: Sam still felt bitter 25 years later. The reflective practice group offered insight and comparative cases, and suggested Sam wrote an account from the mother's perspective.

The following week saw a very different Sam: 'I don't know exactly what was wrong, but I do know, having relived it from this mother's point of view, that she was upset and confused. Because I saw her as a stupid, middle-class bitch who thought she could have everything she wanted her way, I never listened to her properly. I think I'll see demanding mothers in a different way in future.'

Telling the truth?

The narratives we tell and write are perspectival. Looking in through a window at experience objectively to reflect on it from outside is impossible. To be objective is to be 'not influenced by personal feelings or opinions in considering or representing facts; impartial, detached' (*Oxford English Dictionary*). Humans, however open about themselves and their practice, can only perceive and understand from their own viewpoint, broad and empathic and professional as that might be. 'We don't see things as they are, we see them as we are' (Nin, quoted in Epstein 1999, p. 834).

Individual perspectives, values and understanding can be widened and deepened. One can look on the glass and only see one's self reflected, or through it to whatever is the other side as in George Herbert's poem: 'A man that looks on glass, / on it may stay his eye; / or, if he pleaseth, through it pass, / and then the heav'n espy.' Lewis Carroll's Alice does even better: she crawls right through the looking-glass, leaving her stuffy Victorian rule-bound world, entering a world in which everything 'was as different as possible', things are 'all alive' (Carroll [1865] 1954, p. 122), where dynamic connections are made between divergent elements.

A creative leap is required to support widening and deepening of perspective, and the effective ability to mix tacit knowledge with evidence-based or explicit knowledge. The professional arena can be opened up to observation and reflection through the lens of artistic scrutiny. We are still anchored to our own perspective, but these perspectives will be artistically and critically widened. We cannot really pass through the mirror's silvering, and can inevitably reflect only upon ourselves, our own thoughts and experiences. Artistic processes such as writing can, however, enable a harnessing of, for example, material such as memories which we do not know we remember, and greater access into the possible thoughts and experiences of others. The perspectival nature of such writing is acknowledged (that is, they do not purport to be objective or true), and many of the skills used are those of literature.

Professional writers are being heard clearly, both students (for example, Charon 2006; Gomez et al. 2000) and practitioners (Charon 2006; Clough 2002; Helman 2006; Loughran 2004). Samuel Shem says fiction writing has been an essential way of humanising medicine (2002; see further *Annals of Internal Medicine:* Physician-Writers Reflection series).

Writers acutely observe small details and subtle nuances of behaviour and situations. A teacher- or clinician-writer observes details missed by good observant teachers or clinicians (see Charon 2004, 2006). Try it. Observe a student or client walking into your practice place. Capture on paper how they hold themselves, breathe, move their limbs, their characteristic gestures and sayings. What do they remind you of – a cat? A soft deep armchair? A locked filing cabinet?

A writer has the unparalleled privilege also of entering into the life of another. That this person is a character on a page does not make it any less of a insight-creating privilege. Deep understandings can be gained by entering (virtually) another's feeling, thinking, perception and memories. This is writing beyond what you know, and has to be: if you know where writing is going to take you, start at that known point, and write on into the unknown. Try it. Take the person you have just described. Write the conversation they might have had on returning home that night. Remember this is an artistic exercise: do not think about it, let your hand do the writing, free of your normal controlling thought processes. If you add in something about how they got home, where they live or drink, you really are allowing your imagination to take you through the glass. You tap into latent understandings which have possibly not been so fully exercised before.

This is fiction; the writing has been invented imaginatively: it removes the straitjacket of *what really happened*. Writers are therefore free to draw deeply upon their imagination and aesthetic sense, and upon their intuitive knowledge of social and human areas such as relationships, motives, perspective, cause and effect, ethical issues and values.

You bring what you understand and think about this person into the forefront of your mind. It matters not a jot that you do not depict what actually happened, or what your student or client really thought. Medical students write patients' illness stories in the voice and vernacular of the patient, imaginatively and vicariously entering patients' contexts. They 'become the other' through creative writing (Engel et al. 2002, p. 32, 2008).

It is not quiddity we seek – the real nature or essence of a thing – but our experience of it.

Sharing this writing with a colleague can offer effective reflection upon understandings. Rewrite with the fresh insight gained. And perhaps a colleague, also present at the encounter with the patient, might write an account. Reading each other's account will offer the different perspectives from which you unwittingly work.

This method of reflection does not jeopardise professional accuracy of perception (Mattingley 2000). Neither does it impose distorted interpretations about patients (Garro and Mattingley 2000) because its purpose is to explore and express what is already there in clinicians' and educators' understanding and perception. It brings this to the fore to be reflected upon critically and effectively. It also brings to the forefront of attention the perspectival nature of our perception. No one can know *what really happened* in any situation. Perhaps it might become clear that the doctor understood the patient very differently from the nurse, or the teacher might think and write one thing today, reflect upon it perhaps with peer(s), and write something different tomorrow, their perception enhanced by the writing and discussions. Such a collection of stories can build up a composite picture, and what was thought and felt – getting as close as possible to *what really happened*.

Kevin Marsden, a special-school teacher, and Master's in Education reflective practice student, tells a classroom story:

 Malcolm

One morning we were doing number work. Malcolm was struggling to recognise sets of two. He was troubled by the book in front of him and sat slumped on an elbow.

I had one of those 'bright ideas' teachers tend to get. Let's make it more practical. 'Malcolm,' I said. 'Look at Darren. How many eyes has he got?'

Malcolm looked at Darren. Pointing with his finger he slowly counted in his deep voice, 'One ... two'.

'Good, well done,' I said. 'Now look at Debbie, how many eyes has she got?'

Pointing carefully again Malcolm intoned slowly, 'One ... two'.

'That's great, Malcolm, now look at Tony, count his eyes.'

'One ... two.' Let's take this a step further, I said smugly to myself.

'Now Malcolm, look at Matthew. Without counting can you tell me how many eyes he has got?'

Malcolm looked at me as if I had gone mad. 'OK that's fine Malcolm, you just count them like you did the others.'

Relieved he slowly repeated his methodical counting: 'One ... two'.

> There is a magical moment in teaching, when the penny drops, the light goes on, the doors open. Success is achieved. I was starting to worry. We weren't getting there!
>
> 'Malcolm, how many eyes has Naheeda got?' Malcolm counted slowly, as if it was the first pair of eyes he had ever seen. 'One ... two'.
>
> 'Good, you're doing really well.'
>
> We carried on round the class. Eager faces looked up to have their eyes counted. I was growing desperate as we ran out of children. Was I leading Malcolm on an educational wild-goose chase? Were we pursuing an idea that was not yet ready to be caught?
>
> The last pair of eyes was counted. 'One ... two.' The finger carefully went from eye to eye. There was only me left. 'Malcolm,' I said, trying to hide my desperation, 'how many eyes have I got?' Malcolm studied my face carefully. He looked long and hard at my eyes. I waited expectantly in the silence. His brow furrowed. Finally he spoke.
>
> 'Take your glasses off.' (Kevin Marsden)

Kevin read this to his established sub-group of five teachers. They trusted and felt confidence and respect for each other's professional abilities and views. Kevin was able to share his frustrations and sense of failure; the group learned about the methods, joys and problems of special-school teaching. They were able to explore the probability that Malcolm had had a different understanding of his task than did Kevin. Possibly Malcolm thought he was to count the eyes, rather than 'guess' how many each had. To do this he would have had to ask for spectacles to be removed so he could see clearly. The situation of a mismatch between a teacher's intentions and a child's understanding must happen so often.

Why reflective practice now?

The grand stories of patriarchy/patriotism, religion, family and community no longer bind society. We look to counsellors, psychologists, teachers, clerics, police, life partners, general practitioners (GPs) or social workers for essential support. Marriages founder and professionals increasingly experience stress as they now bear the burden previously carried by a nexus of local and family community.

Faith in that great god science has also been shaken: 'Science, in my view, is now at the end of certainty' (Prigogine 1999, p. 26). There has been a powerful frontier (boundary) between science (and scientific professions like medicine) and the arts since the Enlightenment. A blinkered view of what constitutes knowledge and experience cannot be held for much longer.

The assumption that an objective view of the world (Kantian) is 'grown-up', that we should shed our subjective view along with sand and water play, is being questioned (see also Sacks 1985, pp. 1–21). Paul Robertson (Director of the Medici String Quartet) supports this argument from the artistic perspective: 'If any of us are out of touch with any part of ourselves we are in an impoverished state. The dominant culture is scientific, but the scientist who concentrates on this side of themselves exclusively is as impoverished as is the musician or writer who concentrates only on the artistic' (Robertson 1999).

An ethnographer can no longer stand on a mountain top from which authoritatively to map human ways of life (Clifford 1986). Clinicians cannot confidently diagnose and dictate from an objective professional or scientific standpoint; teachers do not know answers; lawyers do not necessarily know what is right and what wrong. The enmeshment of culture and environment is total: no one is objective.

'Since the seventeenth century, Western science has excluded certain expressive modes from its legitimate repertoire: rhetoric (in the name of "plain" transparent signification), fiction (in the name of fact), and subjectivity (in the name of objectivity). The qualities eliminated from science were localised in the category of "literature"' (Clifford 1986, p. 102). These categories have returned from that 300 year marginal position, to be embedded alongside the scientific approach.

Holistic coherent understandings which might support us out of our alienated mess are increasingly entertained. 'We now see the world as *our* world, rather than *the* world' (Reason 1988, p. 28). Complementary healing considers our wholeness, not just within ourselves, but also within our environment and community. 'We seek a knowing-in-action (and thinking-in-action) which encompasses as much of our experience as possible' (Reason 1988, p. 30).

Ideal professionals, gathering data on which to base their pedagogy diagnosis or care, are like social anthropologists. Geertz suggested that successful ethnographers create a 'thick description': a web of 'sort of piled-up structures of inference and implication through which the ethnographer is continually trying to pick his way' ([1973] 1993, p. 7). The reflective practice writer who explores and experiments with different writing approaches, using whatever seems appropriate at the time, is like Lévi-Strauss's *bricoleur* (1966). This knotted nexus has then to be understood and interpreted to some degree: 'a good interpretation of anything – a poem, a person, a history, a ritual, an institution, a society – takes us into the heart of that of which it is the interpretation' (Geertz [1973] 1993, p. 7). An effective reflective practitioner attempts to understand the heart of their practice. Understandings gained in this way, however, are always partial; the deeper the enquiry, the enquirer realises the less they know and understand: *the more you know, the more you know you do not know*. Geertz also stresses that it is vital not to generalise across cases but within them. Having got somewhere near the heart of clients' or students' stories and poetry, practitioners can begin to act upon this understanding.

Professionals writing about their work, sharing it with colleagues in order to offer insight, and relating this to a wider field professionally and politically, are together engaged in an activity rather like Reason's *co-operative enquiry method*, in which researcher and subject collaborate in all the stages of research, including reflecting on the experience and making sense of it (Reason 1988). The practitioner takes a full share of responsibility. There is a similarity with heuristic research (Etherington 2004; Moustakas 1990). All too often professionals act in the mould of traditional researcher; acting *on* people: collecting data, and coming to conclusions in camera.

'In this way, it may be possible to avoid providing care which is dry, barren and – perhaps the greatest sin of all – unimaginative' (Smyth 1996, p. 937). *Through-the-mirror* writing can enable care or education which is alert and alive to the client's or student's needs and wants, whether professed or not. It can enable the practitioner to use their skill, knowledge and experience creatively and lovingly, and look forward with a greater confidence.

Angela Mohtashemi, management consultant, shares reflective writing experience:

> As I help organisations become more effective through better communication and engagement with their employees, I introduce reflective writing wherever I can as a tool for teamwork, learning and development and coaching. The workplace is a tough, manipulative environment where people are often expected to comply without challenge, to 'live the company's values', to 'display the right behaviours' and even to adopt the corporate language. One's sense of self can become fragile and this limits potential. Whenever I have used writing with groups or individuals they have commented on the sense of liberation and the feeling that they are getting to the heart of things.
>
> Sometimes I have run workshops or team sessions specifically to explore reflective writing, sometimes incorporate it into other situations. A writing activity, such as writing about your name, can be a great icebreaker. I recently ran a session on writing for personal and organisational development as part of a leadership course my firm runs jointly with a university business school. The session incorporated learning theory, my own experience, principles of reflective writing and practical activities. These activities were typical of the techniques I use and included free writing and using unfamiliar imagery to look at the daily work experience.
>
> Free writing, although very simple, fulfils many purposes and is often a revelation to people. A number of participants went to their action learning sets
>
> *(Continued)*

(Continued)

keen to use free writing to explore organisational issues before discussing them with the group. They were excited about the patterns that emerged and about the honesty of a conversation with one's self. I encourage people in action learning sets to reflect about the experience afterwards. One wrote to me later:

> I spent almost 2 hrs writing up how I felt during our discussion and how I intended to change my behaviour as a result. It was tremendously thera-peutic and enjoyable, which I found surprising, as I have, until now, been avoid-ing writing down anything about how I feel – so Thank You!

Sue Smith wrote:

> Bringing the issue was like opening a door and seeing a crack of light – and seeing a very small slither [*sic*] of a room. Once the door was opened fully – which happened when I started to look at the amount of change I'd undergone – I could see the room in its entirety – and appreciate how full and intricate the things in there were.

Sue Smith has a tremendous opportunity to change people's lives. Writing helps her find a way to pause and reflect, to argue with herself until she believes what she says and can then find the voice to persuade others. In that way, writing can be a powerful force for change.

> When I first began this work I feared the response would be cynicism and doubts about its relevance. After all, most workplaces are based on rational and 'scientific' management practices: plans, budgets, facts, timelines, blueprints etc. There is little place for emotion and individual expression. My fears were wrong. Every time the response has been very positive and unleashed the power people can have when they bring their whole selves to work. One team member said the writing was 'one of the most exciting, interesting and engaging things I've done since I've been with the firm'.
> (Angela Mohtashemi)

Reflective practice and reflexivity according to the principles and practice outlined here is a valuable developmental process for any professional or student. It can take its non-judgemental camera down to any aspect of practice, with patients, colleagues, administrative and other staff, the interface of home and work, and the impact of experiences in the past on present actions. No feeling, thought or action is too small or too big for this zoom or wide-angle lens.

Read to learn

Cunliffe, A.L. (2009a) Reflexivity, learning and reflexive practice, (Chap23) in S. Armstrong and C. Fukami (eds), *Handbook in Management Learning, Education and Development*. London: Sage.

Davis, M. (2003) Barriers to reflective practice: the changing nature of higher education, *Active Learning in Higher Education*, **4**(3), 243–55.

Fook, J. (2002) *Social Work: Critical Theory and Practice*. London: Sage.

 Write to learn

Each chapter ends with *Write to learn*. These exercises can take very different lengths of time. Some are very affirming, some challenging, all result in positive writing. Each can be done individually or by a facilitated group: many are useful for initial group forming. *How to start writing* preliminaries is useful (see Chapter 6). For now all the advice you really need is:

- This is unplanned, off-the-top-of-the-head writing; try to allow yourself to write anything.
- Whatever you write will be right; there is no critic, red pen poised.
- All that matters here is the writing's content; if you need to adjust grammar and so on, you can – later.
- Ignore the *inner critic* who niggles about proper form and grammar, and even worse, says you cannot write.
- This writing is private, belongs to the writer who will be its first reader.
- No one else need ever read this, unless the writer decides to share it with trusted confidential other(s).
- Writing can be shared fruitfully with a group or confidential trusted other, if this seems appropriate once the writer has read and reflected on it first.

Advice for facilitators

- Each writer reading silently back to themselves before reading to group or partner is vital.
- Participants need to know at the start they will be invited to read out; they can choose not to read if it feels inappropriate.

(Continued)

(Continued)

- Many exercises will occasion laughter, some tears: both are fine.
- These exercises are best done with facilitator giving instructions in numbered order, as participants finish each section.
- I suggest participants complete each section before being given the next.
- Participants do not need to know why they are doing each element: people are usually keen to 'play the game' unburdened with decisions, if they trust the facilitator.

Exercise 1.1   Names

1. Write anything about your name: memories, impressions, likes, hates, what people have said, your nicknames over the years – anything.
2. Write a selection of names you might have preferred to your own.
3. Write a letter to yourself from one of these chosen names.
4. Read back to yourself with care, adding or altering positively.

Exercise 1.2   Milestones

1. List the milestones of your life and/or career, do it quickly without thinking much.
2. Read back to self: delete or add, clarify or expand as you wish.
3. Add some divergent things (for example, when you first really squared up to your head of department).
4. Choose one. Write a short piece about it. If you wish, continue and write about others.
5. Read back to yourself with care, add or delete (without listening to your negative critic).

Exercise 1.3   Insights

1. Write a quick list of 20 words or phrases about your work.
2. Allow yourself to write anything; everything is relevant, even the seeming insignificant.
3. Reread; underline ones which seem to stick out.
4. Choose one. Write it at the top of a fresh page. Write anything which occurs to you.
5. NOBODY else needs read this ever, so allow yourself to write anything.
6. You might write a poem, or an account remembering a particular occasion, or muse ramblingly. Whatever you write will be right.
7. Choose another word from your list, if you wish, and continue writing.
8. Add to your list if more occurs to you.
9. Reread with care, adding or altering, using only a positive approach.

CHAPTER 2

REFLECTION AND REFLEXIVITY

Chapter 2 continues explaining reflection and reflexivity, and how focusing upon ethical values, acute observation and description, and challenging emotions to reflect upon, can help to make sense of experience. Vivid examples of practitioners' reflection deepen and clarify the explanation.

> By three methods we may learn wisdom: first, by reflection, which is noblest; second, by imitation, which is easiest; and third by experience, which is the bitterest. (Confucius, quoted in Hinett 2002, p. v)

> There are in our existence spots of time / ... whence ... our minds
> Are nourished and invisibly repaired; / ... Such moments
> Are scattered everywhere. (Wordsworth [1880] 2004, p. 208)

> How can we know the dancer from the dance? (Yeats 1962, p. 128)

You are watching a film. An arty one starting with a wide-angle lens: a hawk's eye city view. From this height cars and buildings look like toys, and streets and fields make a pattern: pretty but with little human meaning. People are too small to be seen.

The camera zooms: into focus comes one particular street; people walking and talking, everyday interchanges. Closer and closer up to one building, and one window; we pass through the glass into a big secondary school staffroom.

The mind's eye is likened to film. Reflection creates film like a dialogue with the self (see also Attard 2008). We become film-makers and authors of our own lives to stand back for a critical view; 'I didn't see it as a discussion between me and the lecturer I saw it as a discussion with myself' (Wright 2005, p. 514).

A film of professional practice

The camera has entered the school staffroom. The atmosphere is stiff and almost silent; only one staff member, head of maths, is humming to himself, the rest look anxious and jumpy. The headteacher enters and the quiet deepens; she solemnly invites the hummer to her room. He follows her, the tension shifts but does not lessen: staff talk in low voices. This tension has been building for months: since the biology teacher began to suspect the head of maths of sexual relations with a pupil.

The camera pans out, circles at hawk level again, zooms. This time it focuses on a terraced house in a narrow street where there are tiny backyards and no front gardens. A distraught mother has run out of the front room, thrusting her dead baby into the health visitor's arms. The tiny body is cold – so cold. The little girl wants to play with 'dolly', thinking the nurse might be kind and let her; Mummy would not. The health visitor is in anguish, knowing the baby has had an autopsy: a horrifying sight unclothed.

The camera takes us now to a high-rise block of flats deep in London's East End: utterly confusing with walkways, lifts which work sporadically and jerkily, and flat numbers assigned by a dyslexic infant. A grey-haired social worker confusedly studies number after number as the wind whistles, blowing crisp packets to reveal hypodermic needles. She jumps as heavy footsteps interrupt the wind's whistle, her heart missing a beat as a dark shape looms.

What do the practitioners in our films do with the distress, guilt, anxiety, horror, anger, humiliation, which they cannot, or do not, express at work? How do they prevent these powerful feelings from draining energy, disabling them from effective practice? How do they learn from their own feelings, turn those negative energies into positive? How do they learn from each other's mistakes and successes, each other's ideas, experience and wisdom? How do they learn to empathise with another through experiences which they will never know? A man will never know childbirth, for example; how does he learn compassion and understanding to support a mother in travail?

Our films zoomed in from the distant and impersonal to the close and intensely human. *Through-the-mirror* writing can focus on the 'rag and bone shop of the heart' (Yeats 1962, p. 201). We move from the grand ideals of practice, to precise stories of individuals who cry and laugh, shout and tremble, and are involved with clients at the thresholds of life and death, at periods of intense change and development. Our professional heroines and heroes come to terms with powerful emotions, learn from mistakes and successes, and develop empathy.

Reflective practice concerns how practitioners can examine their own stories closely, look at themselves as heroines and heroes in their own real-life films, and perceive colleagues and clients also as heroes and heroines. They take themselves, problems, grief, anxieties, joys, seriously.

Through-the-mirror writing focuses upon detailed stories of practice and life: actions, thoughts, feelings, assumptions, prejudices and engagement with others' point of view. These stories are imaginative creations drawn from experience. Seen as interlocking plots, the problems, anguishes, and joys of practice become comprehensible: to be dealt with creatively and developmentally. The use of the aesthetic imagination provides a screen as wide as life itself, drawing upon all faculties. Attempting to reflect only upon 'what actually happened', and then to subject such an account to rational questions such as 'how might I have done it better?', constrains unnecessarily.

Writing stories, poetry and drama about practice can foster critical reflection upon experience, roles, values and knowledge. Perceiving, recording and discussing life as narrative is a natural human mode, as is understanding of abstract theorised social, cultural and psychological forms and structures. Practice, and its attendant education and research, primarily concern individual people, each of whom, made up of stories of inextricably linked psychological, emotional, spiritual and physical elements, is also inevitably impinged upon by cultural and social forces. Gaining access to all this via narrative can make sense of seemingly unmanageable complexity. Engel et al. (2008) describe how paying attention to narrative enhances medical education.

Vital observation of practice

All the above film plots were written about, reflected upon and discussed in groups by practitioners. The departmental head's affair with a pupil greatly distressed the teacher who wrote about it. Closely involved with pupil, family, colleagues, community, she felt deeply entwined in the drama, but could discuss it with no one. A confidential reflective group was an ideal forum. The story was written in the genre of romantic love, on my suggestion (see Chapter 14). This distance and strong set structure perhaps enabled her to begin. Her Master's in Education sub-group became agog for each episode. Discussions and group support were so valued, the group continued as a special study module the following semester.

The health visitor did prevent the toddler from unwrapping the 'dolly' dead baby; but was distressed at not handling it sensitively enough. The group were able to help her see it through the eyes of the child, and consider carefully how she might have acted rather than just anxiously warding off the toddler.

The black man who approached the social worker in the high-rise block courteously asked if he could help her find her way. The group helped her out of feeling intense shame at her assumptions, and enabled her to consider her habitual state of mind on home visits.

Why practice as screenplay?

Sharing stories with each other must be one of the best ways of exploring and understanding experience. That is, if what we want and need to say is not just *stored*, but held in our minds as *story* (Winter 1988).

Narrative telling is a vital part of our lives: in staffroom, and home kitchen: 'our preferred, perhaps even our obligatory medium for expressing human aspirations and their vicissitudes, our own and those of others. Our stories also impose a structure, a compelling reality on what we experience' (Bruner 2002, p. 89). It is also a 'source of consolation' (Eagleton 1983, p. 185). Stories offer the fictive comfort of structure (beginning, middle and end), and of the closure of our desire. We are involved in an endless search for something lost: God, Lacan's Imaginary, Freud's pre-Oedipal stage, Sartre's 'Being-in-itself', a unity with the mother's body, a sought-after haven where the signified has a direct innate correlation with the signifier:

> Something must be lost or absent in any narrative for it to unfold: if everything stayed in one place there'd be no story to tell. This loss is distressing but exciting as well: desire is stimulated by what we cannot quite possess. (Eagleton 1983, p. 185)

We relate to loss or lack in every story because we want good characters to gain their hearts' desires, the bad to founder. We experience joys and tragedies vicariously. Stories reinforce assumptions about what we might desire and what fear, affirming values and principles. We follow Odysseus past the Sirens holding our breath, and when a fair wind brings him back to Penelope, we will him to shoot his arrow straight to prove he really is her husband; we help Dorothy kill the wicked witch of the West. When Tony Archer's son was on trial for political activity (BBC Radio 4, *The Archers*, autumn 1999), people talked about it in my village, not the latest news or football, until they were satisfied the jury had found him 'not guilty'.

Being reflectively aware is similar to what Einstein called 'an appreciation of the mysterious [which] is the fundamental emotion which stands at the cradle of true art and true science' (1973, p. 80). Socrates is said to have observed 'wonder is the beginning of wisdom', because wonder is an open enquiring state of mind when anything might be possible, when startling inspiration appears as a result of no cognitive logical thought. The sculptor Juan Munoz spoke of an aim of his art 'to make [the viewer] trust for a second that what he wishes to believe is true. And maybe you can spin that into another reality and make him wonder'.

This reality spinning can involve imaginatively entering others' consciousness, empathetically and ethically, as Eagleton points out:

> There would seem to be a need for some special intuitive faculty which allows me to range beyond my own sense-data, transport myself into your emotional innards and empathise with what you are feeling. This is known as the imagination. It makes up for our natural state of isolation from one another. The moral and the aesthetic lie close together, since to be moral is to be able to feel what others are feeling. (2008, p. 19)

The culturally refined Nazis have forever disabused us that the aesthetic necessarily makes us act morally. Rather if we can allow ourselves to be in a state of *mindfulness* (see Chapter 1), *negative capability* (Keats 1818), *willing suspension of disbelief* (Coleridge [1798] 1969), then our moral and ethical faculties will necessarily be brought to the creative process. The Nazis called this *degenerate*, and denigrated, expatriated or murdered those who used it.

Listeners' roles are as important as writers': 'It is the joint effort of author and reader which brings upon the scene that concrete and imaginary object which is the work of the mind. There is no art except for and by others' (Sartre [1948] 1950, pp. 29–30). And:

> so there is an art of listening ... Every narrator is aware from experience that to every narration the listener makes a decisive contribution: a distracted or hostile audience can unnerve any teacher or lecturer: a friendly public sustains. But the individual listener also shares responsibility for that work of art that every narration is: you realise this when you tell something over the telephone, and you freeze, because you miss the visible reactions of the listener ... This is also the chief reason why writers, those who must narrate to a disembodied public, are few. (Levi 1988, p. 35)

Through-the-mirror writers write for *embodied* readers, real people: peer group, supervisor or mentor. My practitioner students say how *re-storying* with colleagues is as essential as initial writing.

Reflective practice allows relationships with students, clients, patients or colleagues to be seen within a range of possible roles. The whole person of the professional relates to the whole client.

The possible roles for professional and client could be seen to be: *I, you* and *her/him*. The client as '*I*' is central to the drama, the subject, hero/heroine: the story told from their point of view. The client as '*you*' is the *other*, while the professional is the teller of the story, whether telling it as 'I' (first person narrative) or 'he/she' (third person narrative). The client as 'her or him' becomes an object: an appropriate role in some circumstances such as research trials when the patient is only a statistic.

This poem explores a family doctor's awareness of patients viewing themselves centre stage, and the way she handles that:

Performance

This is your stage.
Sit down, compose your face.
Lines rehearsed in the waiting room.
Family can't hear you –
'Leave mum she has a headache.'

Headache.
Muscle ache.
Spirit ache.
Tired all the time.
Tired of the time.
Too much time.

Let me perform for you.
Let me touch you,
measure your blood pressure,
measure your worth.
You are worth my time.
When you get home, they'll ask what I said.
Rehearse the lines. (Jo Cannon)

What about practitioners' relationship with themselves (me with myself)? A professional wrote in evaluation: 'Writing weaves connections between my work and the rest of my life, between my inner and outer selves, between the left and the right sides of my brain, between the past and the present.' A trainee said: 'This kind of writing has to have material about who we are and what we stand for.' A medical practitioner wrote: 'I'd considered resigning because I'd been struggling with being a doctor and who it turned me into. Reflective writing has helped me see what was happening – share it with others and begin to find a way through.' Storying and re-storying our lives helps us to keep pace with the way we change and develop over time. 'Who I am' does not and cannot remain stable:

> It is important to view the self as an emergent and changing 'project' not a stable and fixed entity. Over time our view of our self changes, and so, therefore, do the stories we tell about ourselves. In this sense, it is useful to view self-definition as an ongoing narrative project. (Goodson 1998, p. 11)

Through-the-mirror writing helps the writer perceive *the character who is myself* as dynamically evolving, just as the stories this character finds itself within are neither stable nor definite, but 'ongoing narrative projects'. This fluidity is contained within the expression human *being*. Words ending with -ing involve movement and change as in *doing* and *playing*.

Why reflective practice?

Our stories are inextricably intertwined: with themselves and with those of others. We tell and retell, affirming and reaffirming ourselves in our own and each other's eyes (and ears). The accounts slip and merge as we tell, developing new twists and losing ones that have served their turn. This urge to recount and re-create each day is strong; but it is easy to devalue our own stories because they are unimportant compared with those of powerful others such as pop stars, surgeons, politicians: we have lost trust in ourselves, and ownership of our stories.

*Through-the-mirror w*riting is a way of claiming control by expressing and exploring our own and others' stories: crafting and shaping to aid understanding and development. These stories are databanks of skill, knowledge and experience: much of our knowing is in our doing. We can learn from our own and each other's mistakes and successes, each other's ideas, experience and wisdom, and tackle and come to terms with our own problem areas. Although practice is continually aired – over coffee with a colleague – we do not tell each other the things at our cutting edge of difficulty. We often do not even tell these to ourselves.

Discussing reflective writings in depth enables outcomes of reflection to be taken back into practice, improving and developing (Kolb 1984). Reflection reaches the stage when 'words can do no more … / Nothing remains but the act' (Aeschylus 1999, p. 115). This gives a 'different way of being', or as another course participant said: 'It seems like a new country, one which we've all been peering into for a long time.' This insight facilitates developmental change. Davidson reports using a reflective writing approach within an eating disorders unit:

> Through reflection and writing, we can struggle to get a conceptual grip on the situation. With a leap of faith we can open ourselves to honestly experiencing what is going on in our relationships. Even if the resultant understanding and experience is partial, it should yield a point of leverage where something that we can *do* is revealed. And if it transpires what we do does not have the desired result, then at least we have new information with which to enhance our experience and aid further reflection. (1999, p. 122)

Rita Charon (2000c, 2006), general internist and medical professor, reports how sharing reflective writings with patients deepened and clarified understanding; some responded by writing also.

I have realised that we have to make the day-to-day parts of our work more enjoyable and varied. Writing, and the reflection it allows, has brought me a real pleasure – that's why I used to smile and now I can keep that joy and even the intimacy by writing what I've felt or seen and its ironies too. (Clare)

Through-the-mirror writing can increase confidence and ability, by facilitating and enhancing:

- acceptance of, and increased confidence with, the essential complexity, uncertainty and perspectival nature of professional life
- reflexive critique of personal values, ethics, prejudices, boundaries, assumptions about roles and identity, decision-making processes; taken-for-granted structures
- similarly reflexive critique of professional milieus
- awareness of diversity, and struggle against misuse of institutional power and managerialism
- willingness to explore the interrelatedness of the professional and the personal
- sensitive, fruitful review of 'forgotten' areas of practice
- analysis of hesitations, skill and knowledge gaps
- respect for, and trust in, others' and own feelings and emotions
- development of observation and communication abilities
- constructive awareness of collegial relationships
- relief of stress by facing problematic or painful episodes
- identification of learning needs
- communication of experience and expertise with a wide range of colleagues.

Hoping for answers to conundrums is like searching for babyhood security blankets. Reflective practice leads to further searching questions, the opening of fascinating avenues to explore, but few secure answers. Questions like 'What should I have done?' become minor. More questions are thrown up, such as: 'Why did the maths teacher not hide his relationship with the pupil?' 'Perhaps I could have told the toddler a story about the dead baby?' The social worker's walkway story was capped by another who turned to face a threatening young gang and asked them the way (although she knew it): they immediately became kids who communicated with her as a person. This supported the social worker to reassess her attitude to seemingly threatening people.

A paradox concerns effective practice being uncertain. We all know colleagues who cannot say 'I don't know'. Their effectiveness is diminished by inflexible need to know. In order to acquire confidence, effective practitioners:

- let go of certainty, in a safe enough environment
- look for something without knowing what it is
- begin to act without knowing how they should act.

The essential uncertainty associated with reflective practice and reflexivity make it hard for many. 'Certainty goes down as experiential knowledge goes up … Pre-service teachers want answers and methods. They want to be certain. They want to know. In pre-service teacher education, working towards habits of uncertainty and puzzlement needs to be undertaken with modest expectations' (Phillion and Connelly 2004, p. 468). Carl Rogers wrote with empathy and wisdom about education, and said:

> The goal of education, if we are to survive, is the *facilitation of change and learning*. The only person who is educated is the person who has learned how to learn; the person who has learned how to adapt and change; the person who has realised that no knowledge is secure, that only the process of seeking knowledge gives a basis for security. Changingness, a reliance on process rather than on static knowledge is the only thing that makes any sense as a goal for education in the modern world. (Rogers 1969, p. 152)

Experienced effective practice concerns willingness to have faith in your own knowledge, skills and experience; to trust the process you are engaged in (*through-the-mirror* writing, doctoring, teaching, and so on); to relate to students, clients or patients with respect and unconditional positive regard (Rogers 1969; see also Chapter 3).

Willingness to subject every action and thought to reflection *in action* and self-respectful reflection *upon action* (Schon 1983) is required. Reflection *in action* is a hawk in the mind constantly circling, watching and advising on practice. Reflection *upon action* is considering events afterwards (Schon 1983, see also 1987). Self-respect is needed, while opening up to close observation, uncertainty and questioning previously taken-for-granted areas:

- *actions*: what you and others did
- *ideas*: what you thought; what others might have thought
- *feelings*: what you felt, and what others might have felt.

> We live in deeds not years; in thoughts, not breaths;
> In feelings, not in figures on a dial.
> We should count time by heart throbs. He most lives
> Who thinks most – feels the noblest – acts the best. (P.J. Bailey (1816–1902) *Festus*)

'Beween feeling and action there is thought' (Sophocles 1982). Effective actions arise from both feelings and thoughts. Emotions can too easily be marginalised in professional life:

There is something rather odd about trying to get help from health workers who have not worked out their own feelings, or who deny them to themselves and others. Where do all those spontaneous feelings go and who is to say what damage they might be doing to the delicate internal workings of our minds if we continue to repress and suppress them ... The key insights and changes in the way I view myself and my professional work have come through self-reflective work. (Heller 1996, pp. 365, 368)

Ethical values

Stories do social and political work. A story is never just a story – it is a statement of belief, of morality, it speaks about value. (Goodson 1998, p. 12)

Writing a personal narrative of practice is a moral project. (Arthur Frank personal communication; see also 1995)

What are ethical values? How do we discover those we live and work by? More crucially, how do we appraise and develop them? Values inherent in practical wisdom, along with technical knowledge and skill, are foundations of living and working, according to Aristotle, rather than those laid down by our culture: 'A person's actions are not based on the values law seeks to universalise, but on self-reflective values' (Manickavasagam 2000, p. 4). Values have substance only in practice: we are what we do; actions speak louder than words. Professional integrity can be defined as working according to values coherently integrated within daily practice, but many practitioners might never have defined their own values explicitly.

Values become clearer when events are narrated critically in writing: 'stories ha[ve] a key part in educating us into the virtues' (MacIntyre 1985, p. 216). Narrative communicates ethics in a way nothing else can (Charon 2006), for example without stories the meaning of fairness would be difficult to explain (Watson 2003). A qualitative research study examined how stories can shape lawyers' ethics (Economides and O'Leary 2007): the 'findings were illustrative of the subtle way in which narrative both constructs and reinforces particular understandings of professionalism within legal organisations' (p. 12). They concluded: 'Stories can be used to shape morality in contemporary organisations' (p. 6). Economides and O'Leary observed that stories can also be used negatively (for oppression, dissimulation, lying), and that good stories (powerfully persuasive) can also tend to push out true ones (see Twining 2006).

Practitioners cannot know the myriad effects of their actions, or what colleagues and clients feel and think. *Through-the-mirror* writing can, to some extent, open this up.

The family asked to meet me. Their daughter had recovered from meningococcal septicaemia, and they wanted to know why I hadn't diagnosed it … My stomach wrenched with anger and frustration. Can't they see? That's the whole point: two doctors a few hours apart both made the same clinical judgment that this was a viral illness. I felt that their criticisms were unfair …

As the date for our meeting drew closer, that black churning bitterness was still there, and I realised I had to do something … I decided to … write the story of the family's complaint from the point of view of the parents. The first line came easily: 'She nearly died you know. Our daughter nearly died.' At that point my perspective on the complaint changed. I felt the parents' fear, and I understood their terror. They had taken their ill child to a doctor and had trusted him to keep her safe … The child got worse and nearly died. They lost the doctor; they could have lost their daughter.

The complaint wasn't about diagnostic skills or statistical probabilities but about a family trying to make sense of the horror of nearly being ripped apart forever. By thinking about the complaint from the family's point of view, I understood that my role in the meeting wasn't to defend but to listen. (Munno 2006, p. 1092)

Munno's clarity about listening taking precedence over defending his professional judgement lies in his final half-sentence. He reached this conclusion by perceiving from the parents' point of view, using story-writing. His first sentences – 'She nearly died you know. Our daughter nearly died' – changed his perspective on the parents' attitude, and therefore helped him begin to reassess his value judgement as to appropriate action. This remarkable change was enabled by him humbly and honestly putting himself in the parents' position, by harnessing the narrative power of story-writing.

At a senior medical educators' conference (UK Conference of Postgraduate Education Advisers in General Practice, UKCEA) I asked a workshop group to write a list of words about their work: any words. We took some time listening to each list; the items carried such significance. Each then chose one abstract noun (trust, respect, for example) to write reflectively about. They then wrote a narrative about any experience. Allan's abstract noun was *vulnerability*, and he also wrote about missing a diagnosis of meningococcal meningitis, concluding:

I lost some of the confidence I'd had, and have been since more wary of my patients. I sometimes fear my involvement in them compromises my professional judgement and makes me more vulnerable. Perhaps it would be better to be less interested and more detached. Perhaps I would be a better doctor and less 'sloppy' if I maintained a more professional distance.

The group delved deep in discussion about professional responsibility: how relating closely to patients enhanced both clinical practice and personal experience of it, but could increase anxiety. Each participant brought interpretations, perspectives and experience, offering individual insight into the story's implicit meanings, widening understanding. The discussion enabled them to tussle with issues around relationships with patients: relating to them with empathy opened up insight, but entailed vulnerability. Allan found that writing about his loss of confidence and sharing this with trusted peers helped re-establish confidence built on more appropriate values.

On another course, narratives were written as if to be read by children. Lucy Henshall, initially nonplussed, followed my recommendation to write whatever came into her mind, in whatever way. Lucy's story concerned a tricky consultation with a boy presenting with listlessness and stomach pain. By attending carefully to what child and mother expressed, she gave him the confidence to confess his deepening anxiety about his mother's new boyfriend.

> His mother, quieter than I had ever seen her, reached over, took his hand and squeezed it.
> 'It's going to be fine' she whispered, 'We'll work it out together, Bill'.
> Bill didn't look quite as small as he went out, and his Mum didn't seem quite so tall and loud either. It was almost as if, while we had been talking, he had grown taller and she had grown smaller so became much closer than before.

Reflecting later, Lucy felt proud of having valued listening and openness, rather than maintaining professional distance. She had made herself vulnerable and open to being trusted with the sensitive kernel of the problem. The task, to write as if for a child, enabled her to re-experience and re-evaluate the event, and therefore to clarify her implicit values.

These examples are from experienced practitioners. Research shows medical education inhibits rather than facilitates the development of moral reasoning (Patenaude et al. 2003a, 2003b). This leads students, the authors conclude, to regard 'the patient as a problem to solve rather than a unique person who is part of society' (2003a, p. 828). The report did not say whether reflective practice and reflexivity was taught, facilitated and encouraged within that medical school: those students surely need it.

Challenging emotions

Powerful emotions sometimes arise within practice and reflection. Powerful emotions can initially appear to inhibit reflective abilities, however, as Andrew Eastaugh found in research into co-tutoring:

> The idea that my emotions are a source of understanding has an exciting and novel ring for me. Exciting because it opens up the possibility … that the emotional part of me has a value outside my own personal attachment to it …

It is novel because my experience of the world of learning has been that emotions are, at best, merely the icing on top of the cake, for decoration, self-indulgence and treats, but not the real substance. Too much will make you sick and is unnecessary. At their worst they are a serious barrier to the real business of life – should be pushed aside and ignored. (Eastaugh 1998a, p. 48)

Strong feelings are an indicator of ethical values. People become aroused (positively or negatively) when human values are transgressed, opposed or affirmed (examples of values are respect for my personal boundaries, trust in my professional standing, unconditional positive regard for clients (patients, students) despite race, creed or culture). Reflecting upon emotional situations can help to discover ethical values in practice.

Recognising and working with emotions through reflexivity can significantly develop practice. The deaths of Victoria Climbié (Laming 2003) and Baby Peter (www.nhsconfed.org) indicate a failure of practice. Climbié's social workers failed to respond to clear indications of abuse because their defence mechanisms protected them against psychological and emotional stresses of working with violent clients (Ferguson 2005; Cooper and Lousada 2005). In our post-emotional welfare state, professionals increasingly have an instrumental role in the delivery of services rather than being themselves agents of change, support and care (Dean 2004; Le Grand 2006; Ruch 2009). MacIntyre (1985) says managers' activities have become value neutral, concerned with rationality, efficiency and confidence, rather than moral debate or awareness. People are viewed as costs, effects or benefits, rather than feeling humans. These metaphors can lead professionals to perceive service users in terms of specific problems or as theoretical constructs rather than unique people with unique needs (Redmond 2006). A further scandal involved abuse of learning-disabled service users (www.healthcarecommision.org). Another danger of working with violent clients is that workers do sometimes *mirror* the behaviour of clients, and become aggressive themselves (Knott and Scragg 2007).

Anger can prove to be a useful if uncomfortable focus for reflection. Here a senior medical Master's student reflected upon the effect of his reflective practice story-writing and work:

As a result of reflecting upon these incidents I now understand much better how I have been dealing with anger and the effect it was having on me. I felt unable to express anger because I was afraid of making a fool of myself, afraid of losing control and because I want to be well thought of. I feel that if I get angry with someone they will not like me. I want to be liked. I therefore tend to push my anger down inside. I have not been consciously aware of doing this and therefore have not been aware of how much anger I have been carrying. I have therefore not been able to explain the unpleasant feelings I have had when it has begun to rise to the surface.

I now know that it is not possible (or necessarily good) to please everybody all the time. I know the difference between telling someone I am angry and expressing the anger itself. I am able to recognise when I am angry, when I am suppressing it and the feelings that this causes. I feel more able to tell people when I am angry with them and that I can do this articulately. (Rod)

A doctor wrote a vehement and dramatic long-term 'diary' about his relationship with his health authority. Reflecting upon it later, he wrote: 'I am much less emotionally reactive in all these management meetings I have to go to, and certainly not as nervous!' Lindsay Buckell's 'expression of my passionate hatred of the current climate of fear and blame' (Chapter 5) is another.

Keith Collett, a GP (family practitioner) trainer, and supervisor for fellowship application to the British Royal College of General Practitioners, encourages the writing of drafts of medical reports, responses to complaints and so on, so that they can be discussed, reflected upon and redrafted:

This is incredibly useful to prevent registrars [interns] overstating support or condemnation for a patient … They have a chance to reflect on how it will be received by the patient, their relatives, or their solicitor … I encourage the first splenic draft to be written as I feel it has a healing and calming effect, and offers an opportunity for reflection. Too often dictaphones are used and the resultant text signed and sent without reflective reading. (Keith Collett)

Anger is often viewed as inappropriate, beyond the professional boundary. Reflective practice is an appropriate locus for exploring it, and the other seemingly dangerous emotions.

Discussing each other's work, our focus moves naturally between personal development, professional development and writing technique. We work intensely, sometimes sharing deep emotions, but I rarely experience any tension or sense of effort. (Maggie)

I wrote bits of verse which expressed conflicts of loyalty and fears for the future. I read them out and wept, and the silence of our group carried my emotions. (Clare)

Paula Salvio supports teachers in *empathetic enquiry*, a deeper understanding of ethnic minority students. She says teachers must 'travel into our own worlds' in order to 'travel to those of others', and gain empathetic understanding. This process must involve feelings, as 'emotional whiteout' will disable this travel into both our own worlds and those of others (Salvio 1998, p. 49). Cixous described this as feminine writing:

All the feminine texts I've read are very close to the voice, very close to the flesh of language, much more so than masculine texts … perhaps because there's something in them that's freely given, perhaps because they don't rush into meaning, but are straightway at the threshold of feeling. There's tactility in the feminine text, there's touch, and this touch passes through the ear. (1995, p. 175)

Focus on reflection

Mark Purvis and the Death of Simon
The grown-ups stand around watching.
Grown-ups know what to do.
The grown-ups stand around watching.

Is that Simon lying on the pavement?
He has got blondie hair like Simon's.
The grown-ups stand around watching.

A boy has been run over, another kid says.
Is that Simon lying on the pavement? He *was* walking in front of me.
The grown-ups stand around watching.

Mrs Bailey puts a blanket over him – but I can still see his blondie hair.
She looks at me but before she can turn quickly to the other grown-ups,
I can see she's scared.
'Send Mark away.'
What have I done wrong?

The grown-ups know what to do.
They send me away.

I run ahead alone.
Trying to find Simon.
I might not recognise him.
Pulling kids by their shoulders – no that's not him.
I speed up when I hear the ambulance siren.

'Simon's been run over.' Pete Williams said.
I run away, trying hard not to believe him.

How can Pete Williams tell who is lying there,
anyhow I saw *him* looking for *his* brother too.
Surely I would have recognised my own brother.

My teacher says 'Simon will be in his classroom'.
But he isn't, so she smiles and cuddles me, warm and soft.
'It's alright Mark, they call ambulances for sprained ankles these days.'

When he came into the classroom everyone stopped and looked.
He didn't have to tell me.
I said 'Simon's dead,' and he nodded, unable to speak. (Mark Purvis)

Mark (a GP trainer) needed to write about his little brother's death in a professional development situation to free himself from the way the unexplored memory inhibited his ability as a doctor to cope with child deaths. After he had read the poem to the group and we had discussed it, he wrote this:

I had never before in detail talked about what I was feeling at the time when Simon died. Now I have written about it I can and do talk about it.

Simon and I had had an argument about a fortnight before he died. I'd asked Simon not to walk with me to school. You know what it's like, an older brother wants to be with his own friends and doesn't want to be seen taking care of his little brother. Until I did this writing I felt guilty about Simon's death – that it was my fault for not allowing him to walk with me.

In the past my feeling about Simon's death disabled me for dealing with the death of child patients. Everyone finds it difficult; but for me they used to bring all sorts of things to the surface. I remember one child who died, I was totally disabled and unable to cope with consultations with the parents. I cried with them, and told them about Simon and that I was crying for him.

The writing has made me feel completely different about Simon's death, has made me deal with it in a different way. I can now see I wasn't responsible; though my mother still feels very guilty that she didn't drive him to school that day. The time was right for me to write.

I didn't know I was carrying so much guilt. Now I know I don't need to carry it. I will cope differently now when a child patient dies. (Mark Purvis)

Mark Purvis created the character of 9-year-old Mark in his poem. This enabled visiting that so painful scene, observing this bewildered little boy. The poem is so authentic: the voice of the child so consistently, movingly clear, drawing forth empathy in readers. Yet it is fiction, written by a senior and well respected doctor, not a 9-year-old. Can you imagine Mark being able to *talk* about Simon with anything like this power? Writing enabled a private quiet space for this memory to be revisited.

Poetic form is an enabling device (see Chapter 14), being at a remove and clearly not 'true' even when it tells of life events (as poems usually do, one way or another). Poetry draws on a range of devices – such as repetition ('grown-ups'), and cutting away unnecessary words, as in the taut final stanza – which enable deeply painful events to be communicated.

Film-makers use similar devices, such as holding the camera at child height. The reflective practitioner has to be able to reinhabit their own skin at that time in their lives. They also need to experiment with seeing the world through the eyes of another, a student perhaps. The funny thing is that one *can* re-experience an event, or experience another's vicariously. 'The past is [not] a foreign country. They do [not] do things differently there' (Hartley 1953, p. 1). Jean Cocteau vividly describes how he enabled himself to revisit his past; listen to him holding his own camera at child height:

I thought of going along the street from the Rue Blanche to number 45, closing my eyes and letting my right hand trail along the houses and the lamp-posts as I always used to do when I came back from school. The experience did not yield very much and I realised that at that time I was small and that now my hand was placed higher and no longer encountered the same shapes. I began the manoeuvre again.

Thanks to a mere difference of level, and through a phenomenon similar to that whereby a needle rubs against the grooves of a gramophone record, I obtained the music of memory and I discovered everything again: my cape, my leather satchel, the name of the friend who accompanied me, and the name of our teacher, some precise phrases I had said, the marbled cover of my notebook, the timbre of my grand-father's voice, the smell of his beard and the material of the dresses worn by my sister and mother, who were At Home on Tuesdays. (Cocteau [1930] 1968, p. 137)

Re-view

A film or story is a dynamic fresh look through the eyes of more than one actor. Replaying what 'actually' happened is impossible: any retelling is affected by the view of the teller. *Through-the-mirror* can enable exploration of viewpoints and possibilities:

> Stories are a lens through which I view the world to make sense of my experiences and those of my colleagues and patients. In writing some of these stories I am able to focus on complex issues that have previously appeared distorted by time and emotions. Metaphors shed light on subjects that I had been unaware of before, patterns stand out in ways that I had not hitherto understood. (Mark Purvis)

In the film *Blow-up*, a photographer notices figures in park undergrowth in a photograph's corner. These indistinct details, blown-up in size, using photographic development (before digital methods), prove to be a body and a gunman. No detail is potentially too trivial or insignificant to write, think and talk about. Vital life-changing details will go unnoticed, unless they are *blown-up* and focused upon.

Many helping professions facilitate others. Practitioners cannot support others if they are not aware and open themselves (Murray 1982). Bringing the personal into the professional can increase empathy between client and professional (Smyth 1996). Aesthetic experience (such as writing) can leap over the seeming gap between the personal and the professional self, and the seemingly impossible gap between the safe and rehearsed story and possibly dangerous retellings. This can only bring greater unity and wholeness of experience to the practitioner or educator, and greater empathy between them and client. Job satisfaction will increase, and work-related stress decrease. Work takes up the most and best hours of our days; personal satisfaction in it is vital, as Primo Levi says:

Perhaps the most accessible form of freedom, the most subjectively enjoyed, and the most useful to human society consists of being good at your job and therefore taking pleasure in doing it – I really believe that to live happily you have to have something to do, but it shouldn't be too easy, or else something to wish for, but not just any old wish; something there's a hope of achieving. (Levi 1988, p. 139)

The writing, the essential discussions and the writing of additional stories from different angles with the support of the group, is a creative explorative process in its own right: not a tool in professional reflection. Writing is the vehicle for the reflection: reflection *in* writing; course participants do not think and *then* write. Not only does writing enable the most appropriate reflection, but also, as a participant commented, 'one of the values of writing is that you can freeze the film: reflect upon one frame or a short series, then run the film backwards and review a previous scene in the light of reflections upon a later one. This would be difficult to do in talking: it wouldn't make sense; impossible to do during action.'

> I consider writing as a *method of inquiry*, a way of finding out about yourself and your topic. Although we usually think about writing as a mode of 'telling' about the social world, writing is not just a mopping-up activity … Writing is also a way of 'knowing' – a method of discovery and analysis. By writing in different ways, we discover new aspects of our topic and our relationship to it. Form and content are inseparable. (Richardson 2001, p. 34–5)

The psychologist Oliver Sacks studied people who were missing, or effectively missing, part of their brain, and the bizarre things this led to. In *The Man who Mistook his Wife for a Hat*, he studies 'Dr P.' who could see, but had lost 'visual perception, visual imagination and memory, the fundamental powers of visual representation … insofar as they pertained to the personal, the familiar, the concrete'. Sacks concludes:

> Our mental processes, which constitute our being and life, are not just abstract and mechanical, but personal as well – and as such involve not just classifying and categorising, but continual judging and feeling also. If this is missing, we become computer-like, as Dr P. was. And by the same token, if we delete feeling and judging, the personal, from the cognitive sciences, we reduce *them* to something as defective as Dr P. – and we reduce *our* apprehension of the concrete and real … Our cognitive sciences are themselves suffering from an agnosia essentially similar to Dr P.'s. Dr P. may therefore serve as a warning and parable – of what happens to a science which eschews the judgmental, the particular, the personal, and becomes entirely abstract and computational. (Sacks 1985, p. 19)

Reflective practice can learn from Sacks's 'warning and parable', and be open to as much of ourselves as is possible. A reflective practice suffering from agnosia will not get us terribly far.

Effective reflective practice encourages understanding and interpretation of principles, justifications and meanings (Morrison 1996). It involves interrogating both our *explicit* knowledge, such as known and quantifiable evidence-based knowledge, and *implicit* knowledge – 'a collection of information, intuitions and interpretation' (Epstein 1999, p. 834) based on experience and prior knowledge (for further analysis of types of knowledge, see Belenky et al. 1997; Eraut 1994). Implicit knowledge is tried and tested, gained initially from experience, observation, or study. Intimately known, its appropriate application is intuitive. This does not necessarily mean it is right, any more than knowledge gained from randomised control trial research (explicit).

Such re-viewing of knowledge and experience can lead practitioners to perceive a need for change. One of my students stated: 'This is not an academic module, but an assertiveness training course'. Asserting yourself inevitably involves challenging social structures.

One of the greatest benefits to a student in a learning situation, or a client with a practitioner, is the sense of their relatedness to the professional: that they are interested, involved, and care. In medicine this has been called the *placebo effect* of the physician as *healer*: 'the attitude of the doctor can make an appreciable difference to the psychological response of the patient who feels the need to be understood and listened to empathically' (Dixon et al. 1999, p. 310). To give clients confidence in us as professionals, we have to be secure and happy enough ourselves in our roles, and not anxious or inhibited.

How can that happen in overworked, overstressed professions, getting less appreciated daily? One of the ways of being an empathetic, effective practitioner is to be reflexive as well as reflective.

Making sense of experience

Life does not really have a beginning, middle and end (Sartre [1938] 1963): that is the prerogative of literature, of stories of experience. Writing and telling our stories is not straightforward; but if we can have sufficient faith in ourselves, trust in the process, and respectful unconditional positive regard (Rogers 1969) for clients and colleagues to create a beginning, the rest might well follow.

A closely observed event (Wordsworth's 'spot of time'), written about, reflected upon, discussed critically and re-explored through further writings stands metonymically for the whole of that professional's practice. Stories and poems are slices, metonymically revealing the whole of life (for explanation of metonym see About This Book). Here is a reflective practice group evaluation:

> a different way of seeing: many insights, many views
> a sense of wonder at the creativity of so many people I had seen
> only as professional colleagues
>
> I am challenged to see others I meet with new eyes.
> a different way of hearing: many voices, many themes
> I have been moved by the quality of our listening and by the careful
> and gentle hearing of my own emerging voice.
>
> a different way of being: many persons, an experience shared.
> I have found a sense of integration in allowing the creative part of
> myself which I had stifled to energise my life and work.
> there is empowerment for deeper living in the shared silence,
> laughter and tears. (Sheena)

The camera focuses upon a drained doctor at the end of a long week. She reaches into her lowest desk drawer, taking out something which will enable her to cope, to continue to see her profession as growing and worthwhile. It is not a bottle, hypodermic syringe, or pills, but a pad of yellow paper and a pen. She starts to write …

 Read to learn

Bulpitt, H. and Martin, P.J. (2005) Learning about reflection from the student, *Active Learning in Higher Education*, **6**(3), 207–17.

Munno, A. (2006) A complaint which changed my practice, *British Medical Journal*, **332**, 1092.

Osterman, K.F. and Kottkamp, R.B. (2004) *RP for Educators*. 2nd edn. Thousand Oaks, CA: Corwin Press.

 Write to learn

Each chapter ends with *Write to learn*. For straightforward advice, sufficient for the exercises below, see *Write to learn* in Chapter 1, and see Chapter 6 for more advice. Each writing can be shared fruitfully with a group or confidential trusted other, if this seems appropriate once the writer has read and reflected on it first.

Exercise 2.1 The story of your work

1. If your work were a book, film, play or radio programme what would it be? A romantic, detective or fantasy novel, diary, roadmap or atlas, telephone directory, DIY manual, *Desert Island Discs*, reality television show, *Strictly Come Dancing* (*Dancing with the Stars*)? ...
2. Describe it.
3. Reread with positive imaginative insight, add or alter if you wish.

Exercise 2.2 The film of your life

1. Write the title of the film of your life (or work).
2. Write the advertising blurb.
3. Write the cast list.
4. Choose a 'character' from this list, write their name on a fresh sheet and fill the page about them.
5. Choose another 'character' to do the same with, if you wish.
6. In this film, which actor will play 'you'?
7. Where will be the shoot location (you can choose anywhere)?
8. Tell the story of one of the scenes in detail.
9. Write the ending of the film (optional).
10. Reread to yourself with attention, alter and add as you wish.

Exercise 2.3 A spot of time

There are in our existence spots of time / ... whence ... our minds
Are nourished and invisibly repaired; / ... Such moments
Are scattered everywhere. (William Wordsworth, from *The Prelude*)

1. Jot down a very quick list of occasions when you felt nourished, content, affirmed.
2. Choose one, write about it with as much detail as you can remember.
3. Give it a title as if it were a film; write the brief paragraph of film advertising blurb.
4. Read it back to yourself with care, adding or altering positively.
5. Write about another one if you have time.

CHAPTER 3

PRINCIPLES OF REFLECTIVE PRACTICE

Chapter 3 discusses ethical principles and describes a range of possible educational models, explaining why educators need clarity as to the model used, and why *through-the-mirror* reflective writing is effective. It examines forgiveness, knotty issues around ethics and patients, students or clients, and the risk involved in reflection and reflexivity which can partly be deflected by tutors creating safe enough educational environments.

> We teach and write to become what and who we are ... The function [of pedagogy] is to invent the conditions of invention. (Hwu 1998, p. 37)

> A disciple became frustrated at never being taught anything, and never knowing how long meditation would last. The master always rang a bell: sometimes after five minutes, sometimes five hours. The disciple became so infuriated that one day she grabbed and rang the bell when *she* wanted meditation to end. The master bowed to her. She had unwittingly learned what she had needed to learn. (Ancient Zen story)

Reflective practice and reflexivity, approaches which support critique of any aspect of professional life, are founded upon strong coherent ethical principles. They are undertaken by practitioners in moral roles, relying on the quality of ethical attitude and actions. This chapter explains these, and examines the educational principles underlying reflective practice. An understanding of the foundation principles of any course or teaching and learning situation is essential: muddles in the models will lead to dissatisfied non-learning students. This chapter also addresses forgiveness, safety and risk, and ethical attitudes to clients, patients and students.

Ethical principles

The imaginative faculty, which enables writers to enquire into the world, their own experience, and the possible experience of others, is both wise and fundamentally trustworthy. Insight and support are gained by writing if the self is respected, the processes of writing trusted, and reliable confidential readers carefully chosen. *Through-the-mirror* writing works when enquirers take full responsibility for all their actions, including writing and sharing. It is essentially playful and straightforward: the greatest wisdom or inspiration is the simplest. It might seem paradoxical to say taking responsibility can be playful. Most of the values underlying this approach can seem paradoxical: their power lies therein. These values are:

Trust in the processes of our practice (in this case, writing): doubt hinders action. *Through-the-mirror* writing can be trusted to lead to personal insight. Only by trusting our writing hands can we write what needs to be explored and expressed. We cannot write wrongly about our own experience, despite initial hesitance we are the world's best authority on it. This writing takes free-rein: it is in letting go that we find our direction.

Self-respect for our beliefs, actions, feelings, values, identity, is respect for our own integrity. *Through-the-mirror* writing can give confidence we have something vital to express, and can do it well. This is enhanced by knowing it is only for us to read, at least initially: there is no teacher-reader with a red pen. We therefore communicate respectfully with ourselves, tackling inevitable fears, hesitations, and the voice of destructive inner critics. With the certainty gained from learning to respect ourselves, we can be creatively uncertain where we are going.

Responsibility. We are fully responsible for everything we write and our response to it (as we are for all our actions). We have full authority over our writing at every stage, including rereading to ourselves and possibly sharing with a confidential trusted reader. Writing fiction can offer significant insight (for example, Munno 2006; see also Chapter 2), exploring how the situation might have been, or perceived by others: fiction thus gives access to the truth. It is in taking full responsibility for our actions that we gain freedom to understand, explore and experiment with inspirational playful creativity.

Generosity. We willingly give energy, time and commitment to our own personal and professional development through writing in a focused spirit of enquiry. This giving enables us to receive inspiration and experience from others, and from our own enhanced self-understanding.

Positive regard. We write about family and friends, colleagues and students, clients, patients or members of the public. Any feeling can be explored within the privacy of writing, both for cathartic release and in order to understand how and why what happened, and discover appropriate ways to act in the future. This feeling, rather than being directed towards the individuals, is safely contained within the reflective process: unconditional positive regard (Rogers 1969) can be maintained. Expressing and exploring negative memories, thoughts and feelings can facilitate positive experience; celebrating positive ones can be life enhancing.

Reflection and reflexivity: educational processes

Reflective practice is an educative process. Tutors and students relate to each other within particular paradigms or teaching and learning models, whether they are aware of it or not. A range of such models is examined and critiqued below. An understanding of the foundation principles of any course or teaching and learning situation is essential. If *through-the-mirror* methods are used within a wider course, the principles must be consonant.

Tutor–student relationships are addressed. At times the educational process is supported either individually or in a group. At times the practitioner reflects alone in their journal. The contexts in which teaching and learning take place and some ways in which this can be understood and handled are discussed.

Alice did not stop to study her reflection before she went through the looking-glass. Had she done so her reflection would have been a back-to-front image of her accustomed self. Having crawled right through the glass she encountered a world where everything 'was as different as possible' (Carroll [1865] 1954, p. 122). She learned a great deal from the way familiar things and situations being so different ensured she could not take anything for granted. For example, when she wanted to reach an attractive small hill, she bumped into the house again every time. She learned to walk away from anything she wanted to reach, trusting looking-glass methods to get her there (pp. 132–6).

Reflection and reflexivity critique anything taken for granted. We need to walk away from things, to gain perspective. Why? how? what? who? where? and when? need to be asked of everything, constantly. Alice had to ask these questions because nothing worked as she expected; professionals have to push themselves into this state of incredulity.

Through-the-mirror education requires self-respect in both learners and tutors; willingness and ability to work either autonomously or in collaboration, with whomever, as appropriate; and the confidence to ask questions which might lead anywhere. It tends towards the aesthetic rather than the purely functional. The very questioning playfulness, rooted in uncertainty as to where the process will lead, is essentially non-goal-directed (however valuable outcomes might be). Physical (rather than purely cognitive), passionate (rather than purely intellectual), context bound (rather than goal driven), this artistic process requires flair, style and intuition. It is aesthetic; learners and tutors appreciate and explore the nuances in people's sense of themselves, their environment and experience. Winter has defined the imagination and the aesthetic in this context as: 'a universal capacity for the creative interpretation and representation of human experience' (Winter et al. 1999, p. 199).

We are all culture bound – physically, socially, psychologically and spiritually. We might change that culture, but can never make ourselves culture free. Nor can we be fully uncertain, playful or questioning – our lives would fall apart. But we can do a great deal in that direction: in a game of *what if* ...

This section looks at (a) the characters within the teaching and learning situation – the relationship between teacher and learner; and (b) the place in which they are working – the context. It then examines the educational situation at a *meta* level; that is, some of the assumptions both teachers and learners make about the processes in which they are engaged: the plot or storyline of education, which is being constructed with a certain set of characters in a particular place.

Educational relationships

> The role of the teacher is not to tell others what to do, not to issue edicts, nor to assist in the constitution of prophesies, promises, injunctions and programs. The task of the teacher is not to affirm prevailing general politics of teaching but to question critically the self-evident, disturb the habitual, dissipate the familiar and accepted, making the strange familiar and the familiar strange ... The classroom is therefore a place of invention rather than reproduction. (Hwu 1998, p. 33)

Carl Rogers maintains the *relationship* ensures the success or failure of teaching and learning situations:

> The initiation of such learning rests not upon the teaching skills of the leader, not upon scholarly knowledge of the field, not upon curricular planning, not upon use of audiovisual aids, not upon the programmed learning used, not upon lectures and presentations, not upon an abundance of books, though each of these might at one time or another be utilised as an important resource. No, the facilitation of significant learning rests upon certain attitudinal qualities that exist in the personal relationship between the facilitator and the learner. (Rogers 1969, p. 153)

This opinion was borne out by a group of community nurses in training for reflective practitioner facilitation. One said 'the person of the teacher is the vehicle' for the learning, and another that the 'being' of the tutor enables successful teaching. The group had told each other, in pairs, about significant teaching and learning situations in their lives: both effective and dreadful. They animatedly agreed the underlying principles of good teaching are when the tutor:

- is able to create a relationship with each student which feels 'special' even when it is known to be one-way, that is, the student knows the tutor does not feel specially about any particular student
- 'gives of themselves', not just taking on the 'role' of tutor, but being a whole person
- engenders confidence and respect
- wishes to challenge both students and themselves as tutor, at the same time as valuing, being respectful of, being patient with, and offering praise to the students: an unconditional positive regard
- makes the learning pleasurable, clear and significant; to do this they must love their subject.

The group decided destructive teaching qualities were when the tutor:

- has no understanding of or interest in the student
- bullies, humiliates or even abuses the student with personal intrusions, generally wields power negatively
- has a set, inflexible agenda, a mission with no regard of the needs of the student
- lacks confidence in the student as a person
- transfers their own anxiety onto the student.

These lists, created by eight nurses in half an hour, demonstrate how effective teaching is known intuitively from bad, transcending cognitive understanding or articulation of methodological models. The best teachers and practitioners are reflexive and reflective, qualities enhanced and fostered by education.

An educational environment is also vitally important, as is a teacher–student relationship of trust, respect, openness, confidence and security, a *good-enough* relationship: every tutor is human. With sound foundations, inevitable tutor errors and misjudgements are more forgivable and might even prove a learning situation. Peter Abbs laid greater emphasis on students' roles than on tutors' while stressing identical principles:

> Education is not primarily concerned with the accumulation of facts and techniques but rather with the expression and clarification of individual experience. The centre of education resides in the individual. If we are to achieve a genuinely human education we must return again and again to the person before us, the child, the adolescent, the adult, the individual who is ready, however

dimly and in need of however much support, to adventure both further out into his experience and further into it, who is ready, in some part of himself, to risk himself in order to become more than he now is. The teacher, the tutor can provide the conditions and the support for such a journey – but the journey itself can only be made by the assenting and autonomous individual. (Abbs 1974, p. 5)

In an in-service reflexive session, Master's (Medical Science) tutors each drew how we viewed our role as educators, including: a candle, educator lighting the darkness; map and compass, teacher as guide through rough places; a church, initiating others into the holy of holies; a gardener watering a tree, the educator as *enlightened guide* nurtures, supports and initiates the weaker other. My own drawing had my outstretched arms inviting everyone to an exciting party. Alan Bleakley (see also 2000a) adds:

I have always imagined my own teaching in terms of contemporary jazz (post-bop): opening theme with chorus – long improvisation – chorus – coda. I like the idea of strange harmonies, dissonances combined with resonances, melodies that lose themselves in improvisation but are echoed throughout, and then restated at the end of the piece. (Personal communication)

Educational models

Educators are role models (often unwittingly). The above lists show students do not forget model best and worst teachers, possibly spending professional lives unconsciously emulating or avoiding these vital figures. My best teacher was humorous, straightforward, caring but not motherly: a biologist who gave us an impassioned account of earthworms copulating under the moon. My worst teacher, a chalk and talk didact, made a fascinating subject boring with her flat instructive tone: we dared hardly move, cough or hiccup, let alone ask a question. I still think historical romances must be turgid, as she recommended them to widen our understanding. The influence of those two is probably clearly discernable in this book.

I now turn to the terrain we explore together. A country area with no paths can appear a confusion of walls, sheep-tracks and tors. The view from a helicopter would seem to make more sense: walls making comprehensible gated fields, giving clarity to a whole walk. Adult education has been likened to 'moorland', rather than 'field' (Usher et al. 1997). The helicopter view offered by a heuristic model, meta-understanding of the situation, can be useful here. Stephen Rowland (1999, 2000) has suggested that under all circumstances both tutor and students might understand their resources for learning as a triangle of three areas, as in Figure 3.1.

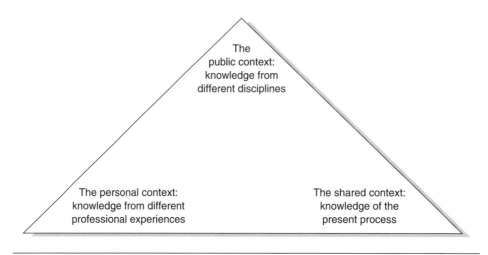

Figure 3.1   Resources for learning (adapted from Rowland 2000, p. 61)

The *public area of knowledge* is, in principle, open to everyone through public texts: government documents, professional or academic publications. Interpretations may vary; if an area is disputed, the text can be referred to as arbiter. Reflective practice must be embedded within this public arena, to prevent it being merely personal confession.

The *personal area of knowledge* is private, known only to individuals. Much reflective practice material belongs in this arena. Knowledge of situations, people, thoughts and feelings involved, belong in individuals' minds. The process of examining this area might be the reflective one of laying any aspect of the situation open to question; or it may be reflexive: questioning one's own impulses, attitudes, assumptions. The individual is the authority.

The *shared area of knowledge* is the 'process of the group (or pair)'s work'. Individuals have personal private stories of their lives (personal area of knowledge). In association with others a shared set of stories, assumptions, principles and so on is created. All remember how they struggled to grasp the difference between reflection and reflexivity; or when Sue shouted at Bob for assuming she was late because of childcare. They have tacitly understood group methods, such as sitting in silence reflecting deeply when appropriate rather than scrambling for immediate answers. This knowledge and understanding is available only to participants: and no member has more information or rights over it than another.

The *shared* area is often missed for reflexive consideration. Yet addressing it, in supervision or group, can be invaluable. People can only learn when they are confident, respected and valued, and to an extent control the process of learning. Exposing the educational process (including tutor's role) to scrutiny can enable participants to take a degree of control: say what they want and do not want. Tutors can act upon such effective feedback, and adapt methods or syllabi according to students' needs and wants.

The focus on *shared*, *personal* or *public* areas will vary. Reflective practice focus is often *personal*, though *public* material develops, extends and critiques ideas, ensuring participants' burgeoning understandings are embedded in wider social, professional and political spheres. My reflective practice students pursued knowledge or theory gaps they encountered, such as about ethics. A reflexive examination of the *shared domain*, the educative process undertaken with the tutor (whether group or one to one) models any teaching and learning process.

Aware tutors can harness and drive these three contexts to their own and students' advantage. Students can use them to broaden their awareness within, and response to, learning situations. Awareness of different ways of functioning within the three contexts can further enhance understanding and ability to maximise teaching and learning efficacy and interest. Within *public* contexts, *reason* comes to the fore. Within *shared* and *personal* contexts, actions, thoughts and feelings are appropriate for consideration. Examining what was done, thought and felt about a specific situation helps explore dark corners in personal professional experience, shared group experiences, and in the political situations in which we work. 'We understand through feeling' (Shem 2002, p. 935). 'Reflective practice is the public recognition and interrogation of the *effects* of *affect* within action' [emphasis in original] (Usher et al. 1997, p. 220).

Unmuddling educational models

Any involvement in education as teacher or learner can only be undertaken from within a particular approach or understanding of the processes. Sometimes people are aware of their own image, metaphor or model of education; sometimes they accept a 'given' model without knowing what it is. In order to be involved in an effective, consistent educational process, tutors and students need to be aware of the model used.

Chalk and talk

A traditional model, recognisable from schooling and much university education, is the banking (Freire 1972), transfer, moulding theory (Fox 1983), or didactic model (Rowland 1999). Teachers who know the answers attempt to funnel them directly into the heads of students who do not know. Tutors retain control; learners are not respected, nor expected to contribute creative ideas. A hierarchically determined system of knowledge and social status is reinforced; the impact and body of knowledge is predetermined.

Rocky path

This has been called the 'exploratory model' (Rowland 1993), or *fofo* way of teaching (f *** off and find out):

> The broad objectives of the work were discussed with the [students] but then they were put in a position of finding their own solutions. (Department of Education and Science 1978, para. 3)

The student is respected (possibly) and given autonomy, but probably insufficient guidance and support; the tutor is not primarily involved in the processes of learning.

Hey presto

We live, teach and learn in a consumer culture with a market orientation in which people, practitioners included, are constantly bombarded with new practices and new ways of being. A time of individuation: difference appears to be celebrated, yet conformity is fostered. We can choose to change and mould our lives (even our bodies) in ways never before possible: to fashion new identities for ourselves. Outward signs (packaging) are important: what things are called, what they look like. Market place metaphors mean we can buy 'care', even 'love', according to palliative care advertisements as I write. 'Trust' is used of those who hold the purse strings. This has had a huge impact upon education. Organisations 'deliver' courses on the assumption that the commodity bought will directly improve their service, as if it were fertiliser.

Competencies, skills and fully developed reflective abilities are needed by practitioners. But in this system they are seen as products or commodities, *things* like bricks or vitamin tablets to be bought with education currency without primary attention being paid to fundamental educational *processes* which enable their development, such as tutor–student relationships and the learning environment (see below).

Teachers are assessed on the *value* they offer consumers. The *objects* students consume are all too often *signs*, communicating social position and worth. *Who I am seen to be* and *What I can get as a result of this course* (for example, a better job) have become more important than the innate value of intellectual enquiry.

Giving reflective practice students set pro formas, lists of prompts, questions or areas will stultify, make for passivity and lack of respect. Professionals need to ask and attempt to answer their own questions, otherwise practice is moulded towards the system's wants and needs.

Testing and checking up whether students have acquired required competencies further endorses this subordinate sense. 'I get the students to ...' manipulates students in a semblance of 'choice'; they only have to paint the right bits the right colours, join up the dots. The 'shopkeeper' delivering the 'package' gains a neat pile of pigeon-hole-sized submissions with predetermined areas accounted for: evidence this, this and this has been 'learned' – products which can then be consumed by both practitioner and assessor. It matters not that this is solely a paper exercise as there is no continuity between course and practice, no one to see practice has changed or developed; what matters is the product, that the neatly ticked boxes look right. This has been called 'surface learning' (Rust 2002).

Our *problems* cannot be *solved*, however many *problem-solving* exercises we undertake. Problems, issues, relationships can all be aired and examined constructively, but to see the process as a straight line from *identification of need* to *problem solved* is effectively to prevent constructive learning. Learning is innately complex.

The values basis of this functional competence model is technical-rational, utilitarian and instrumental. Students are short-changed and manipulated. A full educational process has to be undergone, however painful and expensive. There are no short cuts, no prestidigitation. But this next model, for all its wonderful features, is not The Answer either, for there is no Right Answer.

Path to freedom

Carl Rogers described *personal* liberation in education and psychotherapy (1969). Paolo Freire developed a model of effective education called *problem posing* – a liberating *political* process (1972) (it must be remembered that Freire was working in a politically revolutionary situation in the 1960s):

> [In] authentic reflection men (*sic*) ... begin to single out elements from their 'background awarenesses' and to reflect upon them. These elements are now objects of men's consideration, and, as such, objects of their action and cognition ... The banking method emphasizes permanence and becomes reactionary; problem-posing education – which accepts neither a 'well-behaved' present nor a pre-determined future – roots itself in the dynamic present and becomes revolutionary. (Freire 1972, pp. 35–7)

My students echoed this, calling their course 'consciousness raising'. Such reflective practice can lead to significant change, both to individuals and the organisation upon which they might act. Freire was right that education should be rooted in the present, and should pose problems about our lives here and now: this is the stuff of reflective practice.

Effective reflective practice is critically active and dynamic in a wide sphere. Practitioners question and problematise themselves, their roles and those in authority over them, their political, social and professional situations. They cannot again uncritically accept a situation, nor just moan about it. Reflective practice encourages *action*, and that means more than keeping the fridge in order so the wrong injection is never given again, but questioning appropriate aspects of the system. One participant during her very first 'six-minute' writing realised she had to change her job. She got one more suitable, but also one in which she could and did implement significant change for her staff.

Marx recommended a 'relentless criticism of all existing conditions, relentless in the sense that the criticism is not afraid of its own findings and just as little afraid of conflict with the powers that be' (1962, p. 212). Carr and Kemmis (1986) with their theory of critical social science and *praxis* of *action research* drew upon Marx and Freire. Based on the philosopher Habermas's writing, this is not personal understanding developed by such as Rogers in therapy or psychoanalysis, but political-social understanding (critical theory):

> The purpose of critique then is to provide a form of therapeutic self-knowledge which will liberate individuals from the irrational compulsions of their individual history through a process of critical self-reflection ... Critique is aimed at revealing to individuals how their beliefs and attitudes may be ideological illusions that help to preserve a social order which is alien to their collective experience and needs. By demonstrating how ideological forces generate erroneous self-understandings, ideology critique aims to reveal their deceptive nature and so strip them of their power ... Action research is simply a form of self-reflective inquiry undertaken by participants in social situations in order to improve the rationality and justice of their own practice, their understanding of these practices, and the situations in which these practices are carried out. (Carr and Kemmis 1986, pp. 138–9, 162)

Action research, as its name implies, is more research based than reflective practice, with a 'self-reflective spiral of cycles of planning, acting, observing and reflecting' (Carr and Kemmis 1986, p. 165), but it does offer a model for reflective practice.

So what is the problem? It seems an unwarranted certainty to consider that the 'compulsions of [participants'] individual history' *before* they begin on a 'process of critical self-reflection' are any more 'irrational' than those they will be enabled to arrive at *after* the process. It could also be said that *all* 'beliefs and attitudes may be ideological illusions that help to preserve a social order which is alien to their collective experience and needs', *however* they are acquired – through reflective practice or otherwise.

Freire was certain, in the political sphere, Carl Rogers in the personal (see below), and Carr and Kemmis in both, that progress is taking place towards a particular goal of personal or political productive change and development. This model asserts that reflective practice (or critical action research) automatically brings people from ignorance to knowledge, from political passivity to effective action. But this certainty is based on nothing more than an assumption that a greater understanding of ourselves or the world will make things better. In the personal sphere this model asserts that these can be *self-actualising* processes in which each practitioner will find the *real me*, the *me* they were intended to be.

The very notion of *me* is problematic, however: I am not a static entity, but in the process of being created every day as social and political forces impact upon me; I am a story I tell and retell every day, with fresh facets and new viewpoints each time. I am not so much a thing – static in shape, form and time – but more a verb – not *me* but *to me*.

Reflective practice has, contrariwise to the *path to freedom* model, been accused of encouraging practitioners to accept their lot, however bad: a form of quietism. People can only *take* power, give it to themselves; they cannot be 'empowered' or 'given a voice' by a more powerful other (tutor, for example). Usher adds the weight of his voice to this argument:

> We become active knowing subjects but now we subjectify ourselves rather than being subjected by others. We think we have mastered the power that imposes itself from 'outside' only to find that it is now 'inside'. We have the power, indeed the obligation, to exercise our 'freedom' but we are not thereby empowered to affect our social and political environment. (Usher et al. 1997, p. 87)

Practitioners can become trapped in controlling themselves to work according to the wants and needs of the system, rather than responding to exterior control. Power is a slippery, omnipresent thing, and does not necessarily do what it *appears* to do. Professionals, tutors and curriculum designers have to be sensitive to undercurrents and meta-levels in education: 'the most effective forms of power are those which are not recognised as powerful but as enabling or "em-powering" ... The drive for emancipation may itself become oppressive' (Usher et al. 1997, pp. 87, 190). And:

> Practices of 'freedom' or 'authenticity', or search for a 'real' self are in fact rule-bound examples of governance of self by self through self-surveillance. While advertised as a route to liberty or autonomy, [they] offer strictly coded forms of self-governance and regulation. (Bleakley 2000a, p. 406)

Carr called it 'essentially an enlightenment project' (1995, p. 121); such a project assumes a knowledge of what *rationality* is: we do not have this knowledge. The very notion of *enlightenment* maintains a confidence that the 'light' I am in now is any better than the 'dark' I was in previously, and that what my tutors tell me is 'light' is 'light' indeed for me. What is wrong with the dark anyway?

Reflective practice education is constant reflexive self-examination: actions, thoughts, feelings, motives, assumptions. In order to be critical of my own personal, social and political situation I have to be able to stand outside it to some extent. Of course I cannot do this fully, whatever contortions I attempt. No one can critique one paradigm while within it: no sailor can propel a yacht by blowing into the sails. We all wear culturally tinted lenses through which we view the world: emerald spectacles cannot be removed to see the world, our actions, and those of others as *they really are*. Alice was the only one who managed fully effective reflexivity and critical emancipation: by crawling right through the looking-glass and experiencing herself and her world from the other side – not an action we can imitate.

No tutor (facilitator or supervisor) can guide anyone else towards their own emancipation, no one can have this wisdom or power; nor can it be an aspect of the curriculum. There can be no specific way of working (however wonderful reflective practice may be) which supports another to 'free' themselves from their social, political and psychological constraints. Educative reflective practice can yet lead to greater agency, responsibility, self-understanding and self-confidence.

Through the mirror

The previous models made assumptions which, I have suggested, we need to shed, missed out vital elements which need including, and presuppose a level of unfacilitative certainty. Effective education is based upon both tutor and learner being able to make as many aspects as they can of their situation, and themselves – strange and different – in order to study them.

In this approach learners are encouraged to be as reflexively aware and questioning as possible of social, political and psychological positions, as well as their environment. In this dynamic state, things will appear to be strange, back to front, and to operate in unusual ways: they should do so. A student called it 'making the ordinary extraordinary'. It is this very strange-seemingness or extraordinariness which will enable students to formulate their own questions about the situations in which they find themselves (reflective), and the self they find there (reflexive). These questions are almost bound to be different from the ones they thought they might ask. Spirited enquiry leads to specific, usefully appropriate and meaningful questioning. Interim answers will appear, but as markers along the way rather than finishing posts.

Learners are supported to find ways of discovering what they feel they need to know, from literature, from knowledgeable others whether other students or external authorities, from tutors. This can be as widely understood as the students wish – popular culture, as well as literature, carries vital data.

Many elements of previous models come into play eclectically in *through-the-mirror* learning. There is no comfortable beginning, middle and end, and the *characters* and *places* are not clearly delineated and set. Individuals take on varied roles: tutor as didactic teacher at one point, and equal friend along the way at another; a colleague may be the enemy at one time and fascinating authority at another. Students may think they are well on the way to understanding something, and then realise they have to stand one step back and view the matter from a fresh standpoint and begin all over again with a new set of questions.

Student and tutor are both engaged in a process, and their roles are more equal than in the other models. Knowledge and understanding are seen as something they are constructing together according to the wants and needs of the student. Their relationship and their roles will constantly be under reflexive review.

Ethics and patients, students or clients

Reflective practice raises and airs significant ethical considerations concerning practitioners, the populations with whom they practice, and their organisation. Practitioners may become unexpectedly emotional (for example, angry or distressed), or find unexpected issues to sort out. 'This really made me realise the learner is not in control when exploring new ideas' (John, Master's student). Inexperienced facilitators may find students' reflections may unexpectedly raise issues or emotions of their own. Hargreaves examined the ethics of requiring nurses to undertake this activity (1997; see also Chapters 7 and 8). Ghaye (2007) quotes an angry student nurse:

> My feelings are private – yet I am expected to frame them in prose and submit them to my university. I don't know my lecturers or personal tutor intimately. What right has anyone to ask for such personal information, let alone ask that it be graded by a faceless lecturer? As nurses we respect patients' rights not to disclose their personal feelings. Yet no such right is afforded to students. (Sinclair-Penwarden 2006, p. 12)

Experienced and knowledgeable facilitation and appropriate levels of assessment will enable students and practitioners to find reflection and reflexivity useful to themselves rather than intrusion by 'faceless' examiners, as above (see also Chapters 7 and 8).

Confidential material about the population with whom reflective practitioners work is exposed even when names and details are altered. Practitioners do all in their power to discuss cases with respect. Sometimes the need to release feelings overtakes: a group of doctors falling about with hilarity about a dropped corpse being unpickupable in snow and ice. No disrespect was intended, but the situation was too horrific to be countenanced until some emotion had been released. I understand paramedics and police officers respond in similar ways. Specific issues need to be addressed rather than generalities. As a user of services myself, I would rather think I was discussed among colleagues – in whatever way was appropriate – than feel I was treated merely as a case by an unreflective practitioner.

Reflective practice appropriately addresses ethical practice. Anne Hudson Jones describes how narratives of practice are used to teach 'narrative ethics', offering 'richer ethical discourse for all' (1998, p. 223). Ron Carson says both studying one's own stories and reading literature are ideal ways of studying and maintaining ethical practice: 'literature shapes sensibility by giving form to feelings and by revealing the narrative structure of experiences of love, loss, loyalty and the like' (1994, p. 238). Reflective journals, and discussions, have sensitively and carefully supported student palliative care nurses:

> The diary sessions are in-depth critical discussions and comparisons of clinical situations where logical and rigorous analysis of moral and ethical concepts takes place. Through this analytical process, assumptions made by health care professionals, patients and relatives are uncovered and examined. This leads to the revelation of attitudes, stereotyping, prejudices, preconceptions, philosophical ethics, frames of references, cultural influences, and the nurse's predisposition to act in a certain way: 'reflecting on clinical situations made me aware of my beliefs … and the assumptions I make … the uniqueness of people and their rights'. (Durgahee 1997, p. 143)

This fully rounded reflective process involves emotional responses and synthetic functions, not restricted to the 'logical and rigorous'. Ethical dilemmas may arise concerning a colleague's faulty practice: should it be reported? What does the confidentiality of reflective practice mean? (See Cutcliffe et al. 1998.) What would I have done had my teacher-student (Chapter 2) not said her school was dealing with the teacher's sexual relationship with a pupil? There can be no rules: careful one-to-one discussion is the starting point.

Practitioners bring their whole selves to reflective practice; and that whole person has vulnerabilities. Reflective practice does not shy away from emotional realisation of ethical problems.

Aspects of therapeutic theory and practice are therefore relevant to *through-the-mirror* work. Jane Abercrombie (1993), an academic biologist, brought therapeutic group work principles into higher education teaching. A basic tenet of Carl Rogers (1969) is respect and 'unconditional regard' for the student (see also Chapter 9).

Reflective practice facilitators are not therapists. An understanding of therapeutic ways of working can, however, offer empathetic and facilitative understanding, and greater confidence in handling emotive situations. Therapeutic needs may arise through reflective processes, for which appropriate outside support may be sought. Sutton et al. (2007) report students feeling they had been required 'to splurge our guts' (p. 396) unsupported (see also Chapter 7). Pre-service students are considered by some to uncover material needing therapeutic support. Young students (for example, undergraduates) in my experience tend to tumble in and out of being emotional in reflective practice; I have not experienced them as any more vulnerable, but yet have known extremely experienced doctors break down and need support. I have, though, noticed undergraduates making definite statements about themselves and each other; 'I'm the sort of person who ...', 'that's just like you, you always ... '. Young adults are finding out who they are, and the location of their personal boundaries.

Checks and balances in facilitation can help prevent distress. Facilitators need supervisors/mentors or co-peer mentors (see Chapter 11). Co-facilitating group sessions can enable one to be tutoring while the other observes, reporting back to co-facilitator in after session debriefing. Periods of group reflexivity and an awareness of Rowland's 'shared context' (2000, see below) is invaluable. The group can be facilitated to take responsibility for its own processes, to observe if a member needs extra support or to be handled sensitively and will alert the facilitator if necessary. Each participant has responsibility for sharing distress or anxiety before it becomes too big for the group to handle.

Clear and agreed ground rules of boundaries and confidentiality help (see Chapter 9). Ethical and power issues need addressing in supervision, particularly if the supervisor is also in a position of authority over the practitioner, who may be justifiably cautious about disclosure. Differing assumptions concerning reflective practice and supervision cloud the area. Fowler and Chevannes stress 'there are potential disadvantages in making the assumption that reflective practice should be an integral part of all forms of clinical supervision' (1998, p. 379). Marrow et al., however, write of effective supervision, where the sister of a busy accident and emergency unit offered effective supervision to her staff focusing on reflective diaries, which she read (1997). And Judy Hildebrand describes deeply reflective and reflexive supervision of family therapist trainees (1995).

Forgiveness

Reflective practice can enable a shift in attitude to events, relationships and values in professional life, whether institutional or relative to clients. Forgiving others and oneself can be an element. A connectedness with ourselves, each other and our world tends to have been lost in obsession with evaluation based upon measurement, external success and appearance, and a belief that people can shape their world by making conscious plans. Connectedness has been replaced by anxiety around relationships, and a fear of each other evidenced by such phenomena as road rage.

Mercy has been marginalised as soppy and/or religious. Blake's description of mercy as having a 'human heart' (1958, p. 33) and Portia's powerful plea (Shakespeare's *Merchant of Venice*) are often forgotten. 'Given this situation it is no wonder that people are flocking to various mental health practitioners with chronic guilt, shame, resentment, disease, and feelings of estrangement' (Rowe and Halling 1998, p. 227). The goddess Athene says of forgiveness:

> Let your rage pass into understanding
> As into the coloured clouds of a sunset,
> Promising a fair tomorrow.
> Do not let it fall
> As a rain of sterility and anguish. (Aeschylus 1999, p. 184)

The inability to forgive binds people to negative memories, thoughts and feelings and to vain hopes for the future (see also Rowe et al. 1989). Practitioners find forgiveness for colleagues, clients and themselves through reflective practice. This forgiveness is like dropping a burden, carried often for years; it can come accompanied by grief (Bauer et al. 1992). Forgiveness of oneself and others go hand in hand. The letting go of remorse and hatred or anger with another cannot, however, be planned for or directed by a facilitator. Forgiveness is a gift coming with increased understanding (see Munno 2006; Mark Purvis in Chapter 2).

Risk and safety

> I have come to realise through the process of writing about this incident that reflection is not a cosy process of quiet contemplation. It is an active, dynamic, often threatening process which demands total involvement of self and a commitment to action. In reflective practice there is nowhere to hide. (Susan)

This kind of work comes with its own anxieties, doubts, fears, and fear of risk. Those who gain feel: nothing ventured, nothing gained. Issues of safety and risk are discussed with reference to an educational principles and practice module on a Master in Medical Science course (see Bolton 1999c).

This group had been working together for some time, discussing and learning about education, for the first time they were now to share thinking and understanding in writing. It is one thing to say something tentatively in discussion, and then develop or alter it as the subject evolves and mutates. It is one thing to sit silent, or only venturing the odd expression while the more verbal and confident develop their ideas through discussion. It is quite another to stand by your written words. The group members knew I would ask them to write without forethought, not merely as rational discourse (Mezirow 1991), but from intuitive knowledge, understanding, and memory of experience.

One asked: 'Are we just going to sit here and write? How do I know which incident to choose?' I replied I would facilitate, with every step carefully explained and agreed to. There was a sigh of relief: the facilitation itself would be strong and straightforward. The process of writing explorative and expressive texts, and sharing them (albeit in a well-formed and effectively performing group) needs a supportive, clear, facilitative, interactive tutor, to develop confidence and trust. This work's growth and development can easily feel unsafe and confusing: confirmation of confidentiality and safety is facilitative, and there needs to be respect for uncertainty. Writers need to feel whatever they write is right for them, and will be respected by the rest of the group, as well as seeming contradictions and changes of mind. We also pulled apart my facilitation style and skills, for the sake of their educational understandings; that is not the story here.

The group understood this would be hot writing (improvised, rather than played coolly from pre-planned ideas). They still needed me to explain how to allow words to flow from their pens; after all their heads were empty of ideas, or full of apprehension. They had to trust themselves to write without prior thought: the breath of creative life to poets, novelists, playwrights, autobiographers, but missed out by academic writers. Everyone wrote for six minutes without stopping, putting on the paper whatever was in their heads (like stream of consciousness). This was not for sharing (but could be if the writer so wished): it was to clear our heads; or capture whatever floating thoughts and ideas were there; and to get the pen flowing untroubled (or perhaps feverishly fast) over the page.

> [One group member] has just left the room, obviously upset, and I think that emphasises just how powerful this can be. How does this 'power' get dealt with without leaving more scars? (Liz)

Risk, which the students rightly discerned, is the seat of the power of this writing. Writing, although powerful, is also well paced: people do not normally write more than they are able to cope with. Writers need sufficient time to read and acquaint themselves with their own writing before sharing. From Elaine's journal:

> The facilitation allowing the group to respond to the writings primarily and giving permission not to disclose any part of the writing made the group safe and gave responsibility to its members.

In talk-based discussion groups it is easy to blurt, and regret (Hulatt 1995). Sonya (NHS Senior Nurse Manager) commented in her journal on her own six-minute writing:

> this seemed to spring from nowhere and resulted in me actively seeking a new job!! All based on a few minutes' thought!

We then wrote about 'a time when I learned something vital at work'. Ann (an experienced educator) wrote about a disastrous session with young disadvantaged mothers which she facilitated years previously. From her final portfolio:

> When I began to write this critical incident I started with a series of descriptive words. They mostly related to emotions, both mine and those I had felt from the other people involved in the incident. Then I began to write the story. As I began to write I was unsure about why I had chosen this incident. It had happened some years ago and I felt that as I had discussed the incident with a number of people at the time, I had understood and analysed it sufficiently. Perhaps that was why I used it – perhaps I felt I had the answers ready to be neatly inserted into the story. Nevertheless, I had been instructed to write about the first incident which came to mind and this was the one. As I wrote, the situation was recreated before me. I could see the room, feel the atmosphere, although parts of the sequence of events were hazy in detail. What I did remember and what hit me again was the emotional force of feeling, both those of the women in that room on that day, but more particularly my own feelings. As I wrote I couldn't believe how much there was to put down. I had to force myself to stop after all the others had finished. When I read the piece to the group I was overwhelmed by the emotional force and couldn't complete the reading. All those emotions. And I thought I had 'dealt with' this incident. (Ann)

Through-the-mirror writing can enable attention to less dominant sides of ourselves. This can feel risky because certainties dissolve in such marginal states. These certainties can feel comfortably secure, once questioned in this way they are experienced as professional straitjackets. Within the marginal writing state, the writer loses clarity in a unitary self, begins to perceive alternative selves in the different retellings of the story. Narrators can become the narration, crossing over that threshold of certainty, of knowing how they should respond in given situations into the unknowingness of uncertainty. The feeling of riskiness lies in the possibility of facing issues previously buried as un-faceable, to begin to doubt their practice, become confused (how will I know who I am if I bring my basic practice into question?), need drastically to alter their practice, their world, even the worlds of others.

They do all these things: hopefully. Later they realise the exhilaration and increase in self-confidence and self-determination, though initially they only perceive dangerous uncertainty. Facilitators ensure this happens at a pace and depth, and with sufficiently created boundaries, so 'this "power" gets dealt with without leaving more scars' (Liz, above).

The next stage was to read and discuss writings. I wrote and read alongside the group, though I made it clear I contribute verbally only when appropriate and after everyone else has spoken (I very rarely read my writing). Discussions were carefully facilitated towards reflectivity and reflexivity, within clear guidelines and boundaries set by the group (see Chapter 9).

Jessica's story concerned a knotty, ongoing work situation unflinchingly brought to the group. She took her fresh understandings back to the work situation, and implemented them immediately: 'I don't believe I could have done it without the learning opportunities I have been given' (see Bolton 1999a).

The group also worked without tutors and in co-peer mentoring pairs (see Chapter 11). One commented issues could be brought to co-peer mentoring, impossible to share with the group. Creative, original, helpful suggestions were made to develop core stories (see Chapter 6).

> I surprised myself with both the subject of what I wrote and the power of emotions it provoked. I hadn't realised I had so many unresolved feelings about the incident despite having talked about it to others many times. On reflection I feel that Gillie is right: there is something in the writing that gives another dimension. Seeing the words on the page gives an added intensity to the power of the feelings. There was a lot of honesty in the group this week, although some people understandably chose to use a far less problematic incident than others. I feel I have learned a lot from hearing the others in the group talk through their incidents. What have I learned? … I have learned about the power of the written word. I have thought about trying to do sharing of critical incidents with primary health care teams and feel it could be very valuable. I'm sure every group finds its level of exposure. (Ann)

Ann felt the group were not sufficiently critical in the discussion, that they supported her too much to feel she had acted out of the best intentions. She wanted to face the possibility that having just good intentions was not enough. She noted six weeks later, however:

> I can see that I had still not been able to put this incident behind me and therefore was cross with others for trying to help me to do that. I feel rather embarrassed now by my reactions to the group. It was, of course, not about them but about me ... I can now forgive myself for this incident, understand it and accept that everyone gets it wrong sometimes. (Ann)

Ann later commented how discussions developed as the group gained confidence; making her more positive about depths of reflection reached. Groups need to begin sensitively and be gingerly supportive when discussing such writings. Ann also recognised later the effect her evident emotion had on the group.

Liz rewrote her piece as a series of thought bubbles, thoughts unexpressed in the writing. Elaine's concerned a frustrating consultation with a client, which left her anxious and responsible. Initially she wanted never to reread the writing, nor think about that client. The group suggested, however, she rewrite the event twice fictionally; from the client's point of view; and as win:win, an occasion when both client and nurse felt in agreement about a positive outcome.

> I was amazed at the reduction of anger when I wrote the win:win situation. I was also struck by the lack of centrality of my position in the clinic compared to the wide complex circumstances of the client's life ... Writing a win:win situation enormously reduced the overall anxiety and power which caused both myself and the client to OVERACT and OVER-REACT. (Elaine)

Elaine and Liz stressed in their journals how writing, rewriting and discussion helped them become more objective. Both realised they had inappropriately felt guilt: some responsibility belonged to the client. Writing and discussion: 'helped change my emotional response to the situations and be more mentally open to all options rather than solving it in a specific way' (Elaine's journal).

Marilyn Pietroni gives a useful set of 'nature and aims of professional education' (1995, p. 48):

- to provide a containing environment in which individual practitioners are given the opportunity of recovering or establishing creative individual thought
- to offer partnerships in learning between educators and learners
- to provide a learning environment in which the log-jams and messiness of day-to-day practice can be faced and scrutinised in detail

- to provide continuous workshop environments (Schon's practicum) in which new ideas and approaches can be explored before and after their use (the double-feedback loop)
- to enable the nature of the organisational structures and defences that frame the work to be examined in relation to identified tasks
- to educate for a context of continuous change in which professional categories and languages, and organisational structure, are constantly by definition under erasure.

This chapter has gone some way towards examining some of the ethical values and educational underpinnings of reflective practice: relationships, contexts, structures of assumptions. There is no one way of getting the education business right: eclecticism is a valuable approach. And anyway all the above theories are lenses through which to view situations, rather than how things really are: they are based on metaphorical models, as theories generally are (Cunliffe 2008). But attention to these vital areas, in particular to mutual respect and authority and a genuine openness as to end-product, are likely to enable effective reflective practice: professionals and students *ringing the bell themselves*.

 Read to learn

Cunliffe, A.L. (2009b) The philosopher leader: on relationism, ethics and reflexivity a critical perspective to teaching leadership, *Management Learning*, **40**(1), 87–101.

Durgahee, T. (1997) Reflective practice: nursing ethics through story telling, *Nursing Ethics*, **4**(2), 135–46.

Fox, D. (1983) Personal theories of teaching, *Studies in Higher Education*, **8**(2), 151–63.

 Write to learn

Each chapter ends with *Write to learn*. For straightforward advice, sufficient for the exercises below, see *Write to learn* in Chapter 1, and see Chapter 6 for more advice. Each writing can be shared fruitfully with a group or confidential trusted other, if this seems appropriate once the writer has read and reflected on it first.

(Continued)

(Continued)

Exercise 3.1 Who am I?

1. Complete these sentences – all or as many as you wish, and writing as much as you wish.
2. I am ...
3. I believe ...
4. I want ...
5. I know ...
6. I think ...
7. I wish ...
8. I hope ...
9. I understand ...
10. I wonder ...
11. I imagine ...
12. I'm surprised that ...
13. My dream is ...
14. If I were not a (doctor/psychologist/lawyer/teacher/?), I would be a ...
15. Reread with care. Choose one to write more about.

Exercise 3.2 What and why and when, and how and where and who?

1. Think of your work, a particular aspect, or in general.
2. Respond to these, in whatever way occurs to you (you cannot get this wrong):

   (a) What do I do?
   (b) Why do I do it?
   (c) How do I do it best?
   (d) For whom do I do it?
   (e) When?
   (f) Where?
   (g) What might I rather do?

3. Reread with care. Choose one to write about at greater length.
4. Reread, add, alter or delete positively, as appropriate.

Exercise 3.3 The essence of your work

1. Write an 'unsent' letter to a young child, telling them about your job
2. Reread, remembering the age of your interlocutor, keep it simple
3. I hope you find you have got to the heart of your feeling about your work

CHAPTER 4

THROUGH THE MIRROR

Chapter 4 introduces the *through-the-mirror* approach, gives its three foundations, and suggests effective facilitation for practitioners to gain confidence to enter this area of educational uncertainty. It explains how skilled facilitation of this method supports students and practitioners to gain authority over their own learning and practice.

> Alice was through the glass, and had jumped lightly down into the Looking-Glass room … Then she began looking around and noticed that what could be seen from the old room was quite common and uninteresting, but that all the rest was as different as possible. For instance, the pictures on the wall next the fire seemed to be all alive. (Carroll [1865] 1954, pp. 122–3)

> The sage offered her disciple tea, but did not stop pouring. 'Master, the cup is full!' 'You are just like this cup: overflowing,' the sage replied, 'there is no space for you to learn.' (Story from Chuang Tsu)

Reflection and reflexivity make the ordinary seem extraordinary, 'as different as possible'. And it makes the extraordinary more comprehensible. Actions, interactions, professional episodes, memories from long ago, spirituality, thoughts, ideas and feelings become 'all alive'. Developmental change becomes possible. This chapter discusses *through-the-mirror* reflection and reflexivity, and the role of stories and fiction.

Practitioners open themselves to relating to a wide range, within both their own experience and that of others, through this dynamic process. They recognise many different ways of knowing, all of them valid. Nothing is irrelevant, however insignificant or personal it might appear to be: assumptions as to what is relevant or significant thwart the process.

> When I realised my mother's cancer was terminal I considered resigning my job to help care for her. Realising that wasn't possible I then had to consider how to survive over the next few months. I'd considered resigning because I'd been struggling with being a doctor and who it had turned me into. Creative writing has helped me see what was happening, share it with others and begin to find a way through. I discovered that I could barely engage with my own emotions and fears any more. I had developed a protective shell through which I couldn't feel but which allowed me to keep going. The reality of a very significant loss in my life meant I had to feel it and understand my self again. (Clare)

All aspects of ourselves are interrelated; practice is not undertaken with one part, and personal life another. They might be linked, moreover, by surprising-seeming factors. The apparently insignificant, appearing seemingly out of nowhere, may be central. *Through-the-mirror* processes can enable developmental, aesthetic and creative access.

Professionals need to engage in 'willing suspension of disbelief' (Coleridge [1817] 1992), open themselves to uncertainty about learning needs and possibilities. This uncertainty, or knowledge of lack of knowledge, is an educative space for insight, intuition and credulity, leading to understanding of what was already unwittingly known (see Attard 2008). Alice was instructed by the White Queen in 'living backwards', and told to practise believing up to six impossible things before breakfast every day (Carroll [1865] 1954, p. 173). I congratulated a novelist friend on having made me believe in impossibly extraordinary characters (Glaister 1999); she responded: 'The more you can believe the better'.

Three foundations

- Certain uncertainty
- Serious playfulness
- Unquestioning questioning.

Certain uncertainty: the one certainty is uncertainty. You begin to act when you do not know how you should act. Interim goals arise, rather than one predetermined goal: creative and dynamic situation, though perhaps less comfortable than a clear map. Students or supervisees, used to the safe certainty of structure, may express nervousness or anger born out of anxiety. The responsibility of uncertainty is uncomfortable, until the excitement of discovery takes hold. Students and supervisees often initially express the non-developmental attitude of wishing tutors to take responsibility. Anyone who thinks they know the right answers all the time is bound to be wrong. To people willing to 'not know' all the time, all sorts of things are possible.

Serious playfulness: a playful attitude, and willingness to experiment and adventure, makes uncertainty a positive force. Looking for something without knowing what it is uncovers pertinent questions. An adventurous spirit leads to that trackless moorland which education has come to be, rather than a walled or hedged field (Usher et al. 1997, p. 3). Anything and everything is questioned, leaving no room for self-importance. There is, however, only so much we can do to alter our own situation, that of others, and the wider political one: we recognise our power is *unlimitedly limited*. This playfulness is essentially serious. It can only take place within a safe enough educational environment in which people can feel confident to take risks.

Unquestioning questioning: we accept, unquestioningly, the questioning spirit. Questions determine directions across the moorland, and therefore what might be discovered along the way. These findings beget more questions. We 'risk abandoning previous "truths" and sit with *not knowing*' (Gerber 1994, p. 290). This *non-judgemental critical* process is active and enquiring, rather like the small child's iconoclastic eternal *Why?*

Paradoxically, the way to find out about ourselves is through letting go of ourselves: of everyday assumptions about who we are, in order to be open to the discovery of other possible selves. I discover the myselves of whom I am not habitually aware, the myself I might be, and the selves I am becoming, joining up the dots between these selves (Watson 2006). Only when 'the cup is empty' can anyone receive, hear what is being said, perceive what is happening. Providing students with frameworks to work within might lessen tutor anxiety, but such programming disables students from thinking and exploring for themselves. Research by Baernstein and Fryer-Edwards (2003) showed critical incident reports (CIRs) to be less effective than reflective interviews without writing. This is hardly surprising as CIRs would have been simple responses to guiding questions. Reflective and reflexive beginners such as undergraduates and postgraduates are wonderfully flexible and adventurous if well facilitated. Formalised structure takes the place of experienced knowledgeable facilitation of beginners (Bulman and Schutz 2008). Senior practitioners are more likely to have blocks, having more in their cups to empty before they start.

These oxymorons underpin an aesthetic (Schon's 'artistry', 1983) and ethical approach rather than a logical or instrumental one. Practitioners and students have responsibility to tell and retell their stories in ways appropriate to them: they are the authorities in this work. They create narratives in relation to the stories of others and their social, cultural, professional contexts. Socrates' pedagogic method was based on just such oxymorons; here is Meno struggling with Socrates' ruthless method of enquiry into the nature of 'virtue':

Meno: Socrates, even before I met you they told me that in plain truth you are a
             perplexed man yourself and reduce others to perplexity …

Socrates: It isn't that knowing the answers myself, I perplex other people. The truth
             is rather that I infect them also with the perplexity I feel myself … So with
             virtue now. I don't know what it is. You may have known before you came
             into contact with me, but now you look as if you don't. Nevertheless I am
             ready to carry out, together with you, a joint investigation and inquiry into
             what it is.

Meno: But how will you look for something when you don't in the least know
             what it is? How on earth are you going to set up something you don't
             know as the object of your search? To put it another way, even if you come
             right up against it, how will you know that what you have found is the
             thing you didn't know? (Plato 1958, pp. 127–8)

Facilitating effective reflective practice

Facilitating reflective practice is as uncertain as practising it, like handling
unpredictable fireworks. They will probably go off when the blue touchpaper
is lit; but the direction or how they will explode into colour, light and sound
is unknown. Some facilitators avoid this educative uncertainty by containing
the process within non-reflexive structures.

Through-the-mirror facilitators stay in uncertainty with their participants.
Together they commit themselves to perceiving key stories which shape their
existence, take responsibility for their own part in these narratives, and do
what they can to develop and alter things constructively. Session plans and
learning objectives have to be provisional. The most important achievable
learning objective is active dynamic engagement.

> Looking at the discussion of the previous week and thinking of the Mezirow
> stages finally made the whole thing click into place for me. What is hard about
> the reflection is that it is so multi-layered. Analysis is of the actions, motivations,
> perceptions, etc. of the individual players in the story along with making links
> to other situations in the players' own past histories. But connections are also
> made at a more political and theoretic level of analysis which makes you then
> re-look at the original incident from another angle. No wonder it all takes so
> much time. (Ann)

And no wonder it all takes so much trust in the group, a degree of self-
confidence and faith in the professional self. These also all take time and
nurture. A safe-enough closed environment, agreed way of behaving, and
time limit are required. A safe-enough boundaried confidential space can
facilitate openness, willingness and courage. Course members have said such
as: 'I have been able to be *me!*', 'I have been able to say what I really *think!*',

in evaluation. Perhaps even more pertinently: 'for the first time I have been able to express what I *feel!*'

Courses constrain professionals, or professionals-in-training, to behave in certain ways for a certain time, in a specific place. This has the paradoxical effect of giving them freedom in educative exploration and questioning. Losing responsibility for everyday elements enables responsibility for more fundamental issues, such as values and professional identity. Another paradox.

Dialogue is required, rather than debate or didactic discussion. Debate is oppositional: constructing intellectual arguments to win points. Participants in dialogue attempt to express what they think, feel and experience, and listen and respond attentively, in order to gain access to deeper understandings.

Most training and post-experience courses include elements of reflective practice. A potential danger lies in undertaking it because it is the thing to do, or part of the course. To work it has to be undertaken critically. And facilitation is key to enabling students to find their own confidence and skills:

> [I have sought] out again some of the literature on reflective practice. I realise now how varied this is in quality, scope and depth. On one level some people talk about reflective practice as if it was just a chat about an incident over a cup of coffee. (Ann)

Fear of going through the mirror

Self-protectiveness against exploring unknown aspects of oneself arises from fear of unpalatable selves like *Steppenwolf* (Hesse 1927), Mr Hyde instead of Dr Jekyll (Stevenson [1886] 1984), a withered face in the portrait (Dorian Gray, Wilde [1891] 1949) or a murderous reflection step out of the mirror ('The Student of Prague', 1926 Conrad Veidt film).

Freud theorised our psyches as containing *ego*, *superego* and *id*. *Id* has been seen as 'animal instinct': potentially ungovernable, and in need of control by conscious *ego*s. If *superego* – conscience – fails to direct *ego* appropriately, devil *id* might take over, as Pat Barker (1991) depicted with shell-shock and fugue in the First World War.

Through-the-mirror work can seem transgressive of psychological boundaries to the newcomer. An examination of our taken-for-granted psychological and social structures does not, however, let out ungovernable demons, though the uncertainty it occasions can be uncomfortable. Crossing boundaries is a marginal activity to be undertaken with knowledgeable care by experienced facilitators. Practitioners might find it unsettling to perceive that previously accepted situations and relationships are untenable and need to be rethought. The alternative, however, might be depression and boredom at unquestioning lack of change. When dynamic change *has* to take place, due to the developed understanding of the reflective practitioner, it becomes inevitable and exciting. Reflection and reflexivity generate energy and commitment to change.

Through-the-mirror writing is trustworthy and paced, if allied with carefully facilitated confidential group or paired work. Participants get what they pay for: those willing to express and explore deeply receive the most. Practitioners involve themselves according to strengths, wants and needs. Those not so ready only go as far as they can. There are often those I wish could have taken themselves further: the choice is theirs, whether conscious or not.

Courageously adventuring through the glass, rather than merely gazing on its surface, is personally demanding. It enables unprecedented width of view. It can offer insight into the motives, thoughts and feelings of others, and suggest possible actions never before envisaged. This is likely to change practice, and the relationship of the practitioner to their practice, dynamically: a politically and socially unsettling process.

It can't *transform* practice with *hey presto* magic wands, without deep personal investment. No education can offer straightforward definitive answers, and betterment is never unalloyed. The wish for *transforma-tion* in this way can be as uncritical as Midas's wish that everything he touched might turn to gold. At least he can 'give up smoking for good'. (Duffy 1999, p. 12)

Even if magic wands were to hand, gains based on uncritical, un-thought-through assumptions would prove non-developmental. Myth tells us to take full responsibility for our own lives and learning, to have our eyes clearly open to drawbacks as well as advantages, to errors and blunders as well as successes of our educational journey.

Leslie Boydell (associate director), and Anne McMurray (organisational development consultant) reflect on leadership development:

> The Institute of Public Health in Ireland (North and South) launched its first leadership development programme in January 2002 to build a network of leaders across the island working collaboratively and creatively to reduce health inequalities and improve health and well-being during and beyond the life of the two-year programme. Leadership development requires assessment both of oneself as an individual and challenges faced. Action is based on assessment. Reflection enables learning from experience so that what has been learnt can be integrated into practice (Kolb's learning cycle (1984)).
>
> Reflective practice writing seemed useful for public health practitioners deal-ing with intractable problems of improving population health. We saw its poten-tial both to make sense of leadership challenges, and to reflect on actions. Participants worked in learning sets, formed at the start of the programme, and had developed strong relationships of trust.

Following this workshop participants were asked to make a commitment to write regularly about progress with leadership challenges, what was happening, what they thought and felt. They identified partners with whom to share their writing: logistically a challenge as participants were dispersed throughout Ireland. At the two ensuing events they were asked to share writings, and write more from a new perspective.

The group decided they would like to produce a book; Gillie provided individual consultations to help develop publishable pieces depicting leadership in public health at this time in Ireland, North and South. The book [Denyer et al. 2003; see also Chapter 8] provides very personal and powerful essays, short prose, poetry and metaphor of the participants' views and experience of leadership, development journey, practice and dilemmas faced.

This approach does not suit everyone's learning style. Some found it a valuable learning technique, writing to find out what they think about situations where they do not know how to act or where they have already acted and need to make sense of what has happened. For others, a more interactive style of reflection may be more suitable, as writing is regarded as being a solitary activity (although sharing the writing is an important part of the process). A key leadership activity is to find some way to 'get on the balcony' and find perspective in the middle of action (Heifetz and Linsky 2002, p. 54). As Gillie suggests, reflective practice entails embracing uncertainty. Some people may be more comfortable with this than others.

Two years later, participants from both groups who used the techniques report continuing to find it an invaluable tool to reflection, thinking and planning. It provides a way to develop the leadership discipline of thinking things through, deal with conflict, power and leadership, explore complexity, come to terms with grief, and to unlock organisational and relationship impasses. (Leslie Boydell and Anne McMurray)

Synthesis, as well as analysis

Writing a story or poem is organic, synthesising elements from life's muddles, weaving them to create a coherent communicating artefact. Sharing with peers, and writing new accounts from different angles or perspectives they have suggested, can enable writers and readers to perceive experiences as synthesising multiple stories. If this is associated with reading and discussion of significant related material from wider professional, social and political worlds (journal papers, popular magazines or television programmes, views and opinions of colleagues), then experiences will deepen. This perception takes place because the professional experience is not only examined across a range of levels of reflection (as in Mezirow 1981) but, more importantly, refracted through different lenses, in different lights, and with different senses predominating. Material is also considered from different psychological, social, political, cultural, and spiritual arenas. This process is critical-synthetic, rather than critical-analytic.

Through-the-mirror writing synthesises sources of knowledge, including cognitive understandings of events (the rational discourse of Mezirow 1981, referred to above), intuitive perceptions (feelings), metaphoric and creative understandings, and so on. Feelings and ideas are multifaceted, complex. Writers cannot *know* others' feelings, ideas, experiences but can imaginatively understand by writing fictionally from their perspective. Writers' own feelings and ideas can be explored further by writing fictions in which events are altered in some specific way (such as switching genders). Wider knowledge and opinion can be drawn upon through reading and discussion. A multiplicity of themes can be perceived within a single incident. We know in so many different ways, yet constrain ourselves to a tiny portion of knowledge. Writing fictionally is one way of engaging with this complexity, of being aware of the embeddedness of our knowing in experience.

Writing fictionally, for example from the point of view of the student (patient, client or member of the public), or rewriting giving the thoughts of everyone at key points, can give insight and release of emotion. An allied approach is to collect written stories from other characters in a situation, as Mavis Kirkham (1997) has with a series of births (mother, midwife, doctor, and so on), to give a 360-degree view. Brookfield (1990) describes an exercise in which three people write a critical incident. When each is read, the others try to identify assumptions they perceive to be embedded in the description, thereby gaining access to the writer's values, and the way they are formed or part of their social, political or organisational context.

There are no single answers to such questions as 'How could I have done better?' Yet more questions arise instead, such as 'If I had done this, which I think would have been better, what would the patient/doctor have felt?' As Master's student Ann commented: 'no wonder it all takes so much time!'

Exploring issues in depth and width can take time. Or enlightenment can arrive after 15 minutes' writing. Rereading can enable writer-readers to 'own' depicted experiences, recognise and begin to accept and work on them.

> [Professionals] who learn on courses to take more responsibility for their suc-
> cesses, weaknesses, actions and feelings, and to relate their course functioning
> to their work context are in fact developing competencies that are readily avail-
> able for transfer to their work settings. At worst, staff thus empowered may offer a
> challenge too threatening to be coped with by an unempowered organisation
> and management structure. At best, they can become a stimulating and thoughtful
> resource for their agencies. (Hughes and Pengelly 1995, p. 170)

Or at very best they thoroughly shake up their organisation, or seek a new and much more dynamic post. Here is a health professional with authority over her professional and personal development. Her tough personal situation impinged directly upon professional life; she handled it with courage in the face of pain and uncertainty.

 Ann Williams: professional and personal world collision

My professional and personal worlds collided when my eight-week grandson, Luke died a cot death. For many weeks I lived a double life working as a health visitor and lecturer, and grieving. I had a role of grieving grandmother with professional colleagues who knew that grief follows a structured model, and were willing and able to support me through the stages. It kept the pain at bay, but was not where the grief resolved. My personal world of grief was chaotic.

When the pain became unbearable I jotted down notes: a safe place to record my feelings before they were lost. There were so many adjustments to make, and finding that for the first time I had nothing to offer others in resolving their own grief. The dissonance between my public grief, where the goal of acceptance held sway and the wish to hold on to him in private, to deny his absence, became wider.

I have used reflection professionally to manage difficult situations. As I became stronger I was able to look at my jottings and the story they told, not of Luke but of me. I wanted not just to create an account of my experiences but to share it, to validate Luke's short life and my commitment to him. I submitted an abstract to a Medical Humanities Conference a few months away, the first step in reconciling the two worlds. Presenting a personal account in a professional arena raises all sorts of doubts. My personal account was far removed from the tidy, professional model of grief.

The conference was my chance to peep out from behind barriers grief had helped me build. Creating the story, and reading it with tears running down my face, was powerful but emotional. I have found that I can be more myself professionally than before the conference. I have become aware I had fairly strong ideas about what was acceptable. Now I take more risks with letting clients and colleagues see a more authentic version. It makes life easier for me but whether it makes me a better professional I don't know. The conference really was like setting down a heavy burden. (Ann Williams)

Guidance or control?

Where you start from, and what pedagogical principles you use, affects where you arrive. Appropriate principles are essential: if you start from a place inappropriate to your desired destination, you won't get there (when asked

'How do I get to Dalston', the Londoner in Holborn scratched his head: 'If I wanted to get there I wouldn't start from here!')

Just as there are severe drawbacks in *structuring* practitioners' or students' reflection *for* them, so too there are inherent potential problems in *guiding* it. Reflective practice can effectively be undertaken in discussion groups or pairs of peers, with knowledgeable and skilful *facilitation*. Open discussion can widen reflection and reflexivity politically and socially, *guidance* hedge it in. To be critically reflective and reflexive, practitioners must question and face themselves rather than being directed.

Guided reflection and reflexivity may create effective and self-satisfied workforces. But they may now be regulated from outside (by supervisor and line manager). Practitioners internalise supervisors' instructions. Practice, once private and formed by personal ethical judgements, is now public: open to scrutiny and guidance. Professionals are controlled from without *and* from within.

Authority

An effective reflective practitioner has authority for their own learning. A facilitator's or mentor's role includes the creation of a safe-enough educational environment with clear boundaries. In this space practitioners can be brave enough to stay with uncertainty and self-doubt, gain confidence in their own strength and intelligence to develop significant questions, as well as meet and tackle challenges creatively and insightfully. This learning environment is secure enough for enquirers to take risks, beginning to realise, and wield, the full extent of their responsibility. It is like a window through which sunlight can enter (see Chapter 10), an empty cup with room for new contents such as 'aha' or 'epiphanies'.

Entering this space, realising the necessity of taking ownership of learning, can feel uncomfortable. Practitioners often ask 'Isn't there an easier way?' No there is not, because no tutor can give authority to their student. It has to be taken authoritatively by the learner: flexibly, reflexively, enquiringly, and open to diverse ways of perceiving and knowing. Here is a typical senior practitioner's evaluatory comment at the end of a *through-the-mirror* course:

> I felt to begin with that the course was slightly wacky and flaky – surreal … I felt uncomfortable and a bit insecure at first … But now I feel this process is empow-ering. I was initially afraid it was too self-indulgent.

She had initially expected structure and analysis, but was strong enough for these assumptions not to block her from a totally new educational environment. Participants, whose senior roles involve telling others what to do, often try to block educative uncertainty due to their fear of insecurity. Nine senior doctors initially resembled naughty infant lads recently, using delaying and warding-off tactics. They did not want to be challenged to question the foundation of their responsibility and power. They would happily have given me, their tutor, authority and responsibility to tell them what to do and think. They would rather I artificially structured their learning with little scope for the uncomfortable uncertainty of exploration.

Understanding educative processes in terms of levels or stages of reflection (for example, Mezirow 1981) can unfortunately offer such artificial structures. A leadership student (Cunliffe 2002, p. 55) felt disabled in groupwork, feeling he could not move up Maslow's hierarchy of needs. He felt his basic needs could not be met within the group. His tutor saw this as a rich opportunity for reflexive dialogue about the validity of theories (Maslow's in this case). She was able to encourage him to explore the nature of theories in general and his ready assumption that they represent reality.

Such stages or levels are theories or models: specific ways of perceiving experience. They are designed as an aid to give specific insightful perspective into a part of experience. They give an angle on the picture, but can never represent reality, as Cunliffe's student clearly thought.

Structuring reflection through stages is therefore likely to be unfulfilling: the range of experience is narrowed and participants are disabled from taking authority over their own learning. In certain methods specific areas of experience are dismembered into stages with questions such as: 'What did I do right here?' and 'What could I have done better?' (Atkins and Murphy 1994; Tripp 1995a). In other structured work, a fictitious situation is provided to reflect on.

Appropriate and useful material for reflection within these structures is assumed to be readily accessible, for example: 'practitioners must first select what aspects of the situation to attend to' (Greenwood 1995). Yet the same author realises the reflective process is not so simple, upsetting her previously neat programme: The problems of practice do not present themselves ready labelled for solution; the knotty problems of practice inhere in messy indeterminate situations of uncertainty, instability, uniqueness and value-conflict ... Argyris and Schon remind us that the ego-protecting function, as well as the relative implicitness of some theories-in-use, might make their access through reflective exercises very difficult indeed. (Greenwood 1995, pp. 65–6). A muddle in the model (see Chapter 3).

Another model muddle is the way *learning styles*' approaches are often foundational to courses. The theory describes a restricted number of ways in which people learn. This has its uses, when understood to be a model describing a limited area of experience, open to flux and change. However,

aires have been formed which purport to tell people into which
hey fit. Practitioners then feel justified in taking up the label,
saying, 'Oh I can't do that, I'm not the reflective type'. Self-understanding is
thus restrictively ossified because of the way they understood the
questionnaire, and the mood they were in at the time. The approach used
thus is based on a muddled assumption that the theory, or model, represents
reality. Reynolds (1997) points out that use of such *learning styles*
decontextualises diversity and encourages stereotypical thinking, perpetuating
social inequality.

Such methods, especially when associated with assessment, can lead to
reflection being reduced to 'little more than a mantra rather than a model
of practice' (Kuit et al. 2001, p. 129). Macfarlane and Gourlay (2009) liken
structured reflection to television reality shows. People are organised to
expose themselves and their actions, show their remorse and how they have
developed as a result, with as little educational impact as reality shows.

Here is an account of a *through-the-mirror* writing course in which people took
authority over their own learning. It is written by group member Tom Heller.

 Reflective writing in a group of doctors

Several years ago I wrote a story about a drug addict whom I had looked after
for several years, and read it out to the reflective writing group.

'Sheila', not her real name of course, had deeply affected me. She was exactly
the same age as me, and although she had lived a very different life to mine,
including spells in prostitution, a time in prison for drug running and a serious
opiate addiction, we really liked each other. The other members of the group
remember other 'Sheilas', and how difficult they found them. They gently probe
why I may have chosen this particular story. What role does her age have, might I
have a special empathy with people the same age as me? And is her decision to
run off with Jim reflected in any way by big decisions in my life? Is there an equivalent moment from my own past which, had it been different, would have changed
my whole life? How does Sheila's experience relate to other things in my life? My
own children are making choices for their own lives. Does Sheila, as a teenager,
remind me of one of my own children and their current struggle for detachment
from me and the family hearth? Does this give clues as to why I apparently
became embroiled in her story-web?

By opening myself and my emotions to the group through the writing,
I remained in control of what I disclosed and how deeply I wanted to go. The
continued process of sharing my writing usually gets down to other levels which
individual, personal reflection never approaches. The group immediately estab-
lishes its caring for me and empathises with the difficulty people like Sheila

present to doctors. In general they will help in my quest for further enlightenment, this is the group pattern. The doctors are not competitive or aggressive, they will not laugh at me for getting something wrong, or leave me feeling exposed when delicate emotions are touched on.

The group leader, Gillie, patrols the boundaries and asks the 'naive questions' no one else dares to ask. She pretends to know little about general practice and is an interested outsider. The group makes no suggestions or proposals; there are no conclusions, diagnoses or certainties. Various things are considered, mulled over and the enquiry moves on. This is very different from the formal, often aggressive bog-standard general practice, where the drive for evidence-based, cost-effective interventions and the like leaves little room for philosophical ruminations, experimentation, or following of feelings or hunches.

After the group I felt I really could understand at a greater depth the way Sheila's life has panned out for her, and what is happening in the interaction between her and me during consultations. I felt I learnt as much about myself during the group session as I did about Sheila, and this is useful, if not always comforting. It may have brought up quite disturbing things, which may need resolution in other contexts and at other times. I recognised it is not possible to get help at this level with every patient, but that selective, intensive work of this nature does help me to understand what may be going on for people whom I have some responsibility to try to help. It is a valid and important form of training for all my work, not just for my work with Sheila. It might also help me in my way of being with other people (specifically my own children) at important times of decision.

Why write?

Writing Sheila's story helped me empathise. It doesn't really matter about exact details or chronological precision. Indeed I fantasised and embroidered some events and forgot or changed others to make it into a story rather than a case history. The important feature seems that I was able to see the world through her eyes for a while. The process of writing has clarified many things. What must it be like to live your entire life with a major regret? How can that event have shaped everything else Sheila did and the way she thought and felt about things thereafter? The feelings of guilt, self-loathing, remorse, hatred and despair were immediately transmitted through writing from Sheila's own life in a very direct way into my consciousness. The written product is not especially brilliant, it is just that it responds to the human dimensions of the situation.

By writing it down, I have acknowledged the importance of the story to me and started to consider what happens when two human beings meet. The story has started to make Sheila's life understandable and accessible to me and to any others who take the trouble to read or hear the story.

(Continued)

(Continued)

In the group
We have developed a way of working together that looks at institutional, structural, and especially personal strains involved in our jobs. When we write in the privacy of our own homes we focus naturally on events and situations that have affected us. There is no point in writing about neutral events.

The process of writing gets me in touch, very directly, with my feelings, and I imagine it is the same for the others. Writing, the flow of words and ideas, thoughts and inner feelings ... and then the editing and rewriting, polishing as best I can for presentation to the group, is a ritual I now know will help me sort out and organise my feelings about the subject. It has become less scary to bring these private efforts and lay them bare before the others. The group seems able to accept each other's imperfections and are relieved and strengthened to find that many of them are shared ... and that all of them are understood by the group.

The levels of discussion following presentations acknowledge the human being within the professional concretions; discuss the feelings behind the descriptions; empathise with the situation; ask a few questions to get to the nub of the problem. Ease and joke as well to relieve some of the intensity. All this seems to have been developed unselfconsciously together and they have arrived at levels of intimacy which are indeed supportive.

When I next met Sheila I felt a warmth and understanding had developed and deepened. I felt emboldened to suggest things that might never have been tried if I had not felt the support of this group. (Tom Heller)

 Read to learn

Carson, L. and Fisher, K. (2006) Raising the bar on criticality: students' critical reflection in an internship program, *Journal of Management Education*, **30**(5), 700–23.

Cowan, J. and Westwood, J. (2006) Collaborative and reflective professional development: a pilot, *Active Learning in Higher Education*, **7**(1), 63–71.

Watson, C. (2006) Encounters and directions in research: pages from a simulacrum journal, *Qualitative Inquiry*, **12**(5), 865–85.

Write to learn

Each chapter ends with *Write to learn*. For straightforward advice, sufficient for the exercises below, see *Write to learn* in Chapter 1, and see Chapter 6 for more advice. Each writing can be shared fruitfully with a group or confidential trusted other, if this seems appropriate once the writer has read and reflected on it first.

Exercise 4.1   Positive and negative

1. Write three sentences describing the sort of person you are (no one else need ever see this).
2. What characteristics do you think you excluded: be honest.
3. How many 'nots' are there (for example, I'm not good at numbers), compared to positives?
4. Rewrite these negatives as positives.
5. Reread and reflect positively.

Exercise 4.2   Wild solutions

1. Describe a work problem, occasion, or person which puzzles you.
2. List your hunches about it: go on be wild.
3. Reread and choose one to write more about, thinking: *What If ... .*
4. Reread with loving attention, altering as you wish.

Exercise 4.3   Pay attention to language

1. Write a list of proverbs or clichés (any, for example, 'a stitch in time saves nine', 'locking the stable door after the horse has bolted', 'moving the goalposts').
2. Take each in turn and write what you feel: is it useful, helpful or infuriating when said to you?
3. If possible write by each one whom you associate it with (for example, my mother always said that!)
4. Can you invent a useful new proverb?
5. Read back to yourself, altering or adding as you wish.

CHAPTER 5

WRITING AS REFLECTION

Chapter 5 introduces the theory that *through-the-mirror* writing is itself a reflective and reflexive process, and how it does this by harnessing narrative, story and the power of perceiving from a range of perspectives. In order for it to work, practitioners need to take responsibility for their own learning and writing and find their own vital voice. Among other benefits, it can be a stress reducer.

> We write before knowing what to say and how to say it, and in order to find out, if possible. (Lyotard 1992, p. 119)

> Roland Barthes ... said an *ecrivante* is someone who uses language only as an instrument, an instrument through which a message ... can be transmitted. And an *ecrivain*, a writer, is someone who uses language as an end in itself, as something that in itself has justification. (Llosa 1991, pp. 114–15)

> [Writing] is a bit like looking at the world through a kaleidoscope. You can look at the same scene but find it different every time you turn the viewer. (Diski 2005, p. 31)

Through-the-mirror reflective practice *is* the reflective process, rather than recording what has been thought, using writing processes to find out how and what we need to say, as Lyotard points out above (1992, p. 119). 'Writing no longer merely "captures" reality, it helps "construct" it', as Plummer points out (2001, p. 171). We cannot underestimate the power of writing to aid our mental capacities: 'Writing *is* thinking, writing *is* analysis, writing is indeed a seductive and tangled *method* of discovery ... I used ... writing to think ...

I trust you will ... use writing as a method of inquiry to move into your own impossibility, where anything might happen – and will' (Adams St Pierre 2005, pp. 967, 970, 973, emphasis in original). Writing, discussing, and associated text writing (such as from diverse perspectives) is creative exploration in its own right, 'To write is to measure the depth of things, as well as to come to a sense of one's own depth' (Van Manen 1995, p. 127). *Through-the-mirror* writing facilitates a wider view from a distance, close acute observation, authority over practice, and a critical challenging attitude to assumptions about diversity of perspective, and taken-for-granteds about political, social and cultural norms.

Through-the-mirror writing can create informative, descriptive material from the mass of ideas, hopes, anxieties, fears, memories and images provoked by everyday working life. Window-shoppers filter out unwanted reflections by restricting light sources: cupping their eyes against the glass to focus on the object of interest. Paula (2003) described *through-the-mirror* 'writing as being like self-supervision, like watching the self on video (p. 28). This requires high concentration likened by one student to a long refreshing swim, another to a deeply dreaming sleep. Another student audibly whispered 'disgusting', scribbling hunched over her page: we had all disappeared from her consciousness. Writers interact with and respond to drafts, subjecting them to interpretation and analysis, clarifying and extending understanding, deepening their involvement in the text: 'The only time I know that something is true is at the moment I discover it in the act of writing' (Jean Malaquais, quoted in Exley 1991, p. 64). Reflective practitioners say: 'I didn't know I thought/knew/remembered that until I wrote it'; one said: 'it is an opportunity to inhabit the unknown'.

Laurel Richardson advises a range of writing activities in order to acquire writing confidence and skills, such as joining a creative writing group (Richardson and Adams St. Pierre 2005, pp. 973–6). Elbasch-Lewis runs courses for teachers to enable enquiry, re-storying, appreciation of diversity of voices in education; one student said writing is 'a useful everyday tool enabling me to continually examine assumptions and patterns of living and to maintain a dynamic of ongoing change ... to confront, understand and study ourselves, what we were, what we are now, how we got here ... we didn't expect these to appear in such a significant and lucid way in our stories' (Elbasch-Lewis 2002, pp. 425–6). 'Theology by heart' is a dialogic reflexive writing portfolio method used for theological reflection turning 'life into text' (Graham et al. 2005). A study in medicine concluded: 'we observed that doctors felt the process of writing and talking about the stories was both profound and helpful. The process stimulated clarification of personal values and priorities, created a context for peer support (which doctors often seem to resist), and fostered recognition of opportunities to make constructive changes in their professional lives … Amid so much discussion of what is wrong with medicine, the workshops seemed to help them remember what is right' (Horowitz et al. 2003, p. 774).

Medical students' reflective accounts of memorable consultations in general practice stimulated them to articulate learning experiences and key features of general practice (Svenberg et al. 2007).

To write is to open oneself up to chance, to free oneself from the compulsive linking up of 'meaning, concept, time and truth' that has dominated Western philosophic discourse. Writing involves risk, play, loss of sense and meaning. (Flax 1990, p. 192).

> In everyday life I am sceptical of many things, and scornful of superstition. Writing fiction has taught me to respect what seems to be random, or coincidental; to have faith in small beginnings, and faith that the process of writing has its own alchemy … in writing the sense of touching something both beyond and within myself which I can do in no other way. Only through solitude, the tap of the keys, the discovery of some connection between inner and outer, intellect and emotion, body and spirit – feeling aspects of all these, and of the smallest and most everyday events, fall into place in silence and stillness, striving towards a whole. (Sue Gee; see also Gee 2002)

Perspective

Writing always comes from specific perspectives; the truth it conveys can never be completely objective. Readers might understand something different from what writers intended, particularly in such as email. This could be seen as a different understanding rather than a misunderstanding. Words are not bricks given to interlocutors, with meaning inherent in physical being. Bricks are for building physical structures. Words are for building meaning. String words together and the speaker or writer creates not a solid wall but a permeable evanescent web which looks different in different lights, whose meaning depends on the angle at which it is viewed. And there are a large number of viewpoint angles.

A colleague reported by email she had been badly treated, trying to elicit my support. My opinion of her plummeted because I perceived her extraordinarily self-centred world-view. My sympathy was with her colleagues, since she clearly had no sense of teamwork. Her writing gave a different message than the one she intended. A piece of writing is the joint responsibility of writer and reader; writers cannot determine what readers might infer from their writing. Readers usually do not know, and generally do not need to know, exactly what a writer intended; they make their own sense of a piece of writing. Another reader might have inferred a different set of meanings from her email.

Dialogue with the self is a form of multi-perspectival thinking via writing. Wayne Turnbull (Turnbull and Mullins 2007) developed a strategy for his PhD based upon *The Screwtape Letters*, a clever and funny religious tract by C.S. Lewis (1961a), in which Screwtape and Wormwood, apprentice and master in the art of wickedness, write letters to each other. The traditional PhD tuition model is master and apprentice, but Turnbull's are both himself, he wrote the letters from both of them, formulating and developing his theory, ideas and practice in the process (see Chapter 11).

Taking responsibility

Reflective practitioners write about their own experience for specific others (group or mentor) with whom they are read, discussed and developed. There is full interplay of story, teller and audience, or text, interpretation and intentionality, without alienation (Tyler 1986).

> For me, the group is not about using the writing to analyse my work as a general practitioner. It is about discovering, through the medium of writing, something about my personal and professional relationships – with patients, family, the world, the past etc. Constructing or crafting a piece of writing is part of the discovery process, and reading it is the final act of legitimacy. (Becky)

Writing is increasingly introduced into professional courses (Hatem and Ferrara 2001; Montgomery et al. 2003). Davidson (1999) comments how, on introducing colleagues to reflective writing, they 'say how it helped their writing to know it was acceptable to write in forms of their own creation, and as a way of expressing their experience. The [reflective practice] norm seems more often a feeling of intimidation at the prospect of using a foreign tool with stuffy rules'.

If meanings are formed by language, if signs do not have innate meaning but are in an endless interplay or diffusion of signification, and if writing is more important than the spoken word, then undertaking a conscious process of self-examination through writing must develop awareness of language and meanings.

Many life constraints are constructed around and by us, rather than being bars we can only beat against. Responsibility for my action lies with me. Sartre suggested that unperceived choices always face us, although we rarely perceive our freedom to choose ([1938] 1963): recognising, and taking responsibility for actions is part of reflexivity.

If control can be exerted over everyday elements, then, metonymically some control will have been taken over the larger structures. In deciding to write, tell and take ownership of some of our stories we positively and enjoyably exercise responsibility. Self-expression in writing and critical reading is vital. Paolo Freire (1972) asserted illiteracy spells oppression. The boundaries of our understanding and communication need to be pushed beyond what have for so long been considered its limits. 'In the struggle to reassert feminine values, feminine writing which draws on the unconscious is a key site for bringing about change' (Weedon 1987).

The confidence acquired in *through-the-mirror* writing can spill over. A Master's student described one of her 'benefits and achievements' as 'learning to write with freedom'; I would add: with confidence and authority. Writing can enable supervisory relationships to reach deeper levels. Writing done in private will encapsulate confidential vital material which might be difficult to surface verbally in a session:

> I use writing in my supervision: I require the supervisee to write down from memory a verbatim account of one session, but include their own feelings, ideas, and bodily sensations in the process (counter-transference). I receive it by email before the session, so I have a chance to mull it over. They agree producing this written account is hard work but very rewarding in itself. What I haven't yet done is to review these process recordings to track the progress of a particular patient. (Nathan Field, www.scribblesociety.com)

Fictional dialogue with either characters, or with *internal critics*, or *supervisors* (see Chapter 6) can develop insight and querying of previously unquestioned assumptions and barriers. Dialogues are written like drama script, the hand being allowed to write in the voice of the other alternately with the writer's own habitual voice. The other voice can be similar to the *internal professional supervisor*, recommended by Casement (1990), or the educational supervisor (Turnbull and Mullins 2007). The silence of writing is relatively undemanding, as there is no listening other, and no time limit. Writing can provide *safe* present in which to reflect upon unsafe things:

> Writing is a disinhibition strategy, as it anchors people to a safe present while they re-experience a past event, providing optimum distance possibilities and hence cathartic reset. (Evison 2001, p. 256)

The discipline of writing

Writing goes beyond the emotions of the moment, drawing upon deep experience. It distances (puts out there, onto the paper), but also creates closer contact with emotions, thoughts and experiences. Some of the dynamic, immediate properties of speech can seem to be lost in writing, which can appear to freeze or embalm experiences. Explorative and expressive writing, however, is as dynamic as speech, if not more so: 'The imaginative structuring of experience, then, is not only an intellectual structuring but a response to an emotional challenge – a sort of emotional discipline (Winter et al. 1999, p. 204).

Paradoxically writers have to allow, 'circumstances in which it is safe to be absent-minded (that is, for conscious logic and reason to be absent from one's mind)' (Freud 1950, p. xiii). Writers surrender to 'safe' 'circumstances' of creative 'discipline'. The Church of England Book of Common Prayer offers a similar oxymoron: thy service is perfect freedom. The discipline of creative writing allows greater freedom of exploration and expression than can be obtained without it. A carefully boundaried space is created in workshops, secure and confident enough to enable surrender to the structured discipline of writing. I encourage people to develop safe-enough writing situations in their own space and time. The security to take risks comes from the carefully managed writing and discussion process and the secure enough carefully boundaried educational environment.

> One of the reasons people seem able to open themselves up in these sessions is that Gillie imposes nothing of herself when she suggests the writing. The suggestions for writing and introductory words are very open and opening, with no way of doing it suggested, nor definite subjects, etc. (A student)

Surrendering to creative discipline is neither simple nor straightforward. Insight engendered by expressive exploration can be dynamically unsettling: 'One leaves a piece of one's flesh in the inkpot each time one dips one's pen' (Tolstoy, quoted Exley 1991, p. 25). And 'The progress of any writer is marked by those moments when he manages to outwit his own inner police system. Writers have invented all kinds of *games* to get past their own censorship' (Hughes 1982, p. 7). My methods, such as *six minutes' writing without thinking*, are *games*.

> It's happening – that thing where I dismiss my own thoughts: *No, not that. You'll get stuck if you go with that. That's so dull, you'll bore yourself stupid. Not that, not that, not that.* It makes it so imposssible to get started and then to follow through. It's the Thought Police, as Gillie said Ted Hughes said. I have a whole battalion of them – bobbies on the beat, sergeants in the office, sharp-eyed interrogating inspectors – loads of them. And then there's the Crown Persecution* Service complete with judge and jury and some hopeless, depressed woman from Victim Support as my only ally.
>
> Is it experience that tells me, Don't go there, it'll be dull? Not just dull – something more like, It won't get born. It'll be a messy miscarriage, a deformed foetus that'll die shortly after it slips into the world. Is it experience? In fact, experience tells me, Focus, write, give yourself over to it and whatever comes out will be healthy, with full lungs and kicking limbs.
> *This is what I actually wrote instead of *Prosecution*. (Chris Banks)

One reflective writer described it pleasurably: 'everybody writing alone yet together'. But many find it difficult to go on to create discipline, or permission, in their own space and time.

Penny wrote effectively in the group, but could write nothing at home. I suggested she try somewhere else, or with carefully chosen materials, or at a different time. Penny then wrote two pieces, the first in a café, having bought a shocking pink folder, a new pad and a bright pink pen.

Some find it hard even to begin to think of writing. One new participant looked startled, rummaging in her bag, saying: 'I've only got lipstick.' Many professionals find it difficult to find the time, though are very glad when they do:

> All of us lead busy lives, and a lot of the actual writing is done like naughty chil-
> dren's homework, at the last minute, yet it is also clear that the stories come
> into being in the context of our lives, though they may only be written down in
> haste under a Sunday morning deadline. I think this may be what gives some of
> our efforts an immediacy and seriousness which is occasionally beautiful, and
> always interesting. (Seth)

Many find writing on their own easier, finding the structured discipline of group writing time problematic. And there are those who cannot start at all:

> I know this small group now in a deeper way than I could ever have done in a
> whole course worth of sessions. You [a colleague] look different now. You have
> become a person for me. I'm so glad. I had been so nervous of writing when
> we started, feeling I can't write what comes into my head; I really can't. And
> Gillie said 'fine, we must all write in the way that suits us, you do whatever that
> is'. But having heard all your pieces I can now see how I can do it; I'm going to
> rewrite mine with all my feelings, thoughts, ideas and other things – some of
> them really personal.

Finding the writer's voice

People are often nervous, not realising written expressive ability is as innate as speech. They gain confidence as they gain trust, faith in themselves (that they can do it), and a desire and determination to write. Positive encouragement is facilitative. Beginners will progress from inexpressive, imitative or inauthentic writing, offered positive encouragement.

This *voice* is found with 'willing suspension of disbelief for the moment, which constitutes poetic faith' (Coleridge). Seamus Heaney says 'Finding a voice means that you can get your own feeling into your own words and that your words have the feel of you about them … A voice is like a fingerprint, possessing a constant and unique signature that can, like a fingerprint, be recorded and employed for identification (1980a, p. 43). Ted Hughes likened it to silent, still night-watching for foxes: 'Till, with a sudden sharp hot stink of fox / It enters the dark hole of the head' (1967, pp. 19–20). These passive approaches suggest writers need specific states of mind for inspiration to arrive. Heaney's metaphors are active: 'Between my finger and my thumb / The squat pen rests. / I'll dig with it.' (1980b, pp. 10–11). And:

> Usually you begin by dropping the bucket half way down the shaft and wind-ing up a taking of air. You are missing the real thing until one day the chain draws unexpectedly tight and you have dipped into water that will continue to entice you back. You'll have broken the skin of the pool of yourself. (Heaney 1980a, p. 47)

Hélène Cixous becomes a jewellery thief: 'These pearls, these diamonds, these signifiers that flash with a thousand meanings, I admit it, I have often filched them from my unconscious. The jewellery box … Furtively, I arrive, a little breakin, just once, I rummage, ah! The secrets!' (1991, p. 46).

Writing stories rather than abstractions

Writing narratives can enable grappling with everyday issues, shedding light on feelings (for example, a sense of alienation). Writing an abstract and generalised (non-narrative) piece about mistakes in general offers less access to meaning and understanding. Memorable poems and stories are all about events and people, their thoughts and actions: never only abstract philosophising. Wordsworth's magical poem about daffodils carries a significant message; we understand and remember it because of the illuminatory story in the first stanza: the philosophy, or theory, is embedded. Sartre's philosophy (in *Nausea* ([1938] 1963 pp. 115–16), is part of the story, making the theory memorable and comprehensible.

> We got so much further than I could have thought we might in one short session. We slipped between theory and story in the discussions about the writing. Somehow the stories seemed to open us up to the theory and to clarify it. (Brian)

> Writing about an incident clarifies thought. Instead of a rambling account that moves back and forth in time (which I'm particularly prone to, as I don't have the facility for precise language) writing tends to make one create a sequential story. In doing so, various particulars, or gaps may stand out as one tries to present a story that makes sense. 'The process of writing inevitably leads to a reformulation, added clarity and ideas for further analysis' (Miles and Huberman 1994). (Jane)

William Carlos Williams said 'no ideas but in things' (1951, p. 231): in effective writing, 'things', events, experiences carry or infer 'ideas' and feelings, abstractions are not expressed directly. Writers are exhorted to '*show don't tell*': readers learn from characters, place and actions, rather than from the authorial voice. Do not tell me she is pregnant: show me her ungainly movements, swelling belly, hand to her back as she stops to get breath.

Writing in abstractions is self-protective. Such pieces are sometimes clever. Writers need to be gentled out of being *clever* and into being open.

A role for abstract reflective writing, however, is following on from a story. This next piece was wonderfully useful to a group because it followed the writer's pair of reflective stories. It exemplifies how abstraction can be fruitfully reflective when related *directly* to previous writings. Here is Lindsay Buckell reflecting upon her story:

> So at the end of this I know where I started, and that is being a good creative confident practitioner is about love not fear. It's about looking at what we do and others do with honesty and loving criticism and not with a big stick. It's about learning from the good and bad bits even if it's painful sometimes. It's about the excitement and satisfaction of doing the job a bit better.
>
> Leaving aside the issues of resources, behind a lot of bad practice is fear. Fear of getting it wrong, fear of patients' strong feelings, fear of our own strong feelings, fear of the demons inside us, of change, of saying 'I don't know', of our own inadequacies, of being out of control.
>
> In making more and more rules and edicts perhaps we are in danger of making the fears more powerful. We build the rules, the threats, the edicts into huge castle walls to keep the fears at bay. What if we took the walls down stone by stone and invited the fears to come in? For within our castle walls are the good fairies, the kind caring fairies who have to live alongside the fears. If we dismantle the walls and let the fears come in they wouldn't go away because they are real, and many of them are necessary but they might mingle a bit better with the good fairies. The fears might spice us up a bit and the good fairies – care, compassion, love and laughter – would maybe be able to stretch their wings and fly about a bit better.
>
> What if, in taking down our castle walls, we started with a piece of paper and a pen? (Lindsay Buckell)

Lindsay said: 'When I wrote it, it didn't feel like an abstract piece at all, more an expression of my passionate hatred of the current climate of fear and blame.' Hatred, fear and blame are all abstract, but here they have a strong effective meaning for Lindsay and her readers because she is writing not about hatred, fear and blame in general, but specifically related to the incident which brought these emotions out so forcefully; which she had written previously.

It is a summer's day and I am looking after Simon. He lies, poor young thing, deeply unconscious, the machinery puffs and blows, whirrs and chugs. I am concerned that all the machinery, which is keeping Simon alive, is working right; and yet I love this young man, not sexually or romantically but from somewhere in my middle. I am not accepting that he is as ill as he is, I am not denying it either. I do not believe in a miracle cure, I am simply not engaging with it. I am concerned, at this moment, with looking after him and his machines.

The door opens and the ward sister comes in. She has trust in me that I can nurse her patient. She asks if I would like her to help me turn him. It is a question, not an order, in the way she says it she acknowledges that today Simon is my patient and she is simply offering to help me. She is cheery and competent, not cheery which might suggest avoidance of the situation, she is just present but lightly so. She says 'wouldn't he have hated this'. She is right – he is a diffident and intensely private young man. His mother died of the same disease. He has that depth in people whom personal tragedy has robbed of that illusion we all carry that life is essentially benign. He is quiet and shy, but laughs and chats with the other patients who are all much older than he.

Now he lies, totally dependent, his body exposed to anybody. She is right: he would have hated this. As we turn him she is very careful with the body which is on loan to us, because he can't protect it himself at present, careful to protect his dignity. We talk to him, not across him. In this care of this young man is our understanding that he is still a person with right to care and dignity, whether he knows or not.

In that moment I learned the truth of empathy; I received permission to have empathy with my patients, to believe in their rights as individuals, to allow myself to love them, but as a professional, not as a friend. She didn't talk about it, she didn't analyse it, she simply modelled it and all I'd heard about not getting involved which had never made sense inside me fell away. I understood something profound about the nature of being truly involved in a professional relationship with my patients. (Lindsay Buckell)

Story and fiction

Lindsay's piece is undeniably a story. But is it fiction? Any narrative is inevitably fiction, in that events are reconstructed or recreated from a perspective. Ward sister or patient would tell it differently. Lindsay may, furthermore, have embroidered certain bits, and downplayed others, to make her point persuasively, interestingly and confidentially. My suggested writing theme was 'an aha moment, an epiphany of understanding'; her personal theme, emerging as she wrote, was 'the time I learned about empathy'. All stories could thus be said to be fictions, however much based on memories of actual events. The distinction between fiction or fact (true or false) is one of those artificial binaries which beset modern living. A story is a creative construct, whatever material is drawn upon. All *through-the-mirror* writing is from a practitioner's depth of experience, knowledge and skill, as true as you can get in the way a straight line is true.

A story can re-create with powerful re-presentations of interpersonal relationships. A writer can draw unconsciously on deep professional and personal experience to convey nuances of gesture, speech, intention, memory, thought and feeling. Rereading such an account therefore offers insight to writer and reader. Readers then share insights with the writer, thus expanding the knowledge gained.

Stories and the transmission of culture

Such stories can re-present a picture of unwritten social and professional rules and codes as well as an implicit comment upon them:

> Fiction not only legitimizes emotions and aspirations, it also, again particularly since the appearance of the novel with its devotion to the minutiae of personal relationships, gives models and patterns of acceptable and unacceptable behaviour. I have certainly noticed that those who never read, or have never read, fiction, tend to be obtuse and insensitive in personal relationships. It does really seem as if the consumption of fiction is a part of the necessary education of modern people in the fine points of human relationships. So many examples are given of how people are, how they may be expected to react, and what the harvest is likely to be. (Rockwell 1974, p. 81)

A clash of codes is embedded in Lindsay's sentence: '*We talk to him, not across him*'. Aha, think non-nurse reader I, some nurses would treat this nearly inanimate body as an object; perhaps until this point, Lindsay had only experienced nurses who did exactly that. She responded to my guesses:

> I like what you wrote about it except that the bit that was so unusual and liberating for me was her comment about 'wouldn't he have hated this?' I had, in fact, met many nurses who would treat unconscious patients well – in not talking across them, and so on. What was so unusual was this indication of her deep understanding of him as an individual in that sentence. It joined up with all the other things I wrote about her in her ability to treat patients as individual people, therefore with empathy, rather than as a collective noun patients: i.e. part of the institution and all alike to be worked round as if they were all identikit and those who wouldn't play ball being labelled difficult or manipulative. (Lindsay Buckell)

This issue, and its corollary, has also been reflected upon through reflexive journal writing and discussion by a student palliative care nurse: 'patients must be seen as real people not just patients. Patients need to see nurses as people ... not mere nurses doing their job' (Durgahee 1997, p. 141).

Stories can tell how we might or ought to act, think and feel. Think of the writings informing your thinking: the unloving stupidity of King Lear (Shakespeare); the selfishness of Henry James's Isabel (*Portrait of a Lady*); Agamemnon's monomaniacal stealing of Achilles' girl, Briseis (Homer). The same is true of reflective story writing, such as Lindsay's (see also Winter et al. 1999).

Stories to enable perception and questioning

Stories not only present comprehensible possible ways of being, they create questions. Stories offer understandings, but also lead the reader to want to find out more:

> The truest respect which you can pay to the reader's understanding is to ... leave him something to imagine, in his turn, as well as yourself. (Sterne [1760] 1980, p. 77)

Story-writing allows three-dimensional exploration. Insights often hinge upon small details, such as the sister relating to the patient as a person rather than just another patient. These insightful details often appear unplanned: like the opening of an inner eye. Awareness of detail, inculcated by writing and discussing, increasingly slips into daily practice, making it more aware and reflective:

> This course helped me, encouraging me to be more aware of each day, and making me more observant. (Brimacombe 1996, p. 15)

Novelist Lesley Glaister, whose ideas come from 'my eyes, ears and gut feelings', would advise writers to 'stare, eavesdrop, never stop wondering'. Such awareness inevitably benefits practice. Some professionals do not fully perceive their students, clients, colleagues and environment, but only what they themselves think, just as Virginia Woolf depicted Orlando:

> He opened his eyes, which had been wide open all the time, but had seen only thoughts. (Woolf [1928] 1992, p. 101)

Carefully observed, detailed descriptions are reflective: 'we theorise every time we look at the world' (Goethe 1998). Picasso (n.d.) said 'we must not discriminate between things. Where things are concerned there are no class distinctions'. Awareness of details can enable insight, pushing away assumptions and habitual perspectives and modes of understanding. 'God is in the details' (Verghese 2001, p. 1013). A closely observed event, however small, written about, reflected upon, discussed critically and re-explored through further writings, stands metonymically for the whole of that reflective writer's practice.

Acute observation is required: not the narrowly focused observation skills required by practice, but the detached and impartial detailed observation of a writer. Reflective writers I have trained are amazed at vital details previously missed.

Careful description can create dynamic re-looking, re-observing and re-understanding: 'Writing of narratives in itself is analytical in the sense that practitioners become engaged in conscious efforts to view themselves and their actions with a certain degree of detachment and suspension' (Kim 1999, pp. 1207–8) (see also Chapter 4). Why and how naturally follow from, for example, the precise recollection of a colleague's expression. Take Mark Purvis's simple, but acutely observed rerendering of his little brother's death (Chapter 2). A forgotten memory until the poem was written without forethought; the writing and the subsequent discussions enabled a wealth and depth of insight and learning. This is working 'with stories' rather than 'about them' (Frank 1995, p. 23).

Such reflective approaches are learned experientially. Professionals or students have to be trusted to observe and write with all their faculties wide open. Facilitated discussion about writings is key to their development. This is counter to the view that 'description only serves the process of reflection, covering issues for reflection and noting their context' (Moon 2003, p. 216), and 'is not reflective at all, but merely reports events' (Hatton and Smith 1995, p. 40). This dichotomy between description and analysis is false. Close and careful description inevitably involves analytic sensitivity (see Goethe above).

'Writing as a method of enquiry' (Richardson and Adams St. Pierre 2005) is a method of qualitative research. Watson (2006) and Jasper (2005) both used reflective writing as a research methodology in its own right, Watson using the act of writing her reflective journal as her research.

Autoethnography is a form of research with similar aims and processes, a 'blend of ethnography and autobiographical writing that incorporates elements of one's own experience when writing about others' (Scott-Hoy 2002, p. 276). 'Making the personal political' (Holman Jones 2005), it involves critically examining and rewriting personal narratives, and challenging accepted surrounding stories (Ellis and Bochner 2000; Etherington 2004; Richardson 2001).

Writing to understand from varying perspectives

Stories are fragmentary texts offering narrow experiential slices. *Through-the-mirror* writing widens this. Associated writings deepen the learning for both writers and readers. Lindsay, in her abstract reflective passages, above, worked out what she meant, and gives readers more insight. Bev (Chapter 6) wrote from her own viewpoint, and then from the other protagonist's perspective; she began to grasp forces at work upon them both. Readers not only gain from the story, but can relate it to their own experience. A window of understanding opens not only into Bev's incident, but into their own parallel experiences.

Some reflective writers readily create stories from alternative points of view, or fictions based on their own experience. Others find it less easy. Telling the same story through different characters' eyes is currently common in novels. Jane Rogers's *Mr Wroe's Virgins* (1991), the story of an eighteenth-century religious fanatic, is written through the voice of virgins he abuses. This multi-voiced approach gives the text a depth and roundedness achievable in no other way. Frankenstein (Shelley [1820] 1994) and Dracula (Stoker [1897] 1994) are both also written with the 'I' being taken in turn.

A range of reflective stories and writings are possible around a core story. Professionals are imaginative in devising additional texts. One doctor wrote from the perspective of the sofa on which his patient sat day in and day out: it had quite a story to tell (see Chapters 6 and 14). A butterfly's eye is a myriad of tiny eyes, each recording an image from a different angle. Bodies of reflective writings offer similar textures.

Visualisation can extend perspective. 'We ask participants to write about a landscape they know really well, then to describe their actual classrooms in the language of landscape, then their imaginary classrooms. We then ask them to populate them' (Kemp 2001, p. 350) (see also metaphor, Chapter 8).

Stress

Through-the-mirror writing provides safe enough environments for facing troubling issues, helping reduce anxiety and stress. People regularly cry, are comforted, supported to see events from different and enlightening perspectives, helped to find solutions to problems. This writing can bring painful things to the surface so they can then appropriately be dealt with.

A study of palliative care nurses involved in verbal group reflection (von Klitzing 1999) concluded that over time they reflected less about themselves and more about patients. This might have been because they withdrew and protected themselves in response to increasing stress. This might not have happened if they had *written* as well as discussed.

Many texts explicate the personal development power of writing. Many also describe professional and personal development (for example, Anderson and MacCurdy 2000; Helman 2006; Verghese 2001). Shem uses fiction writing as a resistance against the inhumanity of medicine (2002).

Is reflective writing an art?

Art has always questioned boundaries of existence. Artists and certain ethnographers and philosophers put themselves in situations in which conventional orderliness of everyday systems of thinking is suspended. Artists cross dangerous mental and social barriers to create images that jolt or shock audiences into reassessment. Brecht, for example, set viewers questioning taken-for-granted structures.

The belief that only writers can write, that art is born not made, is erroneous. Poets do not lie around (either luxuriously or starving in garrets) waiting for the muse. Writing is 1 per cent inspiration and 99 per cent perspiration: 'I rewrote the ending of *Farewell to Arms* thirty-nine times before I was satisfied' (Ernest Hemingway, quoted in Exley 1991, p. 13).

People have responsibility for their lives, power is located in each individual rather than in God, government, philosophers. Academic literary criticism is such an authority: policing acceptable language and writing as either literary or non-literary, what form it should take, and who is allowed to create and take part in the discourse (Eagleton 1983). These gods must be overthrown. Quiet powerful internal voices clamour to be heard. Expressive and explorative writing develops confidence, co-operation and collaboration, enables challenging of assumptions about diversity, taken-for-granted unequal or unjust professional structures, encourages skills sharing, the development of team-building, and enhances ability to deal with conflict in an artistic, aesthetic process.

Writing, an ancient power

Writing is first known in the Near East in 3300 BC. A hieratic papyrus from Thebes from about 1850 BC, the teaching of Ptahhotep, says: 'It is good to speak to the future the future will listen.' And we can listen to what was written all those years ago. Writing was considered to belong to the gods, because of this power to enshrine text. Thoth, the ancient Egyptian god of writing, 'knows the mysteries and sets the gods' utterances firm … proclaims all that is forgotten'. Egyptian hieroglyphs were called 'gods' words', were considered to have numinous power as amulets. Stelae were inscribed with magical texts for water to be poured over and drunk to ingest the magic of the texts. 'Damnatio memoriae' was attacking a dead enemy by damaging or erasing their written name: destroying a written name was to deprive its owner of identity and existence. *Through-the-mirror* writers gain power over their practice by naming it in writing, as Usher says 'Theorising is a practice of writing. One writes about the meanings in practice and through writing creates the meanings of practice. Practice is itself always changing hence there are always new meanings to be written about. At the same time, through writing, the meaning of practice is re-created, always cast anew' (1993, p. 100). And Holly 'Writing taps tacit knowledge; it brings into awareness that which we sensed but could not explain (Holly 1989, p. 78).

> I even enjoy the physical holding of the pen, the shaping of the words, and I like the way it unfolds before you, like thought unravelling. The rest of the book is blank; I wonder what the next chapter will be? (Jenny)

 Read to learn

Davidson, B. (1999) Writing as a tool of reflective practice, *Group Analysis*, **32**(1), 109–24.

Richardson, L. and Adams St Pierre, E., (2005) Writing: a method of inquiry, in N. Denzin and Y. Lincoln (eds), *Handbook of Qualitative Research*. 3rd edn. London: Sage, pp. 923–47.

Svenberg, K., Wahlqvist, M. and Mattsson, B. (2007) A memorable consultation: writing reflective accounts articulates students' learning in general practice, *Scandinavian Journal of Primary Health Care*, **25**(2), 75–9.

 Write to learn

Each chapter ends with *Write to learn*. For straightforward advice, sufficient for the exercises below, see *Write to learn* in Chapter 1, and see Chapter 6 for more advice. Each writing can be shared fruitfully with a group or confidential trusted other, if this seems appropriate once the writer has read and reflected on it first.

Exercise 5.1   Truths, lies and fantasies

1. Write one truth about yourself, one wish, and one outright lie.
2. Read back to yourself, adding or altering positively.
3. Write one to write more about.
4. Reread with insight, altering or adding if you wish.
5. If you share this, afterwards choose a wish or lie from someone else's list to borrow for your own list. *(Continued)*

(Continued)

Exercise 5.2   What makes me tick?

1. List 20 (50 or 100, depending on time: repetition is allowed and usefully shows you which items are vital) words or phrases which make you:

   (i)   focused and productive, or
   (ii)   furious, or
   (iii)   happy, or
   (iv)   serene, or
   (v)   lazy and unproductive, or
   (vi)   uncooperative, or
   (vii)   and so on.

2. Reread and order with most important at the top.
3. Choose one to write about further.
4. Read back to yourself with care, adding or altering or leaving well alone.

Exercise 5.3   Another point of view

1. Think of someone you really admire; it does not matter if you do not know them personally.
2. Describe this person briefly.
3. List observations they might make about your work (remember no one else need ever read this).
4. List questions they might ask you about your work.
5. List questions you would like to ask them.
6. Write their reply to you: as a letter (note again contents of brackets in 3).
7. Reread with loving kindness to yourself, and reflect in writing.

SECTION 2

REFLECTION AND REFLEXIVITY: HOW

CHAPTER 6

REFLECTIVE WRITING: A HOW-TO GUIDE

Chapter 6 is an in-depth introduction to reflective writing. It explains the five stages of *through-the-mirror* writing, how to develop them, and why writing is so effective.

> The captain unlocked his word hoard. (*Beowulf and Grendel* 1973, p. 12)

> I learned the science of letters … and this opened before me a wide field for wonder and delight. (Shelley [1820] 1994, p. 119)

A practical guide to writing for both practitioners and facilitators, this chapter helps support the *wonder and delight* of Frankenstein's monster, unpick negative assumptions, and agree that 'cynicism is deadly poison' (York Barr et al. 2006). The *how* of beginning to write is carefully explained, as well as what *through-the-mirror* writing is, for whom, why, and where and when it might be written. Above all it explains: writing is not only an expressive and explorative instrument, but to be wielded and enjoyed for its own sake.

Words, our everyday communicating tool, can be taken for granted so easily. After all we use and misuse them every day, and in the beginning was the Word. Yet writing is an art form, like painting and music. There are many more different ways to write than there are writers, because each develops their own voice. It can have as complex a form, process and set of variations as any other cultural form, say music or algebra. Each writing is an adventure into the writer's own being, and into their culture and society. Reflective writers own their writing, and only share it with readers when they are ready. When shared it becomes a joint journey: reader and writer together. Eeyore expressed his lack of confidence in writing as arrogantly being above such things 'Silly stuff. Nothing in it' (Milne [1928] 1958, p. 153). Many professionals feel threatened by reflective writing, and like Eeyore say it's a silly waste of time. They are covering their fear of failure, a legacy often of bad schooling. But it can be a thoroughly, satisfyingly straightforward process. To be literate and make full use of that literacy requires confidence. Writing does not come readily to many because of early didactic training in proper ways to write: the essay with sequenced argument; sonnet form; the short story's beckoning beginning, slick middle and sting-in-the-tail end; journalism's punchiness. Writing, for most professionals, is for reports: burdensome and long-winded, hated but essential means of justifying work to authorities. Striving to imitate successful writers, to please teachers, editors, line managers is loss of ownership of writing, mislaying of our own voices.

Reflective writers can trust straightforward *through-the-mirror* methods. That hitherto frustrating time of seeming to have an empty head with no writing in it at all can be transformed to writing a telling account. Never again (well, not quite so much) that 'Oh no!' fear of a clean sheet or empty screen. These methods are presented in detail to make the stages and processes clear. Once you have understood the process work out your own approach. Don't reach the stage of frustration, thinking as one reader did that there are 'too many rules, and too much emphasis on controlling time'.

Through-the-mirror writing is creative, a way of gaining access to each practitioner's deep well of experience not always accessible to everyday channels. It is akin to the writing of diarists (Dowrick 2009; Rainer 1978), for personal exploration (Cameron 2002), or the first draft stage used by novelists, poets or playwrights. Writers allow whatever needs to be written, with no forethought, reference to grammar, spelling, punctuation or literary form. Grammar and so on do not matter at this stage: they can so easily be sorted out later if necessary. After all, the ancient Greeks called grammar, logic, and rhetoric *trivium*.

Many find it easier to begin writing in a group, being given the process stage by stage without opportunity for delaying tactics, like anxiety about subject. The *internal critic* doesn't have much opportunity to whisper how useless they are. Some, on the other hand, find writing in a group inhibiting, and are freer alone.

Introduction to *through-the-mirror* writing

Trust the authority of the writing hand.

Through-the-mirror straightforwardly draws on initial writing methods used by professional and experienced writers. *Content* is important, not grammar and other rules. Writers are their own first reader; no one else will read it without their permission. This allows for almost anything to be written uncensored: redrafting or editing can be done before anyone else sees it, if wanted. Every piece of writing is right because an exploration of the writers' own experience. People need to rid themselves of the sense of teachers or editors ready to draw blood with red correcting pens. Each writer has authority over their own expression and exploration; there are no judges or critics. No one can get this writing wrong.

Through-the-mirror writing does not move onto methods required for publication (redrafting, editing), but stays with initial drafting. If this early, intuitive method is skipped, or redrafting and editing focused upon too early, writing is likely to be unreflective, and certainly unreflexive. *Through-the-mirror* writing never bothers about an unknown reader out there, nor about the needs and wants of publication. This material is sometimes progressed to publication stages, processes which might also be personally and professionally fruitful.

Through-the-mirror writing, the heart of reflection and reflexivity, is written primarily for the self. The process matters, not the product. Exploratory and expressive, it is initially only intended to communicate to the writer, and possibly a few trusted confidential others. Undertaken often at speed, it is a dynamic, initially private process of discovery. Speed leaves no gaps for destructive critics to leap in, interrupting flow and destroying confidence. The pen follows the writer's mind in any direction, and might put anything on the paper: insightful, illuminating, funny, mad, bad or even slightly dangerous seeming, occasionally dull. This process can enable burdens to be put down, lightening the writer. It also sometimes seems to come like a flash of lightning out of nowhere. And it can be enlightening.

A valuable mode of expressing, sharing, assessing and developing professional experience, writing is excellent solo, and with colleagues (Rowland 1993), and as a research tool (Winter 1991). Students write to express themselves, store aide-mémoires, present arguments, demonstrate knowledge, explicate experience or create literature. Educators write alongside students to give necessary experience to facilitate, evaluate and assess. Students and colleagues are most ably supported by tutors with first-hand knowledge and experience of the processes themselves (Kuit et al. 2001; Murray 1982).

'Art takes one over a threshold, out of the rut, it questions custom, the "taken-for-granted"; writing taps tacit knowledge – brings into awareness that which we sensed but could not explain' (Holly 1989, p. 75). 'The function of art in the full extent of its expressions includes the deliberate and subversive challenge to everyday understandings and interpretations of events' (Smyth 1996, p. 937).

Writing is private, unlike talking, it can create confidential reflexive dialogues, writer writing, enabling:

- leaps of understanding and connections
- contact with unexamined thoughts and ideas
- exploration of forgotten memories
- expression and exploration of issues of which the writer is aware but unable or unwilling otherwise to articulate, communicate and develop.

Speech or thought can be forgotten, or shift and change like a whisper game, vanishing on the air. Interlocutors often remember conversations differently, each party certain their recollection is correct. Writing leaves clear footprints on the page, aiding progressive thought. Writing stays in the same form to be worked on later. Rewriting and redrafting, to get closer and closer to what needs to be expressed, is self-educative.

- Writing is private. Writers are their own sole interlocutor until ready to share with another: safer than talking. Something said and heard cannot be unsaid, so spoken utterances are severely edited, usually unconsciously. Writing can, to a degree, evade this cutting-room. Greater depth and breadth, and more immediate access are engendered by this privacy.
- Writing can be creative and rewarding, tending to increase self-confidence and be a pleasure in practice.
- Writing can be torn up or burnt unshared with anyone, even the writer themselves, if necessary.
- Writing is longer, slower and more laborious than thinking. Writers are therefore less likely to waffle: in talk when something difficult is pressing to be said, people often say anything in order to put off the painful moment of tackling the issue.
- Imaginative forms such as metaphor are appropriate and readily used, giving indirect access to feelings, thoughts, knowledge, ideas, memories not accessible to non-image contact (Modell 1997; Pennebaker 2000).
- Fiction, a vital element, can protect confidentiality, be less exposing, more dynamic. It can convey ambiguities, complexities and ironic relationships between multiple viewpoints. Re-creation of a situation exactly as it happened is unlikely; it will be recounted as experienced through the writer's own senses, as felt and thought about by them. Accepting narratives are fiction can allow exploration without worrying about getting the *facts* just right.
- Creative processes tend to increase self-confidence and self-esteem.

Why writing?

Suspend your disbelief.

Through-the-mirror writing (as any creativity) is essentially playful (musicians 'play'). Art is not thus denigrated; rather it grows up the role of playing from the purely childish arena to which our modernist culture has relegated it.

> Might we not say that every child at play behaves like a creative writer, in that he creates a world of his own, or, rather rearranges the things of his world in a new way which pleases him? (Freud 1995, p. 54)

Freud reckoned the grown-up version of playing is fantasising. Creative writers surface fantasies and rid us of some of our tensions around fantasies: about which we are ashamed and secretive. We vicariously enjoy writers' fantasies. How much more powerful to write our own, however big or small, in a playful way?

> The sound of pencils on paper
> An occasional sigh, or sniff, a page
> Torn roughly from a notebook, or
> Scrunched and discarded
> I twist a lock of hair around my finger and glance up.
> Someone is frowning,
> Another, smiling …
> Everyone concentrating.
> Time's up. (But this isn't an exam and doesn't feel like one)
> There's a growing excitement – like that moment when someone is about to open the present you've given them …
> My gift to them, theirs to me – words on paper.
> We're sharing very private thoughts …
> Thoughtful silence and lots of laughter too.
> It's a kind of communion. (Becky)

How to start: the five stages

Your writing is a gift to yourself.

Stage 1: The six-minute write

Choose a comfortable uninterrupted place and time, and writing materials you like. Make sure you have everything else you need, like coffee and biscuits.

> Take time to calm down, sit back, change gear. Nice and comfortable in here. Quite a few things I've thought about writing today. Nice to just let things come out and sit on paper for a while. Not quite sure what track I'm on at the moment but don't worry something will come along in a bit. Good technique this. Doesn't matter. No one's going to read this later on – so don't worry about it – so can write anything. (Adam, medical student writing group)

Starting with *six minutes' writing* can help prevent the dither of 'What am I going to write?' by dumping mind-clutter onto the paper. Some of this writing will be useful (or even *diamonds in the dustheap*; Woolf 1979, p. 223) springing from seemingly nowhere, some only shopping lists or scurrilous moans. Stow all safely on paper and the mind is freed to continue. Awareness of anything other than the hand putting words on the paper can inhibit the flow, so allow the writing to follow its own track and leave obeying writing rules (grammar, logical sequencing, and so on) until later.

> I write without thinking much, trying to overcome all kinds of self-criticism, without stopping, without giving any consideration to the style or structure … only putting down on paper everything that can be used as raw material. (Llosa 1991, p. 45)

Begin, like Llosa, by allowing the pen to write:

Six Minutes' Write

1. **Write whatever is in your head**, uncensored.
2. **Write without stopping** for at least six minutes.
3. **Don't stop to think or be critical**, however disconnected it might seem.
4. Allow it to flow with **no thought for spelling, grammar, proper form**.
5. Give yourself permission to **write anything**. You do not even *have* to reread it.
6. Whatever you write will be **right**: it is yours, and anyway no one else need read it.

Lots might be written, or only a little seeming rubbish. It might be lists, poetry, gobbledegook, spirited logical argument: anything at all. *Six minutes' writing* sometimes turns up gold, sometimes dross. It is always useful, however, for beginning to scratch the surface, and for beginning to make marks on the page or screen: a difficult stage for any writer.

Six minutes
I'm clearing out the rubbish
I'm emptying my mind,
The trouble with this task is that
I don't know what I'll find.

I came because I want to write,
I wanted to move on,
And if I keep on writing,
Maybe I can move the stone.

Perhaps what lies beneath is ore,
Of course it may be dross,
But let the chance go just once more,
And all there'll be is loss. (Janet Tipper)

Six minutes

Here I am
Now.
It's hard – Something
I don't know what,
Yet I know
I feel and yet I cannot
Say – or write
the words too slow the thoughts
Who – am I and why I think
that I can come and give.

It's clear – I think – I don't
know, I'm not sure
Will it be OK, can I do
This – I am there – or – here?

So hard, too easy to fill all
the spaces – a thought in
a word it can go to all places!
A life, that is mine, I want
To be known – my heart it is
beating through gates that
are open. (John McAuley)

I always do my 6 minutes, but then I screw it up and throw it away without reading it. I realised when you said you should read it through that while I am doing my 6 minutes, which is complete and utter garbage and can even include a shopping list, weird exclamations and verbal tics, I also have another current slowly going along in my mind which is deciding what to write about in the next bit of writing and then I sit at the end of the 6 minutes and think, oh THAT is what I am supposed to do. Sometimes I don't want to do it and I try to do something different but it is the thing that has appeared in the 6 minutes that is very insistent and demands to be written. (Helen Drucquer 2004, pp. 203–4)

Stage 2: The story

Forget about *grammar*, syntax, spelling – *for now. They block the inspirational flow. Correct them later*.

A story of experience next. *Six-minute writing* has given a generous sense of permission to write anything, respect for whatever is written, and a realisation that words can satisfyingly appear as if from nowhere. It's good to stay with the flow and write a story without rereading the *six minutes' writing* yet: rereading switches writers into responsive reading mode. Stories written immediately following *six minutes* are likely to be significant.

Write straight away about any time in your experience, telling the story simply and allowing it to come in its own order. Focusing on a particular occasion, chosen seemingly at random, is facilitative to reflection. Try to choose the first event which occurs, without striving for significance. The most vital issue might be located or clarified by the seemingly mundane. Alternatively a writing theme may have arisen in *six minutes*. No one else need read this: what matters is capturing what is there to be written.

Write in the same way as *six minutes*, allowing words to arrive on the page without planning or questioning. Don't look over your shoulder, questioning what you write.

Write with a focus: the story of an experience. Try not to question – yet. The most common blocking query is: *why have I chosen this to write about; it's not nearly important enough?!* Everything is important: try to ignore this niggling demon.

Choose the first event which comes to mind. Try not to reject it, for whatever reason. The more anxiously the *right* account is sought, the more the really right one, the one thought of first, will slide away.

Allow 20 to 40 minutes to write. The more time wasted thinking, the less time there will be for writing. I have known some set an alarm clock, and stop when the bell rings. If you find you want to go on, and on, then do – and on ...

Re-create the situation as memory gives it, with as many details as possible, rather than an idealised *what you would rather have happened*, or worrying about *getting the facts right*.

Consider it fiction. Even if it is re-created as closely as possible to the memory, thinking of it as fiction can relieve embarrassment, confidentiality anxiety, fear of getting it wrong. These things happened to a character, which happens to be you-in-the-past. It can also allow experimentation with the hazy edge of memory. Or if it seems less important to explore *what really happened*, considering it fiction can offer freedom of expression.

Do not worry about spelling, grammar, syntax. They usually flow naturally in this kind of vitally charged writing. If infelicities, repetitions or unclarites occur, they are correctable later.

Proper form does not matter. Stories have proper beginnings, middles and ends: life does not. The same sort of glorious muddle of the original is appropriate now. Musings on the event (what you should/should not have said, for example) may arise: let them. Writing is endlessly plastic, and can be altered and tidied up later, before anyone else has to make sense of it, or embarrassingly read innermost feelings. You will probably find, however, it naturally gains a very appropriate pleasing form.

Allow the pen to notice details: tone of voice, clothing, spoken words, seeming incidentals, and feelings. As the experience is replayed, vital details begin to emerge, even if you thought you hadn't remembered them. Write them ALL down.

Allow reactions, emotional responses, feelings.

Refrain from **judgements** at this stage.

Types of writing, and topics for stage 2

Autobiographical narratives, fictional plotted stories, poetry, songs, drama, image exploration (see Chapters 12–14), descriptive passages are all appropriate. Here are some ideas generated by my groups:

changes
a conflict
in control
taking care
a dilemma
a celebration
a moment of joy
a sensitive subject
a time I took a risk
a clash of interests
a conflict of loyalty
a misunderstanding
a frustrated episode
a missed opportunity
a parting or beginning
a case for compassion
an evocative occasion
an extremity of emotion
the most dangerous time
a breach of confidentiality
a time when I was incapacitated
the blowing of the pressure valve.

Bev's story recalled a puzzling episode from some time ago:

Bev's story

I was working on the labour suite in Xmouth. Sister, a bossomly, matronly figure called Miss Lane, with iron grey hair and a face carved in granite. She exuded no warmth but appeared competent and in control. She certainly liked to control her flock of nurses, and also her flock of rams – her doctors.

We were all in fear and awe of her; she had favourites and could be extremely sarcastic and make life difficult for those she did not like and her voice lashed out at people. Unfortunately this extended to the patients and she could be very prejudiced.

The girl was young and unmarried, scared to death and in labour for the first time. An enema was ordered for her – 'high, hot and a hell of a lot' – by Sister Lane. She was subdued and in misery, kept in isolation because she was socially unacceptable.

Her pain was intense and the medication seemed to be slow in appearing and the support she was offered was peripheral and minimal. Sister was in total control and had decided to make this young girl her mission.

I felt excluded and unable to offer support – we all did, we all stood on the periphery – watched and observed what this youngster was subjected to. Sister did the delivery and everything was clinically correct and cold, cold, cold as ice – she allowed no family support into the delivery room.

I don't know what trauma was taken away by this young girl and what processes were set up for her in her future. I do know that the scenario had a profound impact on myself about what to do and how to be with women in labour. About power, dominance, control, exclusion and the withholding of warmth and love to anyone in distress.

From another source years later I learnt that Sister had had a breakdown of some description. Part of me thinks this was divine retribution and another part reflects on what we do to ourselves as human beings when we become so rigid, fixed and inflexible. And part of me reflects that had I made different choices at certain times of my life that could have been me. (Bev Hargreaves)

Stage 3: Read and respond

Trust the process; have faith in yourself.

Reading writing back to yourself is significant. Writing like Stage 2 Stories is often created *in camera*, without the writer really being aware of the content. Reading is then like a dialogue with the self, hearing what the hand had to say, and being able to respond back to it. Reflexive interpretive thoughts might be written in response. Rereading undertaken privately, slowly and respectfully, with responses noted, gives insight.

When the first *dash* is written, reread everything (including, most importantly, *six minutes*) slowly, attentively, and appreciatively, adding or altering if you wish, but being only positive about your writing.

(a) Read with **attention yet openly, non-judgementally**, looking at content rather than form.
(b) Attend with an **openness to divergent connections** previously perceived as separate, or inappropriate together; especially links between *six minutes* and later writing.
(c) Be aware of **underlying links**, fresh understanding and awareness.
(d) **Write additions**, alterations, make deletions.
(e) fill out with **as much detail as possible**, remembering we have **five senses**; smells and sounds as well as what things looked like can give vital clues, as can time of year; discomforts; intuitions; what people said, and the tone of voice they said it in.

Everything is significant.
Ask some of these questions, responding to them in writing:
Is it **puzzling**? Try to work out what and why.
Is it **surprising**? Or different from what you expected?
Are **contrasts** within the story significant?
Does **officialese** or **jargon** conceal anything?
Try not to come to an answer, or even a definitive question – yet.

A participant in a multicultural course for social workers, run by Olwen Summerscales (2006; see Chapter 11), commented on redrafting:

firstly, a summary of the incident … then I redrafted it as a [fairy] story. Noticing how much more emotion came into it, I redrafted it again – this was really powerful, much more reflective. I could see I'd moved on.

Here is an example of Stage 3 writing:

Fiji and reflective practice

It's at 4 o'clock in the morning, when I can't sleep, that's when I get the pen and paper out.

Working as a counsellor at the University of the South Pacific is an idyllic experience in lots of ways: a Rogers and Hammerstein set of tropical colours and scents from my office window. But the sheer cultural complexity of the university community is enough; add to that race, gender, sexuality, status and other aspects of diversity I'm meeting every day and the lack of professional consultation and the isolation from any group of counsellors with Codes of Ethics and Practice is enough to keep me awake. So, I write it all down. The feelings of inadequacy, of excitement, the confusion and doubts, contradictions and discoveries.

Some I've kept, some torn into very small pieces, too awful to reread, the thoughts too negative to carry around any more. Scribbling it all down, in complete privacy acted as a safety valve. I could be my own 'supervisor' and avoid the worst of the isolation. I also started to suggest writing to some of the staff and students who came for counselling. Some were using their third language, English, to speak to me and were thousands of miles from their village in another remote part of the Pacific. The writing gave us the possibility of a bridge.

Mustn't grumble, that so very English maxim is turned on its head. You must grumble, I would say, but do it on paper and in your own language. (Jeannie Wright)

Stage 4: Sharing your writing with a peer(s)

Your writing has the power to influence another, and them you.

Peers' responses can open up fresh avenues. They can support towards deeper levels of reflection, and perceive wider institutional contexts, or on the national social and political stage. Seeking just the right person or people can be worthwhile. E-contact can be a good substitute (see Chapter 11). A colleague might be right, but they or life-partner *might* be *wrong*: emotionally charged relationships may add non-useful complexities without offering different enough perspectives.

Reflecting on a critical incident is still within the confines of one's own perspective. Reflecting with another person, with the written incident before you, can bring added insights. (Jane)

Our discussion may focus on the thoughts, feelings and experiences which led to the piece, on the way it was crafted, or both. The trust we have developed means we may quickly move from empathising deeply with a writer's grief at the death of a loved one to suggesting their piece would be more powerful without the last sentence. (Maggie, Sheena, Clare, Mark, Becky)

Choose a colleague or fellow student with whom to share writing.

- Be positive and supportive; negative opinions are more readily received when preceded by positive.
- Comment on *writing*, not *writer*: considering writings as fiction, reducing possibility of hurt or loss of confidentiality.
- Consider everything read and discussed as confidential.
- Make any particular parameters for the discussion clear to mentor or group.
- Your writing is as wonderful as everyone else's: apologetic competitions are unfruitful.
- Enjoy deepening the reflective process, whether verbally or in writing.

Sometimes reading my work feels exciting; sometimes gratifying; sometimes heartbreaking; sometimes even faintly dangerous. (Becky)

Reading a piece aloud is like writing a song and singing it – it's not just your creation, it's your interpretation, it's putting your own voice out there. (Sheena)

Reading in the group can give the writer the courage to examine painful events in a truthful way. The group holds the writer's hand through a raw and painful life event. (Mark)

I've learned that reflective writing about a difficult event when I am a novice leaves me much more vulnerable than when I write about difficulties in something I am expert at. I have been keeping a reflective journal on these experiences. (Maureen Rappaport)

The next example is by Bev, who reflectively reread her story, wondering about Sister's mental breakdown. Feeling guilty she had not attempted to make things better for the patient, Bev was comforted by her group that there was nothing she, a young student, could have done. But she wanted to understand more clearly what might have been driving this Sister to such cruelty. With the group's encouragement, her reflection led her to decide to attempt fictionally to see the story through Sister's eyes:

 Bev Hargreaves's story from Sister's perspective

I trained in the days when nurses were real nurses – the nurses today don't know what hard work is and are frequently cheeky so need to be kept firmly in their place ...

(Continued)

(Continued)

I remember this young girl came in – she must have been 17 years, arrogant and demanding – I thought I'd soon knock the stuffing out of her, lick her into shape. Anyway it was not right that she should be with the other married mothers so I decided that I would look after her ...

Anyway that's my role, to keep control – control of everything, I'm not here to be liked, I'm here to do a job. (Bev Hargreaves)

Bev's group agreed this is not successfully enlightening fiction, and made further suggestions.

Stage 5: Developing writing

You can't write the wrong thing. Whatever you write will be right – for you.

Writing developmental pieces can deepen and widen understanding. The writer explores: *what would it be like if* …; being the *other*; different endings; or altering other essential aspects. This is often fiction: written to reflect upon deep wells of experiential knowledge and understanding. Psychological benefits of fiction writing are the same as when writers try to stick to what actually happened (Pennebaker 2000). Writing as the *other* is an exploration of the other's experience, not what the writer would think, feel and do if I were them:

Her: You always think of yourself!
Him: I've always been good at empathy!
Her: You!
Him: Yes, putting myself in their place, imagining I'm them.
Her: Yes. If you were them what would YOU be thinking; what would YOU do? You always think of yourself!

Here are some developmental ideas. A group or a mentoring pair will develop their own, appropriate to their own writing:

Give the story a title.

Write about the same event from the viewpoint of client or colleague perhaps: this person will become 'I'.

Try writing from a different, or opposing point of view: observer, friend or foe.

Write from the perspective of *omniscient narrator:* all characters become 'he', 'she', including you.

If you wrote the initial story in the present, try rewriting it in the past, or vice versa.

Rewrite the story with the gender of the main character(s) switched.

Write the next chapter.

Write a commentary on your own or another's text, either as yourself or as one of the characters.

Retell the story with a different ending or focus, for example, happy for sad.

Write what a character is thinking at any one moment.

Write about a (some) missing character(s). Like a photograph, a story is always an unreal and slim slice of reality: think of the area beyond the frame.

Rewrite the story in a different style/genre: newspaper article/fable/narrative poem/children's story/romance/detective/sci-fi/fantasy (see Chapter 14).

Write *thought bubbles* for vital (or puzzling) characters at significant points in the narrative.

Rewrite the story with the focus of control/power altered.

You are a reporter: interview a character from the story.

Take a character who's just left the action; describe what they might be doing/ thinking.

Write a letter to a character, expressing puzzlement/anger/sympathy. Write their reply.

Write a letter or transcribe a telephone conversation between two characters.

List the objects/colours in the story. Are they significant?

List assumptions held by any of the characters in the story.

What themes or patterns relate to others in your life?

What is missed out of this story?

Write a film/dust-jacket blurb for the story.

Continue the story six months/a year later.

Consider asking someone from the *real* situation to write their own version; or interview them.

Explore the area which puzzles you.

Ask what if? Invent your own!

Sometimes writing a further piece can feel difficult, especially if the first has been done in a group, and the second at home/work. Some find it easier to write in their own time and space; others find it awkward or cannot maintain the momentum. Two students once wrote great pieces during a session, received interesting suggestions for development, but merely typed out their original pieces with a few amendments. They came from a culture, I think, where imaginative flair was not expected of students, and could not maintain it in their own time and space without group encouragement.

Still not satisfied she'd understood Sister's bitter cruelty, Bev's group encouraged her to try a different perspective. She concentrated on Sister's past:

 Bev's final story about Sister

I had to write the first chapter: I don't want people to get beyond the shell that I now am. And as I reflect on the hardness, rigidity and controlled automaton that I have become I am upset and scared, scared to remember what used to be – I was in another life and country then and I don't know if I can bear to remember ... to feel again.

Once upon a time there was a bubbly, friendly 5-year-old called Mary Ellen Rose. I had many friends and a special friend called Joe, who became my sweetheart and lifetime partner. He was tall, dark haired, rather serious and intense and we had long involved conversations about the meaning of life – the sort that you have at that age. He was my best friend and eventually my lover.

I don't know when I decided that nursing was for me. It was hard work in those years, but I always wanted to care for anyone who was sick, so young and naive, but so proud of my uniform.

And then the war came and so many of my childhood friends went marching off, including Joe.

I haven't let myself dwell on the last time I was with Joe. I hurt even after all these years. I hurt more and more after the news came – I felt old and cold and grey, a bone-deep coldness that I couldn't shake off – the same coldness I felt when I had the miscarriage which was hushed up and never spoken of ... I had almost forgotten ...

Life had to go on; I never again met anyone I fell in love with, or anyone I have been close to. I have just buried myself in my work. (Bev Hargreaves)

This fictional exploration of Sister's past gave Bev more insight. Rather than considering she had uncovered what had really happened, Bev's fresh understanding concerned the way that past events influence present action. This can be puzzling, or even damaging, to people later, as it was to Bev and the young mother. This psychological insight (for more see Chapter 9), can ease relations in the present, and sometimes support developmental change.

Developing the five stages

These five stages are described and exemplified in an ideal order. They might be undertaken in many different ways and orders. And having experienced all five, reflective writers will work in their own way, adapting the stages, developing them innovatively. There is no end to what can be done creatively with this method, and no set way of doing it. There are also many more ways writing can be used. Here are four examples.

Writing to materially help with practical issues

Sally Jane Shaw used writing to help her decide whether she wanted to change her professional role, from practitioner to lecturer. She made a list of things which prevented her from going for the post, ranging from *Is it really what I want to do?* and *Would I be jumping out of the frying pan into the fire?* to *Would I miss my patients?* and *Don't want to travel.* Under each heading she wrote arguments for and against. As she wrote, more and more insights occurred to her. She realised there were openings other than the two she had felt stuck between, such as remaining a practitioner while developing her additional role of educator. Having thoroughly examined pros and cons, her confidence in her role and ability was reinforced.

Unsent letters

Sally Jane Shaw was struggling with a colleague not pulling his weight. She wrote variously, trying to cope with her anger and frustration. Eventually she wrote a pair of letters, to and from the colleague. The letters were purely for reflection, with no intention of being sent. Here is how she expressed feeling afterwards:

> Reading the reply from Tom has made me cry. I don't know why. I'm crying writing this. I'm overcome with how Tom feels and I think I can identify with how he feels having to keep things locked inside and not lying but not being honest.
>
> I feel like I have opened a wound on Tom.
>
> I feel like I have been cruel not in my letter to him but the thoughts I have had and also some of the discussions I have had with the other team members. I know what we have discussed is right but should we say it to Tom.
>
> The tears are leaving me now but I don't understand why I cried. I did not cry when I was writing the reply but when I read it back to me, Sally, – from the point where, in my fictional letter, Tom says 'I just need you there for a little longer, Sal'. (Sally Jane Shaw)

Sally was able to build a supportive yet developmental relationship with Tom, with him accepting her appropriately pushing, yet not leaning on her. Experiencing feelings fully, crying even, on reading back often happens. Writing can seem to place experiences outside the writer, so rereading seems like hearing an outside communication. Dialogue can create a reflexive distance (Crème and Hunt 2002), useful in embattled work relationships. This distance paradoxically brings the *other* closer and makes them more accessible.

Such writing, whether unsendable fictional letters, or writing as if a playscript, can help towards insight and empathy. Examples are 'oh I see!, he wasn't trying to put me down, but was upset', 'she's not pulling her weight because she doesn't know what she should be doing, and I can help' and 'she seems bossy but like my sister this is her way of coping with lack of confidence'.

Writing to become aware of aspects of ourselves

Writing can enable proper listening to ourselves. Our rushed world tends to cut us off from wider aspects of ourselves. Once different sides are heard, they can be worked with harmoniously, leading to enhanced integrity (that is, with the parts of the self integrated). Thinking of us as containing different voices can be helpful. For example, people say 'I was in two minds about it', 'I don't know what got into me', 'I don't know why that upset me so much', 'I didn't know I had it in me', 'I was able to cope because it was as if it happened to someone else', 'As soon as the music starts my sober self disappears and I party like mad', 'When the time came I just couldn't do it, though I knew beforehand I could', 'I heard myself being really judgemental just like my mother', 'There's this voice tells me all the time I'm rubbish' and 'The knowledge of just what to say came out of the blue'. Writing can enable contact with these hitherto enigmatic selves, to understand their role in my single-seeming self. It can enable us to draw consciously upon the strong elements of ourselves, and find strategies for dealing with the inhibiting and negative.

Sally Jane Shaw dialogued with her *wise self*. She had previously tended to lack confidence in her practice, feel criticised too readily, and unable to withstand unreasonable demands. She began to gain clarity about her professional role, realise she could say 'No', and give opinions. She consistently listened to her *wise self* through writing, eventually realising she could hear and respond to this wisdom during practice as well. She called herself Big Sal and her wise self Little Sal. In this extract she was struggling with work boundaries, feeling pushed and pulled by seniors and losing confidence and clear sense of role. Here is one brief response to a discussion:

> **Little Sal Helped Me Today:**
> Little Sal calmed me today
> Little Sal's voice was clear 'Don't argue the point Big Sal you know you're right but he will not hear this.
> Keep the patient and nurses safe Big Sal
> Keep calm let your voice be heard
> Be clear and non-threatening

Big Sal you may feel you have lost the argument
For maybe he made you look small
No Big Sal you kept calm and kept the nurses and patient safe
Well done Big Sal you heard my voice

Do you know I can now write in my mind at times. I can see things I never saw before. Little Sal talks to me while at work and home. Work is still there but I am much improved at not being pushed and also guilt is far reduced. Through my writing I have looked beyond work. Writing motivates me: Little Sal says I can. (Sally Jane Shaw)

Linda Garbutt: Finding the internal supervisor

Linda has taken the value of a wise inner self a stage further. As a practising therapist and supervisor of other therapists, she researched a theory of the *internal supervisor* for her psychology doctorate (see Chapter 13 for an example of the development of an *internal mentor*, and Chapters 6 and 11 for a Socratic dialogue with an inner supervisor (Turnbull and Mullins 2007).

> The management of practice between external supervision sessions is a key issue for therapists, as well as other professions. The use of an internal supervisor is one means of meeting this challenge. It could also be used by professionals who do not have external supervisors.
>
> An internal supervisor (Casement, 1985, 1990) is a conceptualisation of the process of collecting together knowledge, skills, and awareness from the experiences of training, practice and supervision. It also involves having the capacity to access and consult this resource when working with a client or supervisee. Initially, an internal supervisor will be minimal, until the practitioner has developed the confidence and experience to use the method. I evolved a three-stage model using reflective writing to assist the development and use of an internal supervisor.
>
> The first stage is a piece of generic reflective writing (see above).
>
> The second stage encourages reflection by introducing a direct question to an internal supervisor within reflective writing, such as 'What do you have to say about that, *Internal Supervisor*?' promoting a dialogue between the therapist and their inner self, thoughts and feelings.
>
> The third stage sets out to develop reflexivity, creating necessary distance and space to encourage additional and alternative perspectives. This involves returning to a previous reflection and asking questions including 'What else ...? What was I thinking ...? What was I feeling when ...?' which stimulate reflexivity.
>
> This three-stage model offers one means of becoming a reflective practitioner and developing an internal supervisor at the same time. (Linda Garbutt)

A *through-the-mirror* writing course evaluation

It was a new experience for me to be able to share experiences in the written form in a trusting and stimulating place. I was surprised how easy it was to write about previous experiences, and, once the setting was right, how the ideas flowed. Over the months we laughed, cried and discussed our work together and I found I gained confidence both in my ability to write but also the value of it. Somehow writing it down enabled me to get to the essence of past experiences and events in a way that discussion alone cannot. From the beginning Gillie encouraged us to write whatever came into our heads; this felt very different from the prescriptive writing I had been doing as part of my Masters.

I discovered I wrote about the more profound and painful experiences and sometimes wondered if I wanted to share them; however, whenever I did it was very valuable. (Shirley)

This chapter gives trustworthy writing methods, used by thousands of people. The next chapter gives advice on starting and keeping a *through-the-mirror* journal, using the above writing methods.

 Read to learn

Bolton, G. (2008b) Boundaries of humanity: writing medical humanities, *Arts and Humanities in Higher Education*, **7**(2), 147–65.
Holly, M.L. (1988) Reflective writing and the spirit of enquiry. *Cambridge Journal of Education*, **19**(1), 71–80.
Pavlovich, K., Collins, E. and Jones, G. (2009) Developing students' skills in reflective practice: design and assessment, *Journal of Management Education*, **33**, 37–58.

 Write to learn

Each chapter ends with *Write to learn*. This chapter is stuffed with writing ideas and suggestions; below are some more. Each writing can be shared fruitfully with a group or confidential trusted other, as described above, if this seems appropriate once the writer has read and reflected on it first.

Exercise 6.1   Through the mirror

1. Write for *six minutes* following the flow of your mind, as above, without stopping and without rereading till you've finished.

2. Follow-on writing: write for about 20 minutes about 'A Time in My Experience' as above. Remember this is for you. You need never share it with anyone, or without redrafting it first. Try to choose the first event which comes to mind, even if you have no idea why you have thought of it. Your writing will tell you why it is important. Trust it to do that.

3. Read all your writing to yourself, and alter or adapt as seems good. Are there any connections between the *six minutes' write* and the Follow-on? Note any reflections which occur to you as you read.

Exercise 6.2   Mentoring from a helpful observer

1. Do a *six-minute write*.
2. Think of a puzzling or unsatisfactory work event.
3. Think of an object generally in view in your consulting room/office/classroom/ other, such as:

- your work coffee mug
- work chair
- work mirror
- or similar ...

4. Write a narrative from its point of view (for example, the coffee mug will be 'I') about the event.
5. Reread this to yourself.
6. Now write about the same event from *your* perspective, bearing in mind your object's observations.
7. Reread all your writing with attention; what has this told you about the event?

Exercise 6.3   Really perceiving a person

1. Do a *six-minute write*.
2. Describe a patient/client/student/colleague you know well. They will never see this, so you can write anything (if working with a colleagial group choose someone they do not know).
3. Write phrases, describing these characteristics:

   (a) gesture or movement
   (b) way of walking or sitting
   (c) turn of phrase, or saying
   (d) habitual mode of greeting

(Continued)

(Continued)

    (e) the quality of their speaking voice
    (f)   something about their clothes
    (g) a colour (might not be one they wear)
    (h) a sense of touch – quality of handshake, for example
    (i)   any smell associated with this person
    (j)   any sounds other than voice (for example, keys jangling)
    (k) any taste (perhaps you always have coffee with them)
    (l)   anything or anyone they remind you of
    (m) what they make you feel
    (n) and so on …
    (o) if they were an animal what animal would they be? (phrase)
    (p) if they were a piece of furniture what would they be?
    (q) If they were a season or weather what would they be?
    (r)   a food?
    (s)   a drink?
    (t)   a flower?
    (u) a form of transport?
    (v) and so on …

4. Write as if by this person: a poem, story, letter to someone other than you (for example to their child, mother, or the local newspaper), shopping list, things-to-do list …
5. Read back to yourself with care, altering or adding as you wish.

CHAPTER 7

THE LEARNING JOURNAL

Chapter 7 gives the what, why, how, who and with whom, when, where of learning journals, including ethical values. The difference between logs, diaries and journals is explained, and also appropriate writing materials, types of writing, how to facilitate and assess (or not). The four stages of writing a journal, based on *through-the-mirror* writing processes (see Chapter 6), are explained fully.

> The periods when I undertake this [writing] activity can be unsettling just as much as they can be therapeutic. They are vehicles for me to test out the very basis of my assumptions and re-evaluate significant portions of both personal and professional life. (Sonya)

> I point out that unless they feel sufficiently free to write things in their journals that they would be embarrassed for me to read, then they are probably not using their journals sufficiently well for them to be good examples of reflection. (David Boud 2001, p. 16)

> Try to love the *questions themselves* like locked rooms and like books that are written in a very foreign tongue. Do not now seek the answers, which cannot be given to you. *Live* the questions now. (Rilke [1934] 1993, p. 35)

The learning journal is a relatively unstructured form of reflection and reflexive questioning dialogue. It uses the writing methods explained and exemplified in Chapter 6. Journals are essentially private, yet parts can fruitfully be shared with confidential trusted others in the ways suggested in Chapter 6. Starting and keeping a journal is presented here in a series of four clear stages.

Organic exploration rather than product, journals give a route to tussling with the 'basic practical-moral problem in life [which] is not what to do but what kind of person to be' (Cunliffe, 2009a). They enable engagement of critical faculties about work or course. The most vital enquiry involves seeking more specific and dynamic questions rather than answering existing questions. This chapter covers learning journals: why, what and how, with examples from practitioners, students and lecturers; discussion of assessment and facilitation are in Chapters 8 and 9 respectively.

A learning journal asks a writer directly or indirectly to enquire into:

What you:

- and **others did** on any particular occasion
- **thought**, and what **others might** have thought
- **felt**, and what **others might** have felt
- **believe**, and **how** these beliefs are carried out in your practice
- are **prejudiced** about, take for granted, and unquestioningly assume
- can do about **how all** of the above affects **yourself** and **others**.

(There are many more suggestions below under 'types of writing'.)

A learning journal uses the simple powerful pronoun 'I'. Reflective and reflexive authors are not like Victorian children: best seen (in the credits), but not heard (in the text) (Charmaz and Mitchell 1997).

> Writing a journal calls on students – and [educators] – to relearn a lost language. We are trained to favour academic over expressive language, which includes the use and valuing of the first person singular. Ironically, it seems that the very requirement to write in the first person singular may be an important reason why journals contribute to improved learning. (Moon 1999b, p. 34)

Oddly, Moon herself does not write as 'I' (2004). Stephen Trotter said:

> I initially chose to have my students report *just the facts*, then I slowly found myself more interested in the Journals of students who had violated the rules and strayed into the subjective meadow. The entries were both enlightening and in many instances poignant. I began to see the Journal entries as a mirror of a student's ever-increasing awareness of the act of teaching … I have [also] found that without prior training, entry content is likely to be observational and reactionary rather than reflective. (Trotter 1999)

The 'I' in journal writing is a construction rather than naked exposure of writers themselves, despite most journal writers feeling they are being 'honest'. Journals give writers' perspectives on issues discussed, described, challenged, engaged with in whatever way. They cannot give a final objective picture, and are always open to further interpretation (like narratives, see Chapters 5 and 12).

> I like this idea of writing. I wrote poems in my youth, like we all. Then, writing for what? But now it feels comfortable, like a silent friend, there unquestioning, uncritical. (Rita)

> I think I can see how I changed as well, how I've learnt more self awareness, I've learnt more acceptance, I'm not so rattled by other people's response to me, even if it's unexpected, I think I can accept it and um it's been very, very useful for me to be writing it in a journal. (Student, in Wright 2005, p. 516)

> It was only through reading *Writing Cures* (Bolton et al. 2004) that I discovered that what I had been doing for years as a personal resource was called 'Reflective Practice'. I simply have a large loose-leaf notebook, and take five minutes – or an hour – to write down what's on my mind: anxieties, dreams, experiences, bits from books, puzzling psychotherapy sessions, relationships, ideas … you name it.
>
> The main benefit is that I stop obsessing or ruminating about them, because I begin to disidentify with what's bugging me – get it out of my head and down onto the page; and then I can begin to understand. If I'm too upset, it doesn't work, or I just can't bring myself to write. (Nathan Field)

Logs, diaries and journals

Although these words are often used interchangeably, it is useful to distinguish between them.

Logs straightforwardly record events, calculations or readings as aide-mémoires, like ships' logs. Anorexics, for example, have been requested to keep logs of food intake and symptoms.

Diaries, at the other extreme, can contain anything, be confidantes like Anne Frank's (1947) or Virginia Woolf's (1977, 1978, 1980). One of literature's oldest forms in the West (Blodgett 1991; Simons 1990), diaries were traditionally kept by women who, being more confined, needed confidential interlocutors. Early novels were in diary form (for example, Burney 1898), probably because they created an illusion of illicit reading, diaries generally being written for the self alone. Diaries can be confessor or special friend (Anne Frank called hers Kitty) for a socially trapped woman; or a place of creation such as a writer's (for example, Virginia Woolf). They contain stories of happenings, hopes and fears, memories, thoughts, ideas, and all attendant feelings. They also contain creative material: drafts of poems, stories, plays or dialogues, doodles and sketches (for more on how-to see Bolton 1999a; Rainer 1978).

Journals are records of experiences, thoughts, and feelings about particular aspects of life, or with specific structures. A journal can record anything, and in any way, relative to the issue to which it pertains. These documents (some virtual), might be intended for a wide audience. Politicians, and some artists, intend publication, but most are written for audiences such as tutor, mentor, portfolio group, degree cohort, or examiner. Journal writing has a range of uses. Politicians' journals record their years in office. Victorian travel journals were popular; travel writing still uses this intimate personal form. Qualitative research journals can record material, be a data source, or a process of enquiry itself.

> I now feel quite sad about this journal and the ending of the group. This journal represents for me the space which this course has given me for my 'whole' life so far. It has given me intellectual space and opportunity – physical space from work and social group – spiritual space … also psychological space to rethink my responses, reactions, motivations, expectations and hopes (this passage cut from journal, for personal reasons). I'm more able to take risks and I have thought of things I'd like to do which I've previously not thought as possibilities in the past … (Elaine, Master's student)

> The writing has been a real eye-opener for me. I was sceptical at first, partly because the *reflective journal* has almost become a cliché in nursing education, but also because I was anxious about others reading my gibberish … I will continue to write a log because Gillie was right. Things come out differently when written down. Feelings and thoughts can creep up and surprise you in writing. I will always be grateful to this course for giving me the space to discover this. And when you discover something for yourself you use it! (Ann, Master's student)

The learning journal: an explanation

Learning journals are cornerstones of reflective practice and critical reflexivity. Elements can be discussed with peers, mentors or supervisors, or included in portfolios. Solitary private writing can enable tentative or bold expression and exploration of past, present and future, the discovery of hitherto unknown areas, some even cathartic (Shepherd 2004; Sutton et al. 2007). 'Writing things down without worrying what other people think is the most powerful thing' and 'those who are better able to notice and feel their successes learn more' (Beveridge 1997, p. 42). A student said: 'I must say I like this idea of keeping track of your thoughts.'

A dynamically rewarding process (Boud et al. 1985; English and Gillen 2001), reflective journal writing requires commitment, energy, and sometimes courage. Keeping a professional reflective journal pushed Attard (2008) to question what he previously took for granted, realising that at times 'the more I write, the more confused I feel'. He eventually could tolerate uncertainty sufficiently to appreciate a 'reflexive suspended state of not knowing'.

> By keeping a personal-professional journal you are both the learner and the one who teaches. You can chronicle events as they happen, have a dialogue with facts and interpretations, and learn from experience. A journal can be used for analysis and introspection. Reviewed over time it becomes a dialogue with yourself. Patterns and relationships emerge. Distance makes new perspective possible: deeper levels of insight can form. (Holly 1989, p. 14)

Such insight is not lightly obtained, and could not be facilitated by verbal discussion with a colleague or mentor alone. It is essentially self-dialogic. The writer takes responsibility for discovering personal learning needs, and devises strategies for meeting them. No other person takes responsibility in this dialogue: the writer is face to face with themselves. Writers can thus examine vulnerable areas, their own cutting edge. And it brings its own rewards; students wrote:

> We must first know and understand ourselves before we are at peace internally. We must be at peace internally to participate in our world in an effective manner. When we are at peace we naturally exhibit characteristics of integrity, honesty, openness, and trustworthiness. (Cunliffe 2004, p. 22)

> I came to learn that reflecting on my practice in a meaningful way was key to improving it. This involved articulating and reflecting on my values (espoused and practised) in ways that I had not done before. This process has led to many discoveries, most notably a richer understanding about who 'I' am, and how the values I bring to work affect my role as a practitioner. A necessary part of this process has been to explicitly surface my values as a way of ensuring I practice honestly and congruently. The result has been to create more appropriate strategies of intervention that are *acceptable* and *workable* to my [business consultancy] clients, which has in turn – by means of their own reflective processes – helped them create a more resilient organization. I have also learned that the best way for me to understand my practice is to simply start by articulating what I do. This enabled me to better understand both the nature of my practice and my learning, as well as the nature of my reflection. In this respect, my reflective approach contributed toward my own evolving personal theory of practice. (Shepherd 2006, p. 346)

> From the first few entries I was struck by how quickly I was able to recognize emerging patterns, for example in individual behaviour; similarities in the way

meetings were conducted, who led the discussions and who remained silent; how decisions were made and by whom. This information when combined together helped me develop a holistic picture of the organization which helped me understand how it worked. (Shepherd 2004, p. 202)

Qualitative research journals can record material or be a process of enquiry itself, including findings, thoughts and feelings, colloquial quotes, quantitative data such as tables and figures, and descriptions of focus groups or interviews, or narratives. Journals might be publicly shareable data, or personal and private (Etherington 2004). The research journal itself can be a process of enquiry (Richardson and Adams St. Pierre 2005; Watson 2006): a research methodology in its own right. Watson's research journal (2006) uses the power of narrative to be a 'method of inquiry' (Richardson and Adams St. Pierre 2005). Jasper (2005) found a reflective research journal facilitated creativity, critical thinking, analysis, innovative discovery and provided a trustworthy audit trail. Glaze (2002) and Shepherd (2004) developed reflective PhD journals which can deepen, enrich and enhance research, making it more relevant, applicable, and enjoyable. Here follows an example of a research diary, which is a form of learning journal:

> Masters in Higher Education students were encouraged to keep a research diary of observations and interpretations of their teaching; accounts of thinking in response to discussions critical responses to literature; evaluative comments about the course itself and so on. Private documents, no one else, including the tutors, had any rights of access. The material might be used in informal course seminars; as a basis for later publications; or to identify issues for further exploration with other participants or course tutors. The research diaries were also a major source of material for a portfolio of work relating to each module …
>
> We were concerned these portfolios be viewed as working documents, for thinking through ideas about practice, rather than final products … Of immediate importance was that participants should see their own regular writing as a fundamental part of the enquiry process.
>
> Writing to explore professional values underlying practice is not easy. Such values are always difficult to express. Their articulation needs to be retraced as they become questioned and new experience brought to bear. Thus we expect participants to refine ideas in one portfolio which may initially have been raised earlier, pursuing themes of enquiry across consecutive portfolios. (Rowland and Barton 1994, p. 371)

Ethical values

Journals significantly develop and enhance awareness of ethical values used in practice (rather than espoused values). This purpose has been explicit with palliative care nurses: 'the students are helped to realise there is no magic formula for ethical decision-making. Instead, the process of writing followed by group discourse enables the analysis of relevant and important factors to be considered in morally challenging decisions' (Durgahee 1997, pp. 140–1). Fins et al. (2003) used journals similarly with palliative medicine students. Observing and reflecting on psychosocial and ethical issues and patient-centred advocacy in 'highly empathic and emotional' (p. 308) journals, students share unique perspectives with peers. Journals have facilitated reflection upon emotional response to family medicine (Howard 1997). These practices counteract a tacit medical and healthcare attitude of detachment and, Shem (2002) would say, inhumanity.

Discovering values in practice, by examining assumptions underlying actions, can be uncomfortable (assumptions might prove to be prejudices). A journal needs to be private for this genuinely to take place. The writer gains courage to enter normally no-go reflexive areas, relinquishing certainty for a time in what Winnicott (1971) called 'the play space'. Winnicott also called it a 'transitional space': a place between innermost thoughts and feelings, and the world of actions, events and other people. Normally we protectively hide private thoughts and feelings. In the 'play space' (the gap between imagination and reality, if you like) the two can be played with (see Preface, 'Mind the gap'). Journal writers become *bricoleurs* (Levi-Strauss 1966) or stone-wallers, choosing bits from their thoughts and experiences, fisting them for size and shape, and creating possible constructions and models. In speculating about ideas which are neither right nor wrong, writers try out experimental ideas, values, positions. They discover possible selves: the self is not a concrete discernible thing, but an evanescent collection of possibilities.

Journals can be 'a process of integration' for *containment*, and *therapeutic space*: a 'space to explore and confirm' (Best 1996, p. 298) experiences and emotions, however bad. These can be reviewed more safely later: the material will have remained the same, but the writer will have moved on and be able to reassess the situation, their feelings and thoughts.

The thing

A journal is an object, a possession. I recommend appropriate and pleasurable investment. Mine are A5 notebooks, neat and contained for unruly thoughts and adventures. In the past I used A4 loose-leaf folders containing handwritten or typed sheets, letters, newspaper cuttings, journal papers, pictures, and all sorts. I write with 2B rubber-tipped pencils: I never rub out, but I might; a soft pencil whispers to the page. One nursing group had between them: a suede covered book, one decorated with bright children's pictures, one plain but a glorious red, another a shocking pink folder and pen.

Pen feels more permanent than pencil, fountain pen more professional and sophisticated than biro. Coloured pens and paper for particular emotions and feelings can take writing in unforeseen directions, as can different sizes of paper: A1 for anger, shopping list pad for low confidence. Typing can create different reflections from handwriting: watching print appear on the screen can invite organised and deliberate analytic revision. Discover what's best for you.

> I feel comfortable writing longhand when it's about me my personal stuff. When I'm on the keyboard it's for somebody else to read, it's an essay, it's an assignment it's a letter and that's how I kind of keep a demarcation between my stuff and more public stuff. (A student, in Wright 2005, p. 517)

Types of writing

A journal can contain any writing, in any order, for no reason other than the writing comes out that way. It might contain free-flow *six-minute* writing (see Chapter 6), stories of practice, fictional stories, poems, musings or reflections on what, why, how, when, who, why, dialogues with the self, fictional dialogues with others such as patients, clients or students, analysis of motives and actions, philosophising on such as ethics, evaluation or assessment of practice, description, fantasy used to aid insight, cathartic writing, unsent letters, extended metaphors, visualisation, ethnography, mindmaps, sketches, cartoons, descriptions of dance or diagrams. Or it might be drawings, or collage (cut out pictures or extracts from magazines and so on). Experiment! These methods are explained in different chapters of *Reflective Practice*. Experienced journal writers allow the most appropriate to present itself naturally. Ownership and responsibility for writing offer development of understanding.

Rereading, and reflecting, are significant, and sometimes challenging (Sutton et al. 2007). Some journal writers leave space to return and make reflexive notes in a different colour, others reread and continue to write on later fresh pages. A left-hand column reflective journal (Argyris 1991; Megginson and Whitaker 2003) records events in two columns, the right focuses on the event, the left on what did not happen: thoughts, feelings or impulses to action. Here are two students' astonished responses to being asked to keep journals, followed by an example of dynamic journal facilitation:

> To have the chance to write what we really think rather than just quote some other old dude? Unheard of! Students actually have original thought that is worth reading? Never! And to think that a lecturer was interested in my opinion of class, and my reflections on the topic is really rather empowering and invigorating …

It amazes me that I took this paper because I wanted an easy ride this semester. Well what a ride it has been. Twelve weeks down the track, and I am a different person. I am a person with a purpose, but also a person who recognises that I am in charge of my own destiny. I recognise that I have faults, but I also recognise that they are fixable, adaptable and that they are worth working on …

It's funny to think that a class I nearly withdrew from in the first week has resulted in a change of life: I am now volunteering and choosing a different career path that has low pay but much more enjoyment. Two things that six months ago, I would never have picked. (Students, in Pavlovich et al. 2009, pp. 54–6)

 Management consultancy coaching

I have recently been coaching a new consultant, a recent and very bright graduate, who was working on a complex and difficult business change project. He was often overwhelmed with the challenges of becoming a consultant, the change between work and studying and staying away from home at the client site as well as understanding the company he was working for and the complexity of organisational politics. The journal I encouraged him to keep became a survival mechanism for him and a rich source of learning. The following extract, which is a free word association, gives a strong sense of how his perception of the culture of the company merges with his own state of mind:

NewCo pointless old tired stale dark cold unfriendly confusion anxious bleak stagnant slow protracted conflict going round in circles repeat same old parochial trivial dread going through the motions denial escape fight withdraw individual shell distance myself scared bitten stress pedantic process machine automation indecisive conflict avoidance stupid panic macho picking holes unhelpful barrier don't care apathy ridiculous smallminded prejudiced siloed blinkered unappreciative arrogant waste of space obstruction denial deaf clueless machine hierarchical fragment disintegrate plural infighting political playing games Machiavellian agenda effort failure antagonism conflict embarrassment hide away secretive behind closed doors inefficient paper-pushing overly complex dispersed resentful bitter stuck repeat. (Angela Mohtashemi)

How to write: the four stages

An effective way to start and continue writing is systematically outlined in Chapter 6, and writing suggestions in all this book's chapters are appropriate to the journal, depending on needs, wants and situation. Each journal writer develops appropriate format and ordering. Spaces might be left for later reflections in a different colour, or previous writings might be interrogated on fresh later pages. Here are the four stages.

Through-the-mirror journal writing stage 1

Write the *Six-minute mind clearing exercise* (see Chapter 6).
  Now write an account of an experience (10–20 minutes).

- Allow an event to surface in your mind, rather than reaching for the most *critical*. Often the *uncritical* episode, routine, everyday, or seemingly insignificant element most needs dwelling upon. Paradoxically, and crucially, these might be harder to focus upon than the significant. Or it might be a puzzling occasion.
- Write about the occasion as descriptively as you can, including all detail.
- Give it a title as if it were a story or film.

Through-the-mirror journal writing stage 2

Reread all you've written and reflexively ask questions like these:

- What strikes you particularly about this story?
- What have you missed out? Go back and put it in, however insignificant it seems.
- What do you feel (and felt then)?
- What did you think (and thought then, but perhaps did not say)?
- What assumptions have you made?
- What does it tell you about your ethical values in action (for example, respect for the disadvantaged)?
- How is power handled, and the relative status and roles of those involved?
- How has any power imbalance affected you, or the other person?
- What is the balance of responsibility between peers; how could it be different?
- What do misunderstandings or non-understandings tell you about communication?
- What do you find challenging?

Through-the-mirror journal writing stage 3

Write a further account, attempting to gain wider perspective.

- Write the story again as if from the point of view of the other person (student, client, patient, colleague, other).
- Or, if there is no other significant person, or far too many, write a further account from an omniscient observer, such as from the perspective of your coffee mug, who observes everything.
- Or invent your own way of reflexive re-storying, or choose another from the list in Chapter 6.
- Ask similar questions to those in stage 2.

Through-the-mirror journal writing stage 4

Reread your journal (the next day or after perhaps three months) and ask yourself:

- Where has this taken you?
- What patterns can you perceive, such as repeated behaviour?
- What do you notice about the language, particularly about non-peers?
- Is there a *de*structively self-critical voice in your writing? Make it *con*structively critical.
- Where might further explorations go?
- Why, how, when, with whom?
- What challenges does all this present you with?

Here is a journal extract example.

A letter to my patients

I am listening, really I am.

I have to be honest, though – sometimes it's hard to pay attention. If my focus seems to shift away from you to the clock, or the door, or the computer, please don't think it's because I don't care.

Let me tell you something, my friend. I've got problems, too. Sometimes my problems are bigger than yours and I'm hanging on by my fingernails. But I'm the one with the desk and the prescription pad.

And what am I doing while you struggle to explain yourself to me? I'm holding myself together, is what I'm doing. I might distractedly put my hand up to my face while your words hover between us. Just checking I'm in one piece.

I'm not painting my toenails, that's for sure.

I'm not snuggled up under my duvet, drifting off to sleep.

I'm not licking a rapidly melting chocolate ice cream cone.

I'm sitting here, listening to you.

So make the most of me. (Becky Ship)

Becky (family doctor) explained: '"I distractedly put my hand up to my face" to ensure my *work mask* was uncracked and unslipped, to protect my vulnerable private face'.

When keeping a journal, remember:

- This is for *you*: write somewhere private.
- Date entries: you will not remember.
- Make entries soon after significant events: you will forget.
- Try different writing forms: explorative, descriptive, devil's advocate, story (see Chapter 12), poetry (see Chapter 14), metaphor exploration (see Chapter 13), anecdote, reflective musing, vignettes, portraits, lists, interview yourself …

- It is worth filling out notes taken during teaching/learning sessions.
- You can try developing previously half-expressed arguments or opinions.
- Changes of opinion are significant; explore them.
- The journal will help you examine things difficult to understand or do.

Facilitation of writing

Learning journals, cornerstones of reflective practice and critical reflexivity, are often required for courses or portfolios, and are best introduced and supported by experienced, skilled education, and trusted confidential facilitation (for more, see Chapter 9). Students are often reported as finding journal writing difficult or impossible (for example, Chirema 2007); this may happen if the process is not taught and facilitated well. 'The act of writing alone does not move pre-service (student) teachers beyond a preoccupation with themselves toward a broader conceptualisation of critical enquiry' (Hoover 1994, p. 92). Students wrote about day-to-day frustrations and problems but journals did not seem to 'encourage reflectivity, particularly thinking about teaching and learning in light of theory, contextual factors, and ethical issues' (Hoover 1994, p. 92).

Writers must have authority over and responsibility for their journal. Educator's roles are therefore to introduce the subject fully, yet be carefully consistent about who owns both writing process and product.

Deeply reflective writing and understanding does not come readily to graduates of our schools and universities. The barriers are high (Newton 1996). Without clear experienced facilitation students remain 'stuck and searching for new ideas' (Kruse 1997, p. 56); they also need facilitation in how to write (see Chapter 6) to begin to grasp the rewards, and lessen their fear. Morrison successfully introduced higher degree students to in-depth reflective journal writing. 'They were initially prisoners of their own expectations and perceptions, [yet] the process has been an enabling and liberating experience' (Morrison 1996, pp. 323–4). Introduced and facilitated with knowledge and skill, journals repay the time and effort.

Journals have varied aims and objectives on different programmes. Journals are often integral elements of courses and focus on students maximizing learning from that course (for example, Crème 2008; Cunliffe 2004). At the other end of the spectrum are practitioner journals and portfolios used to develop practice. There are many variations. Learning journals are supported, facilitated and unassessed according to Howard (1997) and Carson and Fisher (2006). Stedmon et al. (2003) report private ones used as the basis of assessed reflective essays, and ones facilitated and used in appraisal process. Others inform reflective tutorials or seminars (for example, Charon 2006; Kember et al. 1996; Stedmon et al. 2003). Pavlovich et al. (2009) report online journals, all of which are read by tutors who respond and grade formatively using a marking schedule. Journals are knowledgeably facilitated and a version or elements transposed for assessment (for example, Beveridge 1997; Bolton 1994). Varner and Peck (2003) have used them as effective, satisfactory examination substitutes for many years. Diaries are used as dialogue between doctor and patient (for example, Charon 2006), nurse and patient (for example, Love 1996).

Whatever their role, journals need to be knowledgeably taught and facilitated with clear and explicit rationale; full details should be given in course and module handbooks (Sutton et al. 2007) when appropriate. Varner and Peck (2003), for example, have successfully taught and assessed semi-structured journals for seven years because they have developed consistent, clear methodology understood by all concerned. They find journals encourage students to be self-directed, more able to create their own focus, gain an intelligent interaction with assignment contents, to be able to anchor their new learning in experience, so they can solve actual problems (for assessment issues, see Chapter 8). A project in which university tutors kept learning journals reported how experienced facilitation of their group meetings had significant positive impact on learning (Cowan and Westwood 2006).

Journal-keeping students may need support with whatever material arises (Bennett-Levy et al. 2001; Sutton et al. 2007). Students can feel destabilised if journals' purposes are to discourage certainty about knowledge and practice and enable questioning of assumptions about roles, knowledge and skills base, ownership of power and influence, and ethical values. Practitioners keeping reflective journals as part of portfolio learning, or solo professional development, will need experienced mentors.

A company's employees kept journals called thinkbooks: 'participants were asked to record significant events, make observations on their performance, analyse their actions, draw conclusions, note learning points, and make suggestions for further action' (Rigano and Edwards 1998, p. 436). Realising the journal's impact after three months, Vincent's daily entries changed from 'organising daily routine ... to a process of reflection leading to growth' (ibid. p. 440). Vincent carefully structured this process himself, using readings and other texts on effective behaviour such as de Bono. The researchers concluded Vincent's success stemmed from owning the process. Realising he needed to share his reflections to develop further, Vincent's company offered facilitated reflective writing in work time.

Journal writing needs to be understood at first hand to be facilitated. Legal educators are advised to keep journals (Hinett 2002). Lecturers applying to be registered practitioners of the UK Higher Education Academy, are required to keep reflective journals. Kuit et al. (2001) report a successful journal keeping 'action learning set' for academic staff. Seven experienced university teachers gained significant personal and professional development writing similar journals to those they required of students: 'I have found that being required to put pen to paper encouraged me to spend more time on my reflection and to structure my thinking more carefully' (Cowan and Westwood 2006, p. 65). Practising what they preached significantly improved their organisation and facilitation of students' reflection. They report a colleague, who required written reflection from his students, yet declined to join the experiment saying:

> I have discussed this with (another member) who says I am a reflective practitioner. I think I need to talk about things with someone … I can write a journal in my head when I am gardening or even in bed or sitting in a traffic jam – perhaps I need a tape recorder but if this works for me does it need to be written?? [*sic*] (Ibid. p. 64)

The paper's authors make no comment as to how successfully his students created and used journal-writing.

Modelling reflexivity

Student journals can and should push *tutors* to meaningful reflexivity. Ann Cunliffe describes an experience:

> It means being critically reflexive about our own teaching practices and the voices we might silence ... The journal excerpt below caused me to do some critically reflexive questioning of my own:
>
>> The process of questioning ones assumptions and values is disconcerting and tortuous. It is uncomfortable to truly look inwards and then reflect on all the assumptions and values that one has built over almost a lifetime. I have always assumed that my values and goals were just right for me and proceeded almost with single-minded purpose to achieve them. There was no reason for me to question them. Yet, I have been *forced* to be conscious [italics added] of this process over the past weeks especially as I become increasingly aware of the applicability of the course material to myself.
>
> Although this student talked about the relative and non-absolute nature of knowledge and voice, the language he used struck me: have I 'forced' others? Have I acted inconsistently by claiming students must consider multiple perspectives? I need to look at my own teaching practices to ensure I am enacting the values I espouse. (Cunliffe 2004, p. 419)

When to write a journal

When you want to, when you need to. Any or every time you can find five minutes or more without interruption. The most creative times might paradoxically be when your cognitive powers are at lowest ebb: midnight or 4 a.m.

> 'Aren't you going to bed *yet* Mum? Are you *still* working?'
> 'No, I'm not working. I'm just writing.'

Write about an event at the right time for you. Left too late, events lose impact and interest: attempted too soon they may be too raw:

> If the experience is very close, I feel inhibited … If the closeness of the real reality, of the living reality, is to have a persuasive effect on my imagination, I need a distance, a distance in time and space. (Llosa 1991, p. 44)

For and with whom

A learning journal is primarily *for* its writer: as internal dialogue for their own reflexivity, reflection, and therefore development. Some or all of it might be shared with peers, tutors or supervisor, or for assessment. For critical learning, writers need to own and be responsible for all writing and discussion. Learning cannot be given by another, it can only be taken by the learner. There are three possible responders to journals: peer, tutor or self.

Journals can be used in mentoring relationships, and can contain reflections on personal objectives set in association with mentor or supervisor (Gray 2007). Journals available for reading by another, or even for assessment, are qualitatively different from private arenas for students or professionals to engage in critical reflexivity and reflection: it is 'misleading, confusing and risky' to treat all forms of journal writing as equivalent to each other (Boud 2001, p. 16).

Co-peer mentoring (paired support), each confidentially reading other's material and supportively commenting is valuable (see Chapter 11). My students shared and discussed otherwise undiscussably confidential material coming close to personal boundaries. Not only extremely satisfying to students, who met over coffee somewhere nice, it took the pressure off their fully stretched tutor. Small trusting, trusted confidential groups or pairs can offer developmental possibilities (Crème 2008; Orem 2001): they need very careful facilitation in order to feel safe enough and therefore effective. Some courses use web-based participant sharing. Boud (1998) suggests peer-feedback is valuable and closely related to self-assessment.

Peers discussing journals need to be clear about their purpose. These are sensitive areas, requiring agreed boundaries and scope. They need to be critical and confronting enough without being like assessors, and they need listening and empathetic responding skills. Peer-sharing of learning journals becomes a route of learning essential interpersonal skills as well.

Dialoguing with journals

Journals often inform dialogic work with supervisor, tutor, or mentor. Managed well this can be valuable for deeply critical reflexivity (Cunliffe 2004; Gray 2007), create and deepen understanding and trust (Meath Lang 1996; Wright 2005), give a sense of respect and being valued (Crème 2008; Wright 2005), and can inform seminar work (Charon 2000b; Kember et al. 1996). Students are more ready to read tutors' comments in journals properly, and act upon them, than those on other assignments (Kathpalia and Heah 2008). A trusting tutorial relationship is key to students' ability to communicate confidential personal material and value written dialogue (Wright 2005). Journal dialogue can be useful in cross-cultural communication, in increasing language facility and fostering critical thinking (Hancock 1998).

Journal dialogue can be meaningfully developmental, Cunliffe (2004) helps students understand a critically reflexive 'inside-out' stance by questioning and commenting such as:

> 'Have you thought about ... ? Are there other possible interpretations? Might this be interpreted as a defensive statement? How might you do this? Is there an implicit power issue here? How might the language you use(d) in this instance influence/have influenced the response of ... ? Might this behavior be self-sealing? How might this relate to the reading by __?' In other words, my comments are aimed at helping students ask further questions, explore possibilities, or make connections (practical or theoretical). (2004, p. 422)

Responding to journals, particularly on the document itself, has to be undertaken skilfully and sensitively, with awareness and experience. Dialogue journals have a direct teaching function, different from keeping a private confidential journal.

Here an education lecturer describes journal dialoguing with students:

 Julie Hughes: 'I didn't have a voice until I joined this group'

I engaged in journal dialogue with all new teachers individually throughout. Groups take time to be comfortable with in-depth self-disclosure and self-analysis, particularly in writing. All dialogue was handwritten, personal and dated, sometimes with coloured pens, stickers or illustrative drawings. A sense of expectancy and trust emerged, facilitative to dialogue and reflection. In the second semester two students per week shared their journals with the group, writing for self and each other: 'I do like the idea of sharing our journals with peers'.

Dialogue reflection and refraction represented multiple perspectives and perceptions, suggesting resistance to the reproduction of self as mirror image. Journal writers found they could be somebody else, reinvent self as teacher and dialoguer (having a dramatic effect upon classroom practices for some). In adopting different narrative voices and genres they were able to challenge and talk back to themselves reflectively, though some writers felt it was their role to 'entertain' their readers with comedic narrative style. Some writers struggled with content and writing style: dialogue can be intrusive, enforcing censorship. Sensitivity is vital to encourage honest reflection and risk-taking in dialogue. Writers and listeners re-story narratives by offering multiple perspectives. Probing and adding information in dialogue allowed other voices to come into play, and create awareness that meanings were being made in conscious and unconscious ways. Language choices and assumptions were probed, and individual and social identities challenged.

Reflective practice can destabilise former certainties (Harrison 2004, p. 177). Maclure (2003) suggests we need new metaphors representing the layering of realities. Dialogue journals offer a tapestry always in the process of becoming. As experimental representation (Richardson 1992, p. 213) they are a transgressive and open writing genre always partial and situational, always temporal and contingent. There is no 'getting it right', they *get it differently*.

Dialogue journal writing demands the blurring of boundaries and literacies. Dialogues of participation 'as a gradual "coming to know"' (Winter 2003, p. 120) are dependent in part upon social assembly and an understanding for writing as a social and politicised practice (Clark and Ivanič 1997). Dialogue journals offer recognition of the plural and multiple text and challenge institutional norms of reflective writing. (Julie Hughes)

Where to write?

Anywhere: by a lake, in bed, perhaps difficult on a bike. This, from an academic counselling department head, was written in a café:

A student tells me she is experiencing severe insomnia, and I feel helpless, feeling only inner compassion. A colleague, in the canteen, looking ashen, laments his own bureaucratic burden and his impotence about finding any end to it. Again, I can only feel for him, sit in silent solidarity. Sometimes, with a client, while listening to a complex narrative of inescapable suffering, I will become aware of some stillness, in me, between us, a sensed original sanity. Is this what is meant by a wounded healer? Wounded, yes. Healer, I'm not so sure. If counsellors become tame, professionalised, 'audit-minded' rule-keepers, how can they free? If I can't overturn my adversity, de-oppress myself, practise what I teach, and practise what I feel, who can? (Feltham 2004)

Assessment of journals

Journals can be used inappropriately if read or assessed by superiors (see Chapter 8). Perceived enforced confession or disclosure of professional or personal material can lead to discomfort, lack of trust, or 'laundered' material (Ghaye 2007; Sinclair-Penwarden 2006; Sutton et al. 2007). Nursing students constrain writing to a very narrow range they perceive to be acceptable (Hargreaves 2004), or create reflective material retrospectively for assessment (Clegg et al. 2002, see also Chapter 8). Students are negative about 'forced RP' (Hobbs 2007, p. 409), and so 'fake it' (Hobbs 2007, p. 411). Knowing they are to be assessed, students can tend to write 'strategic journal entries' (Pecheone et al. 2005), or display journal entries to please tutors (Hobbs 2007). Students are too rarely taught and supported in how to write reflexively (for example, Platzer et al. 1997; Trotter 1999), and are often given structures to work within, and sometimes over-leading and repetitive prompts which show lack of respect, and inhibit honesty and imagination because they only lead to certain types of answers (for example, Hobbs 2007).

Graded assessment tends to prevent genuine examination of feelings, thoughts, ideas, prejudices, attitudes. Students tend to see required assessed journals as a waste of time with 'no real meaning for themselves' (Hobbs 2007, p. 412). For this reason Brookfield (1995) says journal material is and should be non-assessible.

Hargreaves (2004) asserts that nursing students' journals, when read by tutors, display only three types of story perceived to be legitimate. In *valedictory* narratives, a difficult situation is improved, the student-writer-hero recognises a problem, turns the situation round and 'wins the day'. *Condemnatory* narratives have negative outcomes: poor responses are made to a crisis, no one 'wins' and the narrator feels guilty and/or angry. In *redemptive* narratives inappropriate attitudes can be expressed if redeemed: the student-writer-hero learns from her mistakes and thus improves professional practice. Hargreaves suggests a solution of students writing fictionally, that is, not ostensibly about their own experience.

Journal writing enables an ongoing self-dialogue with otherwise quiet or silent voices within (see Chapter 6; Bolton 1999a; Rowan 1990): knowledge, intuition, analysis, inspiration and feelings. It enables standing back, taking a long reflective look, and allowing fresh views to form: a route to *loving and living the questions themselves* (Rilke [1934] 1993).

> This writing process is really helpful. It enabled me to find a synthesis of all those things going round and round in my head. (Priti)

Learning journals can be the locus of effective learning. How can prof-essional and academic course designers find out if their students are learning, and if so, how much? Furthermore, teaching a wide-ranging, deeply personal process like this is tricky, how do tutors know they are teaching well? These are issues of assessment and evaluation, tackled in Chapter 8.

 Read to learn

Crème, P. (2008) A space for academic play: student learning journals as transitional writing, *Arts and Humanities in Higher Education,* **7**(1), 49–64.

Cunliffe, A. (2004) On becoming a critically reflexive practitioner, *Journal of Management Education,* **28**(4), 407–26.

Holly, M.L. (1989) *Writing to Grow: Keeping a Personal-Professional Journal,* Portsmouth, NH: Heinemann.

Varner, D. and Peck, S. (2003) Learning from learning journals: the benefits and challenges of using learning journal assignments, *Journal of Management Education,* **27**(1), 52–77.

 Write to learn

Each chapter ends with *write to learn*. For straightforward advice, sufficient for the exercises below, see *write to learn* in Chapter 1, and see Chapter 6 for more advice. Each writing can be shared fruitfully with a group or confidential trusted other, if this seems appropriate once the writer has read and reflected on it first.

Exercise 7.1   Have a proper look

1. Do a *six-minute write* (see Chapter 6).
2. Describe entering your office or place of work.
3. Focus your mind on what you observe as you arrive. Note everything, remembering you have five senses.
4. Reread to yourself.
5. Mark five things which strike you most: do not ask why these.
6. Choose one to write more about.
7. Write a further reflective piece about what you would like to change about (a) things in this space, (b) the way you use or respond to this space.
8. Reread your writing with care and write more or alter or adapt as appropriate.

(Continued)

(Continued)

Exercise 7.2   Take an even closer look

1. Do a *six-minute write* (see Chapter 6).
2. Write about entering the workroom or place of a colleague you admire.
3. Note what you observe as you arrive: remember you have five senses.
4. Reread to yourself.
5. Mark the five things which strike you most: do not ask why these.
6. Choose one, write more about it.
7. Compare this with your own work space observations. What does this make you think and feel?
8. Reread your writing with care and write more or alter or adapt if you wish.

Exercise 7.3   Rethinking your space

1. Do a *six-minute write* (see Chapter 6).
2. Think of an object you have on your desk or near it (picture, ornament, shell, ...).
3. Describe it.
4. Write why you think you have it there.
5. Now imagine: this object is in another room, different from yours. Describe the room, and how it feels for you to be in it.
6. Reread all your writing including the *six minutes*. Alter, add, reflect.

CHAPTER 8

ASSESSMENT AND EVALUATION

Chapter 8 tussles in particular with assessment. Moral, ethical and practical issues around the contested area of assessing reflection and reflexivity are presented. Assessment solutions created by many authorities are suggested. The fascinating area of evaluation is explained and discussed with innovative and effective methods described.

> We start from the Latin root of the word assessment: 'to sit beside'. This classical meaning reflects the values being promoted in critically reflective learning as collaborative rather than inspectorial. (Brockbank and McGill 1998, p. 100)

> What I wanted, in contrast to faux evaluations, was something that could sink its hooks into my classes, something with wings and talons that could sweep down and snatch both me and my students by the shoulders and shake us out of our collective passivity to the point that we either shrieked with pain at the terror of plummeting to our deaths or else clung to it for survival until we could glide back down to some more stable literary terra firma. (Babcock 2007, p. 513)

Assessment is a complex moral and ethical act, needing to be just, accurate, fair, impartial, and based upon appropriate critical criteria. Knowing something is to be examined can change its nature, as well as attitudes to it; the very process of examination can also change it, a principle common in many disciplines including sciences. Assessment of reflective practice is sometimes at the extreme end we could call *Gillie's Cat*: opening the box will knock over the poison and kill the cat; if you do not open the box how do you know the cat is dead? The struggle is to find out what's going on, while keeping students' focus on learning rather than achieving the highest grade. Educative processes need to drive assessment, not the other way round. It is probably the biggest conundrum in curriculum development.

There are many approaches to critical reflection and reflexivity, and a wide range of aims and objectives, many of which use reflection and reflexivity for specific purposes within defined areas of curricula or professional development. Some do not need assessment, some only need evidence reflection has been undertaken, some have clearly enunciated agreed assessment criteria. To continue our animal metaphor, reflective practice is a many headed creature with many functions, aims and uses. Why and how assessment might be feasible, useful, ethical and moral is discussed in this chapter.

Evaluation, a way of gaining feedback on programmes (summative) and enabling communication between tutor and students to improve student experience (formative), is far less ethically loaded. This chapter looks at effective evaluation using dynamic ways of perceiving and understanding.

Assessment

Assessment of reflection and reflexivity is much discussed. Reflection and reflexivity are process based, and assessment product based: a paradigmatic *muddle in the model* (see Chapter 3). Awareness of assessment can inevitably at best alter, or at worst corrupt any reflective or reflexive process. The creation of reflective products for assessment has been likened to television reality shows (Macfarlane and Gourlay 2009): students are required to expose emotions, insecurities, inabilities, how they discovered the true road to redemption, and their remorse at the error of previous ignorance. 'Governance of the soul' is demanded, and fictional conformism is the likely result.

Assessment can have positive pedagogical impact, it is argued, giving positive messages about the importance of the activity (Crème 2005; Pavlovich et al. 2009). Other authorities go further, saying students will not value reflection and reflexivity without assessment (Bulman and Schutz 2008). Yet private unassessed writing can lead to significant insight, materially and positively affecting final assessments (Carson and Fisher 2006). When used, assessment requirements and criteria in keeping with course aims and objectives need to be open to students (Sutton et al. 2007). Moon (1999a) maintains detailed assessment criteria can play a central part in the success of journal writing, providing structure and foundation for what is expected. This is an example of assessment driving the educational process. Good tuition, facilitation and support in writing (see Chapters 6 and 7) can be all students need to enable and encourage developmental reflection and reflexivity.

Many courses use reflective, reflexive journals dialogically (see 'Julie Hughes' in Chapter 7): tutors can evaluate students' progress, and help them. Students can value relationships with tutors who read and respond (Carson and Fisher 2006; Cunliffe 2004; Wright 2005). A confidential, trusting, non-inspectorial relationship with tutors is essential. This dialogic process will create a *different* sort of journal to the purely private. A journal to be read by tutors can never be personally explorative or expressive or experimental, however good the tutor–student relationship. These curricula presumably do not require such processes.

Reflective practice and reflexivity, as reported in the literature, seem to have a range of aims, requiring different attitudes to assessment. At one extreme practitioners and students are enabled to critically develop work practice. The other focuses on maximising student critical attitude and response to a course of study (business studies, for example, but any educational programme).

In this latter approach, journals can develop students' ability to question their actions, knowledge, ideas, feelings, prejudices, assumptions, and so on, about their course. Dialogic journals enhance communication and understanding between tutor and student (see also 'Evaluation' below). With this clear focus towards a specific shared area of experience, and exposure of personal expression and exploration not expected, if undertaken in a manner consonant with the pedagogical principles of the course, assessment design is tricky but possible. Journals are even used as substitutes for examinations (Varner and Peck 2003), and portfolios containing reflective and reflexive elements are common and effective for assessment (for example, Groom and Maunonen-Eskelinen 2006). Such journals give good access into students' thinking and quality of learning. Students invest personality and self-image (Varner and Peck 2003) and are asked to use individual voices honestly and take risks in journals' contents (Crème 2005). Marking is therefore time-consuming and difficult, forcing uncomfortable value judgements (Varner and Peck 2003), as their subjective nature defies the standardised criteria of more objective forms of assessment (Pavlovich et al. 2009).

Moon lists assessment criteria and discusses the 'need to decide whether the student is being assessed on content or on the writing, the process of the writing, or the product of the learning' (1999b, p. 34). Crème (2005, p. 290) also identifies guidelines for assessment. A good record of study she claims is (a) comprehensive as it meets requirements of an introduction, conclusion and demonstrates syllabus coverage; (b) shows understanding of the material, with the ability to select, summarise, analyse and show relationships between concepts, both within the course and outside of it; (c) shows self-awareness of the writer as learner, both in relation to the ideas on the course, and to course activities, processes and colleagues; and (d) demonstrates that the writer is prepared to take risks with the material in relation to their own political and intellectual position. Embedded in these guidelines is a mix of cognitive skills in knowing what content should be selected as important, while also writing in a manner that emotionally and holistically connects the student with the context. Further assessment criteria and scales can be found in Fenwick (2001). These approaches all sidestep *Gillie's cat* conundrum of assessment (see above).

Journals are in danger of being at best useless, at worst harmful when written for assessment, if the process is not handled with experience and care founded on congruent pedagogical principles (see Chapters 3 and 7). Some 'assessment regimes … kill off the qualities that the work itself was designed to foster' (Crème 2005, p. 291). And 'learning journals cannot be successful if students write them with the sense that they will be judged in the same way as an essay' (Crème 2005, p. 294). David Boud (2001) stresses the clear distinction between writing for learning and writing for assessment. His course contained 'a self-assessment statement that draws from, but is distinct from, students' confidential learning portfolios' (2001, p. 16; see also Crème 2005). Brookfield also sees a danger 'students come to see journals as mandated disclosures focused on eliciting the right kind of revelations' (1995, p. 100).

Non or indirect assessment

Assessment of knowledge, 'or skill or competence that can be learnt through instrumental reasoning' (Ixer 1999, p. 520) is reasonably straightforward and appropriate to test practical knowledge or skill. But not for such as *through-the-mirror* reflection, which develops and nurtures critical attitudes, responses, understanding and acceptance, many of which are deeply challenging both personally and professionally.

My Master's in Medical Science students drew upon private journals and writings for assessment without submitting 'raw reflection' (Boud 1998); Brockbank and McGill (1998) report similar. The reflective course element was formative, only needing to prove they'd kept a journal. With a manageable sized group, using *through-the-mirror* methods, I was able to perceive the fruits of their reflection, offer support and facilitation where needed, and be satisfied they were using critical reflection and reflexivity appropriately for their needs and wants. For graded assessment they discussed and set criteria themselves with tutors, giving them authority and some degree of ownership over the process. Where students are involved in criteria development, there is greater congruence between student and tutor mark (Hinett 2002).

Other authorities also consider graded assessment inappropriate. David Boud (1998) says assessment destroys reflection, disabling students from involving themselves in the 'raw' process. Assessed formal learning contexts with clear boundaries are inappropriate to a dynamic practice, which needs to be unboundaried. Assessed formal learning contexts can only too readily lead to instrumental or rule-following strategies, which apart from stultifying the reflection can also unethically seek inappropriate levels of disclosure and confession. Teachers, coaches or counsellors should only have access to whatever thoughts or feelings reflective practitioners choose to reveal (Boud et al. 1985).

'There is a real danger that creating assessment criteria will have the effect of killing off the spontaneity and individuality of the exercise' (Beveridge 1997, p. 42; see also Rust (2002). He feels tutors are in a cleft stick: without assessment students do not see the process as being sufficiently worthwhile; the effect of it, however, can be to prevent them from expressing themselves freely. Students with non-English mother tongue write journals in English so they can be assessed, thereby reducing the expressive nature of the document (Wright 2005). Scott does not mince words: 'Reflection *can be* a particularly invasive means of reinforcing institutional authority ... Those who assign and assess reflective writing should be mindful of the dispositions toward authority that this practice might foster in time' (2005, p. 27). These authorities point to a major muddle in the pedagogical model (see Chapter 3).

Assessment inappropriate to the type of reflection and reflexivity can damage or even destroy the desired process, and give restricted inaccurate results as written material can be affected by assessment requirements (Hinett 2002; Pavlovich et al. 2009). Students naturally react against unethical demands for 'forced RP' (Hobbs 2007, p. 409), personal details and thoughts by an impersonal assessment system (Ghaye 2007; Sutton et al. 2007). They therefore 'fake it' (Hobbs 2007, p. 411), offer 'laundered' material (Ghaye 2007; Sinclair-Penwarden 2006; Sutton et al. 2007), write within a very narrow range they perceive to be acceptable, and lie about their experience (Hargreaves 2004), some create reflective material retrospectively (Clegg et al. 2002; also see Chapter 7).

Unmuddling models

These examples show inconsistency as to what reflection is, what model of pedagogy it works within, and therefore what model of assessment, assessment substitute or none at all is appropriate. The method of assessment (if there is assessment) has to be appropriate, and in harmony with the curriculum. Like has to go with like; just as sugar and fruit make lovely cakes, but horrid savoury pies. Redmond maintains: 'the appearance of *the ability to reflect* as an assessable category on a competency checklist can only be regarded as a retrograde step, lacking any basic comprehension of the concept' (2006, p. xiii, emphasis in original). Ixer adds:

If reflection is to be regarded as a core facet of individual professional competence, then we need to know far more about its structure, substance and nature … none of the work on reflection thus far has effectively tackled issues of oppression in the teaching and learning environment … A particularly loud note of caution must be sounded that some commentators still inherently endorse reflection as a skill or competence that can be learnt through instrumental reasoning. This leads to the assumption that course planners need only structure assessment in such a way as to encompass a new outcome called 'reflection' … It is clearly the case that the nature of reflection does not fit the competence model … The fear is that reflection will become seen as a self-indulgent or 'soft' subject that cannot be afforded, that standards will fall, and that users will receive a poorer service as a result. (1999, p. 514)

Grasping on to one element of a model without realising that the whole model has to be consistent throughout, might mean throwing the baby out with the bath water:

The increasing prevalence of standards, high-stakes testing, and outcomes assessment obscure the value of reflection, and much else, from fields of vision … There is a risk that the value of teacher reflection will be diminished and overwhelmed by standards. How will the habits of reflection and questioning survive under … the pressures of standards-driven curriculum … Will the habits of reflection that we seek to develop in future teachers become devalued simply because they are difficult to evaluate, summarise, and report? (Ward and McCotter 2004, p. 244)

Assessment solutions

Self and/or peer assessment is effectively used by many bodies, and is also a reflective process in itself (Bryan and Clegg 2006; Hinett 2002). Ken Martin's students set their own assessment criteria, and their work is then submitted to three-way *triadic assessment* by (a) self, (b) peers and (c) tutors:

Once we have agreed on assessment criteria, triadic assessment becomes possible. Class discussions defining criteria are usually terrific, each group seems to bring out something new, though students find it difficult. The usual criteria are flagged up but debating definitions drives home the problems with interpretation of language and difficulties with objectivity and validity [my experience of positive engagement in this tussle is similar]. The exercise concentrates the mind and provides the real stimulus for triadic assessment. This term's exercise produced two new points that could form part of the definition of critical analysis. One was the use of metaphors in critical analysis.

Self-assessment is usually quite acceptable to students, though many find it difficult criticising peers, and being self-critical initially; some find it empowering.

However, many students get very thoughtful, honest, accurate and insightful about their own work very quickly. It can help refine ideas and boost esteem. The standard of reflective practice and reflexivity is certainly helped by self-assessment. I think that including 'insightful comments in self assessment' as part of the 'reflective practice' criterion has given it a higher profile. In a small way, perhaps, triadic assessment opens that 'secret garden' of assessment to some scrutiny and collaborative analysis. (Ken Martin)

Winter's solution is *patchwork text* assessment (2003). A series of fragments created over time from students' learning experience is synthesised into a final submission: 'an essentially creative process of discovering [and presenting] links between matters that may seem to be separate' (Winter 2003, p. 121). Tutors in business, social work, nursing, sociology and Greek tragedy say this developed academic rigour, commitment, motivation driven learning rather than to pass examinations, willingness to take risks and tackle complexities and dilemmas, ability to think independently and present critical arguments, integration of personal and professional issues, critical reading and varied writing abilities. It also allows assessment of the *process* of learning, as well as the *product* (Smith and Winter 2003), though 'the most difficult aspect has been persuading myself to "let go", release students to really take ownership' (McKenzie 2003, p. 160).

Winter et al. do not tackle the issue of assessment affecting, or even destroying, the students' confidence in expressing themselves freely and exploratively, nor the ethical problem. They blandly conclude 'in the end these difficulties can be resolved, and they are essentially not very different from the problems of academic assessment in general (Winter et al. 1999, p. 148).

A dynamic form of reflection is used with university design students; material for assessment is developed organically from reflective course work. Here is how Sapochnic grapples with the assessment conundrum:

Writing is a learning and assessment strategy in the interpersonal/study skills component of a graphic design first-year undergraduate skills module (50 students). Reflectivity is modelled in all workshop activities (e.g., discussing issues in pairs – foursomes – whole group; career planning undertaken by students working in pairs interviewing each other on their strengths, weaknesses, goals and strategies), and prompt sheets at the end of every activity invite students to reflect on outcomes, surprises, satisfactions, dissatisfactions, and possible future strategies. These reflections are collated, annotated and transcribed at the end of the module by students as an essay submission. Writing thus becomes artefact-making. The objective is not the artefact itself (writing), but learning by reflections on the process of producing it.

Most submissions praise the learning thus made, but this enthusiasm might be partly due to possibly unconscious needs to satisfy tutor/readers. Nevertheless, many students engage with and explore issues of uncertainty, not necessarily suggesting improvements to learning practice, but often recognising dilemmas. Such accounts are usually very honest, preoccupied with how to manage reflections (e.g., feeling insecure to speak up in group activities; a wish to lead in teamwork) and also quite moving.

My assessing criteria is subjective: grading is difficult. I pass (I do not grade) those sufficiently comprehensive papers where engagement with the writing – even if not with the activity – has taken place, and to feedback in writing by posing further questions ('You state x was the case. Why might that be?'; 'How could you have done y differently?'; 'Would you consider a pattern in your performance through all the activities?', etc.). This process is lengthy (i.e., uneconomical within current time resources) but, I believe, essential. Having found a reflective voice, the student must be responded to in an equally reflective manner.

I trust that ongoing reflection based on written submissions, my own teaching diary, the photographs I take during and after some events (e.g., teams building towers with newspapers) and the module feedback forms, will assist me to refine, develop or discard this approach. (Carlos Sapochnik)

Evaluation

Evaluation is coming to understand the principles, methods, processes and outcomes of a particular situation. At best a highly sophisticated examination, Bloom et al. (1956) identified evaluation as the highest form of achievement in their *taxonomy of education objectives*. It is used in education to gain feedback on programmes (summative) and communication between tutor and students to improve student experience (formative). Summative evaluations give participants' experience of the whole course; formative evaluations are undertaken at the end of each session, and help form the remainder of the course.

Formative evaluation enables students to tackle and share thoughts and feelings regularly, rather than brood and complain too late. Facilitators gain valuable insight about students' responses to courses from learning journals, metaphor exercises (Linn et al. 2007; see also Chapter 13), and other journals such as for practice attachments (Svenberg et al. 2007). Co-peer mentoring (see also Chapter 11) can enable participants to communicate and discuss ideas and feelings with one peer before sharing with tutor and/or group.

Patricia Hedberg (2009) describes and illustrates reflexive course evaluation periods at the end of each course session. She concludes:

> Most often student reactions are positive and encouraging. This can create a different type of danger, however, one where the process easily becomes a mutual exchange of platitudes. That is not its purpose. All thoughts and feelings are welcome regardless of their praise or pain. What is difficult, I find, is being willing

to express any reaction without sounding like you are trying to ingratiate yourself or meet others' expectations. During a reactions and impressions session, for instance, I keep the focus on reflections rather than on making the instructor feel better. It is much more important to hear what others are thinking or feeling, what frustrates someone, or whether they are engaged. We simply listen to each other with no judgments or further comments necessary. Sometimes it is enough to write or voice your impressions. Nothing more needs to be said or done at that moment. (Hedberg 2009, pp. 30–1; see also Chapter 9)

Like Hedberg, I allowed my Master's students unstructured reflexive space at the end of each session, taking the (occasionally) very rough with the (occasionally) very smooth and everything in between. Brookfield's classroom critical incident questionnaire (1995) is for end-of-session reflexive evaluations. Matt Babcock developed a 'liberating and destabilizing tool for pedagogical intervention' (2007, p. 514; also see above), for a university introductory literature course. His 'Learning Log … if implemented consistently, not only enhances the personal political and ideological communion of teachers and students but also raises the collective awareness concerning classroom dynamics and methods to higher levels'. For 5–10 minutes at the end of each class he and his students free-write 'What have I learned or not learned today?' (p. 514), and then read them to each other. Initially the students offer 'meek verbatim summaries' (p. 515), then by week three there develops the 'class's transformation into symbiotic community of learners and teachers which depends on each individual's willingness to take up, cast off, and exchange those titles at any moment' (p. 516). Of course 'the teacher's reactions to log entries are crucial'. He responded to students' submissions, dialoguing with them dynamically and critically reflexively addressing his own teaching and course design, with positive results. 'The Log … intervened and transformed the physical, intellectual, and interpersonal environment in which my students and I read, wrote, lived, and learned.' (p. 518)

For summative evaluation, my short-course participants write anonymously what was good on one paper, and on another what could have been better. When we have sufficient time, they spread out the positive sheets separately from the negative, and read all, marking each negatively, positively or with a comment. Comments can be transferred to flip chart or typed up and fed back as part of final evaluation. Or they write brief (10-minute) evaluative stories, using the same approach for evaluation as for the course. We read back with no comments, an affirming and warm way to end: the stories tend to refer to the life of the group as a whole. An anonymous form to be handed in is needed to elicit negative points.

Drawing formative evaluations, pioneered in Sydney universities for a range of disciplines and courses (McKenzie et al. 1998), gave different information, inventively and informatively, from participants' written evaluations. One drew a juggler juggling a variety of commitments, another drew someone falling at the last of a succession of high hurdles. Anonymity can be obtained by, for example, a postbox to collect evaluations. I think the evaluation process needs to be useful to participants, rather than just a chore.

Students' reflective writing can itself offer course evaluation and material for tutor reflexivity. Beveridge developed course structures in the light of students' reflective journal material (1997). Here is an example of tutor reflexivity, enabled by reflective journals used as a form of evaluation:

> What we have learned about our students led us to take action on the elementary science methods course ... Interestingly our finding that methods students lack an understanding of first graders' abilities mirrors our lack of understanding of the preservice teachers. While our students were observing, writing about, and discussing the actions of first graders and their teacher, we were learning about them. (Abell et al. 1998, p. 506)

A simple evaluation I have used at the end of a residential is: invent a word which describes this course; now invent a short dictionary definition. Here are some:

> Spontographarsis: release through instant writing; Refreat: a place and time to think and write; Connectifection: the process of finding and connecting realities in the search for truth; Cariyumminess: the process of writing to reveal one's inner thoughts and feelings: the revealing of one's soul (from the Welsh *caru*: to love); Writology: writing one's thoughts down on paper as a way of exploring feelings; Writtance: the process of putting one's thoughts on paper and getting rid of them; Inkathinkalink: with the ink from our pens we think and link our memories and lives with our friends and mentors in a chain of magic pens. The tutor waves her magic wand and says INKATHINKALINKA! (Royal College of General Practitioners (East Anglia Faculty) annual course).

The knotty issue of which comes first, horse or cart, in assessment has tremendous implications for teaching and facilitation methods. Appropriate methods to initiate and foster critical reflection and reflexivity are presented in depth in Chapter 9.

 Read to learn

Babcock, M.J. (2007) Learning logs in introductory literature courses, *Teaching in Higher Education*, **12**(4), 513–23.
Bleakley, A. (2000a) Adrift without a lifebelt: reflective self-assessment in a postmodern age, *Teaching in Higher Education*, **5**(4), 405–18.

Crème, P. (2005) Should student learning journals be assessed? *Arts and Humanities in Higher Education*, **30**(3), 287–96.

Thorpe, M. (2000) Encouraging students to reflect as part of the assignment process. Student responses and tutor feedback, *Active Learning in Higher Education*, 1(1), 79–92.

 ## Write to learn

Each chapter ends with *Write to learn*. For straightforward advice, sufficient for the exercises below, see *Write to learn* in Chapter 1, and see Chapter 6 for more advice. Each writing can be shared fruitfully with a group or confidential trusted other, if this seems appropriate once the writer has read and reflected on it first.

Exercise 8.1   Assessment and spiders' webs

1. Do a *six-minute write* (see Chapter 6).
2. Write 'assessment', boxed in the middle of a page.
3. Write words or phrases which arise in relation to this word anywhere on the page, allowing them to cluster; these elements might be all sorts: frustrations, facts, opinions ...
4. Read back your spider to yourself, adding, deleting or filling out as you wish; list the words/phrases, or join them up into a piece of prose.
5. Note down any thoughts arising about this knotty subject as a result.
6. Read back to yourself with care; you might like to use it to write a more finished piece to share with colleagues.
7. This method can be used with *any* key word boxed in the centre.

Exercise 8.2   Evaluations

1. This exercise can be used with groups at a course end. Participants can either read their lists to the whole group, or if you want to invite negative criticism ask for them to be returned anonymously.
2. Participants each write a list in response to: 'You are leaving this course now and going on a journey. What are you packing in your bag to take with you from here?'
3. I have often associated this final evaluation with an opening exercise before the course first session: 'You have come to this place of education after a long

(Continued)

(Continued)

journey, what do you bring with you?' Participants write a range of things from 'a pen', to 'hope'. They then each read out, so those who have only thought of practical items gain insight. It means they are then prepared imaginatively for the final evaluation 'bag packing' exercise.

Exercise 8.3   Final evaluation

Participants can be given a sheet with these printed, with enough space between for them to respond:

1. What engaged you most?
2. What was helpful?
3. What was unhelpful?
4. What were you surprised by, or was unexpected?
5. What did you give to yourself?
6. What will you take back for the future?

CHAPTER 9

GROUP PROCESSES AND FACILITATION

Chapter 9 gives detailed advice on facilitating *through-the-mirror* reflective writing, groupwork, and mentoring. Principles, how to decide what a group should do and how, ground rules and boundaries, and so on are all authoritatively explained. Who holds authority and power in this work, how to make best use of silence, and psychological processes, are intriguingly described.

> *Socrates*:   It isn't that knowing the answers myself, I perplex other people. The truth is rather that I infect them also with the perplexity I feel myself. (Plato 1958, p. 128)

> No man can reveal to you aught but that which already lies half asleep in the dawning of your knowledge … If he is indeed wise he does not bid you enter the house of his wisdom, but rather leads you to the threshold of your own mind. (Gibran [1926] 1994, p. 67)

> An unbending tree is easily broken. Students say afterwards to wise tutors: we did it ourselves. (Adapted from Lao Tsu 1973)

A group has to be formed with care, looked after knowledgeably, and terminated thoughtfully. The facilitation role is key (Boyer et al. 2006; Trelfa 2005), but needs to be non-dominant and low key in order to succeed. A tutor offers tuition in how to start, and supports the process; their primary role is to create a facilitative environment for the group to enable its own process.

This chapter offers detailed *how* to facilitate others to undertake the development they need at their own safe-enough pace: a very particular skill.

Reflection and still less reflexivity have not been valued in our technologically and digitally based culture where market place, machine, and computer metaphors are paramount. They have been ghettoised as *soft and fluffy* (feminine), a waste of valuable professional time, because they cannot readily be subjected to the masculine processes of commodification, reduction to component mechanical parts, nor tested by tick boxes. Reflection and reflexivity are sophisticated human processes, requiring sophisticated educative support.

The word 'education' comes from the Latin *educare* meaning 'to lead out' (*Oxford English Dictionary*): a reflective facilitator does not so much lead students, as create an environment where they lead themselves. The responsibility for reflection and reflexivity has to come from practitioner, not tutor. Because this is really hard, many students try to dodge the responsibility, defensively complaining tutors should take authority and teach, that facilitative approaches are *flaky*. One reason for defendedness is that such significant learning involves emotion as well as cognitive engagement. Some imagine they can be filled with education without engaging themselves (see Chapter 3). Despite these defended attitudes and stalling at having to face responsibility, a reflective environment created by skilled experienced facilitation enables practitioners or students to adopt a reflective stance naturally (Bulpitt and Martin 2005).

Facilitation needs commitment, skill, knowledge, willingness to work from the heart (Horsfall 2008), and experience to know how to be the strong 'holder of the space for the group' (Miller 2005). This last can be demanding: enabling people to come into close and dynamic reflexive and reflective relationship safely and confidentially, can require facilitators to hold groups' anxiety, fear or embarrassment until they are assuaged (Miller 2005). Facilitators will also have to decide when they need to break confidentiality for ethical reasons. They might, for example, learn from written or verbal contributions about abuse or other unethical practices needing to be dealt with by authorities beyond the group.

Facilitators need to *model* reflexivity and reflection effectively: to *be* reflexive and reflective as well as teach and facilitate them skilfully (Hedberg 2009). The facilitator has to *be* and *do* what they *say*, being reflexively aware, for example, of the voices they might silence (Cunliffe 2004). There has to be a coherence between teaching others how to take a critical stance and taking a critical stance ourselves. (Cunliffe 2004; Noddings 1992). The tutor can be seen as one who 'stands with' the learner as 'enlightened witness' (hooks 2003, p. 89)

A good facilitator joins in a search for demanding questions, but wisely does not know the answers. The role involves constant awareness of both verbal and non-verbal contributions, and fine judgements as to the timing and wording of reactions and suggestions. Low key and unobtrusive, possibly not noticed by some participants, the role is vital.

Reflection is a real key to change, but facilitating good reflective learning experiences is probably more difficult than many anticipate. (Ann)

Facilitators *and* participants will find this chapter useful. Participants can anticipate and support group processes productively, and gain more, by being aware of their own role, and that of others, and alert to possibilities and potential (see later in this chapter). An effective group is run *for*, and largely *by*, its members. Participants are encouraged to consider and express what they want and need from the start, to discover and meet their own learning needs. We learn from our tutors, teachers and lecturers; we can learn far more from our peers. Group members need to feel confident enough to engage in deep and wide-ranging enquiry. Facilitators keep them within boundaries and prevent straying, time-keep, support a reasonable balance of contribution from everyone, and so on.

The facilitator is there to facilitate, to lead from the inside: to support the group to get what they want, or collaboratively create appropriate objectives. Occasionally a member leaves, wanting something materially different from the others, or they stay and collaboratively modify group aims. In one of my groups years ago, a participant was not willing to write, only to talk about how writing can help, despite the clear pre-course information. He disrupted the whole day. I should have been firmer about aims and objectives, and elicited group support in enabling him either to leave or participate.

The examples in *Reflective Practice* are of stand-alone courses or modules. *Through-the-mirror* work can be an invaluable element of longer courses as long as the overall principles of the course are consonant. How to check for consonance and why this is so important is discussed fully in Chapters 3 and 11.

Groups always have *hidden curricula*. It is important to be aware of this, and how everyone brings expectations, hopes and fears, productive or harmful unspoken elements. And groups often learn something completely different from what the tutor intends, sometimes far more valuable. Groups initially test boundaries, deciding how they wish to function, and what they wish to do. Trust, respect and confidence will increase in each meeting, if facilitators support, listen and – facilitate (which means to make easier, or 'help forward' (*Oxford English Dictionary*)).

Writing in this way, and sharing it, can be deeply personal; feelings and emotions can be raw and exposed. Confidences normally only drawn forth by supervision, therapy, or deeply trusted friendships can be shared. Careful facilitation and confidentiality make all the difference.

During the course's monthly meetings, [professionals] contribute by reading aloud pieces written in the intervening weeks. This can be a subject of the member's own choosing or one suggested by the group. These are kept intentionally vague, such as a *time of uncertainty*. Each piece is discussed. An observer seeing the group in action, with members enthralled and, at times, moved by both sadness and mirth, would appreciate that the age-old art of storytelling is alive and well. In these meetings people's prevalent emotions are laid bare, whether of humour, pain, cynicism or sadness.

This course has encouraged me to be more aware and observant of each day. Emotionally charged events no longer make me gulp and bottle up. I now tend to write about what has happened and how I feel about it. I now keep a jottings pad on my desk and even a notebook in my car. I can be seen scribbling away in a lay-by. (Brimacombe 1996)

It is easy for [practitioners] to work in almost total professional isolation, even in a friendly partnership, and it can be hard to admit to mistakes, vulnerability, sadness and even occasionally, joy. If you can commit some of these thoughts to paper, then not only can it be personally therapeutic, but by sharing them with others you may bring insights that can strike a chord and be of benefit to others. (Purdy 1996)

A course facilitator juggles with co-ordinating these three areas:

Needs of the group

Needs of the individual   *Needs of the task/organisation*

Principles

I felt like I'd been given something – real parts of other people. (Elaine)

There are six foundation principles for a facilitator to model, which will support participants to work fruitfully, positively, safely and confidentially. These six are: responsibility, trust, self respect, generosity, positive regard, valuing diversity (see also Chapter 3).

Responsibility: each group member writer has authority over the writings they bring to the group, and for all other contributions such as utterances (which might be words, or perhaps a groan or laugh) and bodily presence (sitting alert, or slouching bored-looking, for example). They are responsible for their own ethical behaviour in the group.

Trust in the group process and writing. Trust can seem an oddly circular thing: how can I trust before knowing my facilitator, or the process to which I'm introduced, is trustworthy? Once I know it's trustworthy of course I'll trust it. A leaning towards trust can start the positive spiral: a willingness to trust enough to get the business going. After that trust breeds trust, and helps heal any break.

Self-respect for our beliefs, actions, feelings, values, identity, is respect for our own integrity. *Through-the-mirror* writing and discussions draw upon our personal core values, as well as ones we did not know were important. It will only work through integrity, which is a sense of wholeness (integratedness), fostered by respect for our own thoughts, ideas, inspirations, values and feelings.

Generosity is the spirit of give and take. No one wins these discussions, no one fails. Everyone gives what they can, and is willing to listen positively and receive, even if it is novel, surprising, and sometimes even outside previously constructed personal comfort zones.

Positive regard is the facilitator's open attitude towards each participant and their contribution, however diverse. A wide range of experiences will be shared within the group, some negative and even shameful: confidence, confidentiality and respect need to be fostered (unless a vital agreed boundary is transgressed: see below).

Valuing diversity is vital, and 'should be engraved on every teacher's heart' (Brookfield 1990, p. 69; also Burns and Sinfield 2004). An awareness of how groups can be marginalised or individuals excluded (Cunliffe 2009a), of inclusivity and empathetic supportiveness with regard to such as non-traditional students and widening access and participation, are essential elements (Zepke et al. 2003). Wright's (2005) study found reflective journals written in English, despite this not being their writers' mother tongue; their learning from the process would have been negated: this should not happen.

Dialogue between facilitators and group members, whether written (see Chapter 7), electronic (see Chapter 11), or verbal is a powerful route to developing reflexivity and reflective abilities and skills (Cunliffe 2009b; Hedberg 2009). The tutor modeling confidential reflective and reflexive attitudes is essential, if time consuming and challenging (Thorpe 2000). It also requires understanding where enquiry processes can take people. There are no short cuts, but this chapter contains information and advice.

Ground rules and boundaries

A group can be powerfully facilitative if it can create its own rules: a relatively safe warm island in life's choppy sea. Issues can be raised tentatively or hesitatingly, aired supportively, and then appropriately taken into the big world. Facilitators create a safe enough space with firm boundaries where people can do this work, knowing 'we did it ourselves'. Participants share a specific part of themselves and their lives with each other. Miranda (Shakespeare's *The Tempest*) first met other people just when she was ready for a greater width of contact and experiences; she responded: 'O brave new world, that has such people in it' (V. i. ll. 183–4).

Many ingredients create appropriate boundaries to engender confidence and relative safety. Two are:

- members taking each other as they experience them within the closed culture of the group
- members relating to and supporting each other through discussions of the writing without seeking to question beyond the boundaries of that writing, and the group.

Both help participants write about and share important issues. Participants do not relate to each other as *doctor* or *senior lecturer*, but Sue or Phil. They do not expose *themselves*, but their writing. They will have had time to write, reread and think about sharing their writing beforehand. It can be helpful if participants recognise the particular nature of the narrated 'I'. In a narrated story, the protagonist, or 'I', will be presented from a particular perspective, involved in a specific segment of experience. This cannot be a true account, because it cannot represent all points of view, nor recount all actions with their repercussions and causes. A narrated story (whether written or spoken) is a construction; it might be based on an actual experience, but it cannot represent that experience in any full width or depth. So the 'I' is the story first person, a character representing a part perhaps, an element possibly of the narrator's experience. It is not the person of the narrator baring their soul. Discussions will then focus on what the writer intended to share with the group: on what happened in the writing rather than in the whole personal hinterland of the account. This can help protect from unintentional disclosure.

If writings are considered as fiction, there is no '*really*': characters do not walk beyond the page and do anything. A question will sometimes stray, but often accompanied by such as: 'I'm going to ask you this; please don't answer if you don't want to, but I think it might help.' A group respects a 'no', just as a decision not to read a piece because it feels too personal is respected. Trust, and a sense of safety, is fostered by *confidentiality*. Belonging to such a group, hearing important reflective material, is a privilege. The writings belong to the writers, and the discussions to the group; neither should be shared outside the group without express permission. I remember one group even requesting nothing be shared with life-partners.

- A sense of group *boundaries* helps create confidence. The group needs to set these at their first meeting. Many professional groups choose to focus solely upon work issues, for example.
- *Respect and mutual trust* are facilitative. An attitude of 'unconditional positive regard' (Rogers 1969) can be modelled by the facilitator. A disagreement can be undertaken in a spirit of mutual respect. Discussions will be constructive and friendly if comments are either generally positive, or if negative elements are expressed gently, along with definite appropriate constructive suggestions.

Group function

A great deal of hassle, disappointment, and possibly pain is avoided by initially discussing more or less what participants are there for, how they are going to do it, why, where and when. The group is likely to be organic, with working aims, objectives, duration, patterns and relationships developing over time, but some initial agreement helps. Some things will be determined in advance, especially if the sessions are part of a course. But these circumstances can make it even more vital to create a safe enough, clear enough space for people to feel confident to work in. Working reflexively and reflectively will be new to many who expect traditional teacher-led classes (see Chapter 3).

How many sessions needs to be decided, unless this is set as part of a wider course or degree. Six sessions can be agreed, to be reviewed at sessions four and five. Three sessions is the minimum for people to grasp the process and begin to tackle it fruitfully, to begin to understand, trust and take responsibility for their own reflection and reflexivity. Reflective practice writing groups generally offer support in professional and personal explorations and expressions to:

- understand more clearly the import and implications of specific experiences
- discover learning needs
- enable the sharing of sensitive issues with involved, supportive disinterested colleagues (that is, not such as line-managers)
- reinforce the self-confidence and self-esteem which writing tends to bring
- support the occasional loss of confidence, writer's block, and lost way.

The group is *not*:

- *a writers' workshop*, in which the form rather than the content of the writings are constructively criticised in order to help the writer improve the text (for example, story, poem or play) with publication in mind: the content of the writing is not considered in such a forum
- *a therapeutic writing group*, where the content of the writing is focused upon, but in order to support the writer in psychotherapeutic explorations
- *a chat group*, where the writings are read out, and the response might be: 'how nice, now that reminds me how my Auntie Gwen used to …'.

The life of a group

A closed group with the same members at each meeting (allowing for occasional absences) can enable, with skilled facilitation, trust and confidence, as well as listening, understanding and creative insightful response. The experience of being in a group is different at different stages: a courtly dance, then jive, quickstep, country dance or tarantella.

A group can be seen to be a story authored by all group members, and to have a classic 'plot' structure of *Meeting, Falling in love, Lovers' tiff* (or *Conflict*), *Kiss and make up* (or *Conflict resolution*), *Mission* 'lovers win over their parents (or don't)', *End* 'lovers sail off into the sunset (or die)' and *Mourning*. What makes a story a story is the way the characters, events and the readers' view of them change and develop. A group does not just get better and better; the duration and shape of the 'plot' will vary for different groups (*Romeo and Juliet*, or a cheap romance):

The Stages in the Life of a Group

- At *meeting* members begin to see themselves as a group rather than a collection of individuals. They find out about each other; the lovers tentatively become a couple rather than just individuals. Relationships are characterised by reserve, avoidance of conflict and politeness; few personal risks are taken, and views and feelings are withheld.
- *Falling in love* is the initial stage of excitement and beginning of commitment.
- *Conflict* is the traditional 'middle day' phenomenon when the group has constituted itself and perhaps felt rather congratulatory. Members provisionally sort out roles, flex role muscles and jockey for leadership perhaps, or push preferred objectives. People can become quite badly hurt in this process if not handled carefully. Argument is a route to finding out more about boundaries and each other; an important stage, engendering creative thinking, such as: Precisely what are we doing here? Who am I in this group? What do I want to get out of it? People may be defensive, assertive, distrustful, suspicious and do not listen to each other.
- *Conflict resolution* is creating group identity and rules, developing commitment, as well as wanting to nurture and care for both group and each other. Participants are supportive, receptive, and attempt to avoid conflict.
- In *mission* the group has tackled each other, uncovered quite a few prejudices to sidestep, and strengths and skills to harness. They have a reasonable group feel for who they are, what it is they are doing, why and how, when and where they are doing it. They work well together, have mutual understanding and are doing whatever it was they set out to do; or something else which has become more important. They are open (enough), trusting, forbearing, supportive, listening well, and willing to take risks.
- *End* is when the group has done its work and moves on gracefully: with regret and optimism about the next stage for each. Members leave: once more individuals. A 'rite of passage', such as a shared lunch, can ease the parting.
- Facilitators might not be aware of *mourning*. An effective supportive group is bound to leave a sense of regret at its passing.

These stages are simplistic, as for any model. The stages will probably get mixed up, and earlier stages, even if undergone thoroughly, may recur. Conflict may arise at any time and need to be dealt with (lovers continue to tiff, kiss and make up). New rules and guidelines may be discussed. The group may even go back to elements of the first stage and need to get to know each other again in areas which seemed unimportant at *meeting*. *Mission* is reached after at least some elements of the previous stages. All the relationships depicted are within the boundaries of the group: individuals meeting outside the group's boundaries may knife each other or jump into bed.

> The group has enabled me to share my writing over the last six years in a supportive and creative environment. This has helped me to both explore and make sense of some of the experiences and challenges of my life. I have improved my confidence and ability to write creatively and have been enriched by the range and depth of poetry and prose which each member has brought to the group. (Shirley)

> There have been times when I've brought a piece of writing and decided not to read it – the circumstances have simply not been 'right'. And this feels acceptable – comfortable – because the group is sensitive to the mood engendered by each person's writing. I think we have learned to 'hear' better and this has informed our writing. The whole process is evolving all the time. (Becky)

> I find the process of listening to someone read intensely moving, knowing something of the life from which the writing comes. It helps me know the person more fully. It really is a unique way of sharing. (Sheena)

> The space created by the group is: supportive, constructive, safe, facilitative, confidential, free from jargon and (almost) free from b****cks. (Mark)

Characters

A group, just like a story, also relies on character: the talkative and exuberant, the shy and quiet, the silent but anguished, dominant and bossy, analytic reasoner, facilitative, divergently creative thinker, moaner, kindly and motherly, frustrated rescuer, frightened pupil, babbler, lurker, catalyst, logical structurer, teacher's pet. Troubles sometimes arise when a group contains two or more habitually dominant people; different problems arise when too many are shy and quiet (or even worse, anguished and quiet). Facilitators can gently and subtly encourage members to try new roles.

Different roles may be played in different groups, as in life: mum one minute, teacher or lover the next. A Master's student, described as 'facilitative' in a reflexive group discussion, was astonished, a bit fearful and kept referring to it. We supported her in thinking it was all right for her to be facilitative, to valuably extend her notion of herself and her skills and experience. Until then she had assumed a whacky role, with creative ideas but had to have the more serious elements of the course explained carefully. The 'game', leading to this enlightenment, was participants likening each other to animals. We then gently and cautiously teased out what we thought our metaphorical animals might signify.

The facilitator also assumes roles as appropriate and with discretion, being a 'good enough facilitator', taking on each character just 'enough' of the time. He or she may be:

- *Teacher*: giving a keynote talk on an essential issue. Participants usually like this, but too much of it makes for a passive group who do not take responsibility for their learning at other times (as in the *chalk and talk model* in Chapter 3).
- *Instructor*: for a set task. The group undertaking to do what they are told is useful when needed for demanding tasks, such as writing to a certain theme for a certain length of time. Responsibility for everything else is removed, freeing them to be creatively explorative and expressive in their writing. This should be in an environment of enough trust and support, otherwise the writing will not be worth the paper it is written upon.
- *Interpreter*: the facilitator reflecting back a contribution, repeating it in his or her own words in order to clarify and ensure it has been heard. This can increase member confidence, but must be used with care as it can irritate, or reduce members' autonomy. The facilitator might also interpret behaviours, or make connections or linkages between concepts or ideas. This pattern-making or pattern-perceiving can be creative and constructive.
- *Devil's advocate/confronter*: appropriate in certain circumstances. Groups need to be challenged enough. The facilitator must be reasonably confident in the way the individual may respond. Tears and anger can be very fruitful, but not when engendered by mistake.
- *Compatriot/discloser*. Groups in which members reveal themselves, but facilitators never do will not work. Nor should they cross boundaries by revealing all their cupboarded skeletons, taking up the group's emotional space and time.
- *Consultant*. The facilitator may respond to a particular wish or need of the group for some information or advice from his or her knowledge and experience.
- *Neutral chairperson*: part of the time makes sure the group keeps to the point, to time, that everyone has a say, the subject is appropriately and thoroughly aired, that sexism, racism, big white chiefism do not happen, the ground rules are respected, the discussion is appropriately recorded, and so on. Chairpeople are not primarily involved in discussions or activities.

- *Participant*: opposite to chairperson, a useful role on occasion. It creates a warm, coherent sense; the skill is not to lose sight of essential facilitator roles. Members new to group processes think facilitators are participants much of the time, without noticing the chairing, interpretive, confronting and some directive functions.
- *Manager*: undertakes essential but unexciting organisational and management tasks, ensuring participants arrive at the right time and place and with the right papers and expectations.

These roles are delineated here simplistically; in practice boundaries are blurred. Groups rarely perceive experienced facilitators moving between them. Shifting appropriately and smoothly is not straightforward. Problems can arise when participants expect one role from their facilitator and they are in another; even a skilful tutor can confuse, anger, alienate or devalue at times.

Authority and power

The facilitator is always in an authoritative role, powerful even. A group trusts him or her to retain awareness of this, and wield it responsibly, confidentially and ethically. Forgetting and playing *participant* too much is as dangerous as becoming *dictator*. Hughes and Pengelly add:

> Trainers need to give considerable thought to what backing they need to enable them to face the full extent of their managerial authority and of the potential impact of this on the functioning of participants. The more they know about their own authority, the less are they likely either to deny it and collude with participants in avoiding powerful learning experiences, or wield it unthinkingly and impose rigid, unresponsive courses. Our argument has been that the more open trainers are about the extent and limits of their own authority, the more open they can be to the professional and personal authority of course participants. (1995, pp. 169–70)

Facilitators can make errors, which need careful handling. A university therapist wrote about a childhood bereavement at a day course. The small group sat stunned at the privilege of hearing such limpid, clear writing full of meaning, clearly of such value to themselves and the writer. The writer said he could never have intended to write it, and would not have done so if I had not forgotten to mention to the whole group they would be asked if they would like to read their writing to their group of six. I was on poor form, my daughter seriously injured in hospital and my mother having just died. He had felt secure in the privacy of paper and pen. On this occasion I was lucky: he forgave me, and they all benefited from him reading it. Here follows an example of a tutor ensuring her students retain their own authority within a group:

> Critical reflection encourages the questioning of traditional classroom authority. Changing the way authority plays out in the classroom may disturb some students, and it will likely challenge the teacher to question assumptions about his or her own role ... When I asked for anyone [MBA-level course] to share their reactions to the class one evening, a student volunteered how much money the entire class had wasted sitting through three useless classes full of vague discussions of the purpose of business and management. He wanted concrete and structured solutions: 'Where were the facts and answers?' Nodding to acknowledge I heard him, I personally was shocked by his strong assertions, troubled by his assumptions that all agreed with him, and more than a little worried that he was right. Vying for time, I asked others for their thoughts while I quietly figured out how I would respond. Then, I remembered I did not need to respond. That was not my job. So I was silent and left a space for learning. Some felt the need to rescue me, uncomfortable with open conflict.
>
> Students rallied around the course, sharing how much their thinking had changed and how they had brought ideas into their work environments to prove relevance and worth. What happened most profoundly is that we all learned during this reflective process. Others had certainly felt the same as the student who originally spoke, but were afraid to voice their thoughts. It was a raw, honest moment of frustration and a great learning opportunity. We were open to sharing our ideas and opinions and thoughts, even to challenging our beliefs about learning. This looked like critical reflection to me, and it was an example of how we shaped our meaning through public reflection. (Hedberg 2009, pp. 30–1)

Despite such challenges, most often student reactions are positive and encouraging. This can create a different type of danger, however, one where the process easily becomes a mutual exchange of platitudes. That is not its purpose. All thoughts and feelings are welcome regardless of their praise or pain. What is difficult, I find, is being willing to express any reaction without sounding like you are trying to ingratiate yourself or meet others' expectations. During a reactions and impressions session, for instance, I keep the focus on reflections rather than on making the instructor feel better. It is much more important to hear what others are thinking or feeling, what frustrates someone or whether they are engaged. We simply listen to each other with no judgements or further comments necessary. Sometimes it is enough to write or voice your impressions. Nothing more needs to be said or done at that moment.

Silence

Silence is powerful in any group, particularly an interactive confidential group discussing deeply held principles and vital experiences. Skilled facilitation wields silence powerfully: tutors who are fearful of it miss an invaluable resource. 'The leader must learn to allow for different sorts of silence – the reflective, the anxious, the embarrassed or puzzled' (Abercrombie 1993, p. 118), the thoughtful, angry or portentous (for a useful exploration, see Rowland 1993, pp. 87–107). If participants do not feel responsible for their group, and lack authority over their own contribution, silence can be experienced as confronting and aggressive.

Silence, handled wisely and carefully, can be used fruitfully for deep reflection when members are facilitated to feel responsible for their group. If no one in the group has anything particular they need to say, then no one needs to speak. The silence is broken when someone has something to say, however tentative. A silence might be used, for example, to allow previous words to sink in, and an appropriate ensuing response sought. Understandings and clarities do not necessarily emerge through argument or discourse.

When a participant has read their writing, a silence might well ensue: this can be fruitful, allowing listeners to marshal their thoughts and feelings before speaking. The one who has just read their writing needs to perceive this brief silence as positive. A new anxious group needs the facilitator to support listeners to say something positive quickly, having heard a piece, as new writers feel exposed on reading their work. A participant rather than facilitator breaking this silence tends to increase group responsibility for the discussion. I never break the silence when someone's read their writing; the discussion belongs to the group, and needs to be started by them. If I, as facilitator, break the silence, undue weight is placed on my words.

More can be said by silence than words: 'a long heavy silence promises danger, just as much as a lot of empty outcries' (Sophocles 1982, l. 1382), and Aeschylus pointed out that safety and discretion can reside in silence: 'Long ago we learned to keep our mouths shut/Where silence is good health, speech can be fatal' (1999, p. 29).

> Sharing our writing weaves connections between us. The special attentiveness as we listen to someone reading their work, and especially in the silence afterwards. There is special pleasure in witnessing each other's writing develop, each in their own way. There is excitement in discovering unfamiliar aspects of people: sensual, lyrical writing by one known for their cynicism, well-crafted, poignant pieces by another who joined the group believing they couldn't write. (Maggie)

> Silence is but a feeling silence. Someone has just finished reading their contribution – perhaps a difficult encounter with a patient or a partner or even memories of training and hospital days which still have the power to hurt. The group has lived through that moment with the speaker, shared the emotions, and for a few minutes there is nothing to say. We are amazed at the power of each other's writing. Certainly when we come down to discuss, with Gillie's help, there are ways that the writing could be made

more telling, but the inspiration comes from the group. It is not afraid to face the feelings aroused daily in medical practice and is learning in the safety of the group to translate them into words. (Naomi)

Psychological processes

A reflexive reflective facilitator is an educator, not a therapist or analyst; certain insightful understandings can however be borrowed from psychotherapeutic theory and practice, and the boundary between the two is not always clear. 'It is helpful and probably essential that coaches and mentors [facilitators and tutors] have some awareness of psychological processes' (Garvey et al. 2009, p. 165).

Ideas about interpersonal dynamics are useful. We *transfer* onto others elements of other relationships. It's worth bearing this in mind all the time as it is so common: we all do it. Facilitators can receive bewilderingly inappropriate emotions if participants transfer feelings which, for example, belong to their parents, or long-ago school teachers. In *counter-transference* facilitators react similarly inappropriately, treating a disruptive member like a naughty son, for example. *Projection* is when emotions are projected inappropriately: 'I'm sure you are getting at me', might mean 'I really wish I could get at you'. In *introjection*, feelings, such as anger, are swallowed and not expressed, possibly leading to bottled feelings erupting inappropriately heavily later. All these happen all the time in everyday life. A facilitator has responsibility to take them into account. Awareness can explain why anger or tears erupt out of nowhere, disrupting the whole group process.

A mentee recently anxiously told me about a group where a participant had launched a blistering attack at the beginning, expressing dissatisfaction with the group process and wanting *to be taught*. After discussion he realised the student was transferring onto him, as group leader, negative feelings about teachers: she had become the naughty angry school child. An experienced facilitator knows such behaviour is not personal, and is able to continue calmly explaining the process and continue the session. The group will then take over and control the obstreperous member: they do not want their time wasted by a naughty school child (see also Hedberg 2009 above).

Group management

Groups do not happen, they are created and nurtured. There are a number of seemingly small details which can greatly facilitate members to take responsibility for their own group functions, giving them authority and confidence to share tentative, border ideas, feelings and memories. The role of the facilitator is key in creating an appropriate environment for which an understanding of the following elements is useful:

- *Participants need to know each other's names.* Beginning the first session with a warm-up exercise (see below) helps people feel integrated and involved. A second session could begin with a few minutes allowed for those who do not know a name asking the person across the circle. It is quick and leads to laughter and companionship, as several people speak at once.
- A *formative evaluation* or *reflexive period* to conclude each session, to check on group satisfaction, personal sense of involvement, needs and wants (for excellent examples, see Hedberg 2009). Groups can examine their own processes critically. Careful facilitation is required to help people to stand outside themselves and their group for a space, in order to be more aware of the rules, values, unspoken assumptions and so on they bring to the sessions. It can enable appropriate redefining of group boundaries and rules.
- *Timing*: beginning and ending when expected. Time needs allocating carefully so each participant has their share to read and discuss their writing. Confidence in *time sharing* and *time boundaries* fosters respect, responsibility and security, and the best use of everyone's energy.
- *Variety of group size and organisation* aids dynamics. Short periods of paired and small-group work during sessions can enable a situation of closer trust: quiet or well-defended participants contribute more, and dominant ones less.
- Awareness of the range of roles (*characters*) participants and facilitator can take on, as well as transference, projection and so on (see above).
- *Verbal contributions from as many group members as possible* and as appropriate. Less voluble or silent members can be encouraged to speak, and dominant ones encouraged to listen by mixing the group format with periods of reflexivity, paired work, small-group work, plenary, as well as appropriate subtle facilitation to help participant awareness of the value of the contribution of every member.
- *Problematic participants* can usually be coped with *by the group* with careful facilitation, leading to greater group cohesion.
- *Open questions*: 'How did you feel about that?', not closed, 'Did that make you angry?'
- *Use of personal pronouns.* People say 'you', meaning 'I' (instead of saying '*I* get tired ...', people sometimes say '*You* get tired of saying it over and over again'), 'we' instead of 'I' (an assumption the group agrees with the speaker). The use of 'I' by each speaker can help the group own and be responsible for what each says.
- Using individuals' *names* appropriately increases inclusion and value.
- An awareness of the power of *sub-groups*.

(Continued)

(Continued)

- *Non-verbal communications* (facial expression, posture, gesture, blushing, sweating, laughter, crying, and so on) are very informative.
- *Who comments first, and when* after a reading? It is never me: as facilitator I can readily dominate and inhibit participant contributions. I speak after everyone else, having asked for a quick response for the sake of a new writer. A deeply thoughtful pause as the group reflect on what they have heard and want to say, can prelude a fruitful discussion in an established, confident group, to which I add a few final words.
- *The door-knob*. Just as the session ends participants may blurt out disturbing or vital information, invariably needing time. Firm time boundaries, aiming to finish in advance of time, and a reflexive formative evaluatory period at session end can help.
- *Listening to, commenting on, and eliciting comments* reflectively on the written experiences of others is a skill to be fostered, enabled and modelled by facilitation.
- *Learning how to take the comments and discussions of others*, about writings, needs practice and confidence building. Facilitative, stretching or surprising points come from participants not just the facilitator. I have been asked: 'Now are you going to psychoanalyse me?' Group and facilitator have the responsibility to support writers in extending and clarifying their *own* ideas, not impose views.

Housekeeping

I keep six honest serving men
  (They taught me all I knew);
Their names are What and Why and When
  And How and Where and Who. (Kipling 1902, p. 83)

These 'honest serving men' have served me well for years, too. I call them *can-opener questions*. Used as a checklist in planning and writing, they help ensure I have covered everything. Here are some practical considerations they have suggested, to help facilitators in group management processes:

- *How*: King Arthur thought *sitting in a circle* helps everyone to feel equal. A centre table can be a barrier. A circle of comfortable chairs can create more confident intimacy. When only schoolroom chairs are available, packing people in close round a table is good. They all lean forward, creating a gathered circle.

- *Where*: *the right number of chairs* for everyone makes the group feel complete; it is worth removing the unneeded chairs. Leaving the chair of an absent but expected member can retain a sense of their presence. A group referred to Jenny's empty chair as if she were there, then, when she came in apologetically but expectedly late, slipping into her waiting chair she felt warm and wanted.
- *What*: *necessary equipment*, such as an overhead projector, being in place beforehand saves wastage of valuable time.
- *When*: *punctuality and regular attendance* can offer a sense of respect to the group and its work, as well as saving time and frustration.
- *Who*: *group size* affects dynamics considerably. Eight is a lovely number; twelve an ideal maximum; four is too few when some cannot come (but may be perfect for a short introductory one-off session).
- *How*: *funds* – who pays what, when, how, how much, to whom (if appropriate).
- *Where*: *venue* – is it right? Can you make it more right if it's not perfect?
- *When*: *coffee time* – important because people get to know each other. But when, where, how long?
- *When*: *timing* – people like to know at the beginning when they will get their breaks (coffee, tea, lunch) and when they will finish. Energy and commitment are parcelled unconsciously for the allotted time: extra time can be useless as energy is used up; finishing early leaves frustrated unused energy.
- *Why*: this chapter doesn't cover *Why?* – all the rest of the book does that.

Maureen Rappaport, medical lecturer, reflects on her teaching:

How can I arrange a series of teaching sessions, or one session, where others feel safe to expose parts of themselves and explore their own experiences, their cutting edges of learning, a place where the learning is raw, but a place we learn from? The edge is where our professional experiences, grounded and guided by mentors, cut into our own beliefs, and values, and boy, do they hurt.

I have been experimenting with different groups and various methods. It is hard to keep the group focused on the writing and meanings and not on making their peers 'feel better'. I, too, have to fight against my natural tendencies to 'save' my students when they express difficult feelings and emotions, although I am perfectly comfortable sharing my uncomfortable feelings with them.

Finding my own voice in writing has been so powerful: I'm afraid of smothering others'. It's time to listen to students' and residents' voices, through poetry and literature and writing among other things. The residents teach me so much. I hope I give as much back to them. It's like the magic between my patients and I. I look up at their sharp minds and clever reason. What do I want to learn?

It never ceases to amaze me that the residents (registrar or trainee doctors) are more self-aware and more self-reflective than I give them credit for. I ask them to write about a meaningful event in their training (20 minutes of keeping the hand moving). Here is Al, 1st year family medicine resident's writing:

> I met an amazing patient recently. I was called down to emergency on my surgery rotation. I was to see a 24-year-old woman with cerebral palsy. When I first saw this African-American with short black hair I thought she was a he, so I got confused.
>
> I approached the patient, introduced myself and began my history. It was obvious that the patient was bound to a bed all her life. She couldn't speak clearly and mumbled her words. It was obvious she depended on others for her care. I began asking her father questions. After awhile she mumbled something and her father started laughing. When I asked what she said, he said, 'she says why don't you just ask me the questions?'
>
> I was shocked and ashamed. I apologised to her and began our conversation. Although difficult to understand I made out her words and realised how direct and concise she was. She was also witty and kept cracking up her dad. At one point I had to stop my 'history' and said, 'I'm sorry, but I just have to say you are one of the most inspiring and amazing people I have ever met'. Despite all the crap in medicine, just the fact that I got to meet her makes it all worth it.
>
> Al (Maureen Rappaport)

Drumming

A skilled facilitator, just like any expert practitioner, is not generally conscious of the kinds of issues covered in this chapter: they work intuitively (or with phronesis, see Frank 2004). But even an expert facilitator makes mistakes, has to learn a new method or technique. It can feel dangerous: emotions, feelings and opinions can be expressed and felt with vigour when groups focus on vital issues as in *through-the-mirror* reflection. A participant said: 'The responsibility for encouraging reflection is awesome.' If effective learning is to take place, that level of responsibility needs to be taken:

> Effective learning is therefore dependent, at least in part, on access to that world of feeling and phantasy, which allows structures of meaning to be recognised, and to be open to change, in a way which facilitates a different (and perhaps more constructive) professional response. Great emphasis is placed ... on the learning environment, particularly on the need for space and for containment ... High value is given to creating a space which is some-what apart from the everyday world, where a reflective mode and a slower pace is promoted, and where it is permissible to allow vulnerability to surface (a view somewhat at odds with the dominant ideas of competence and 'mastery'). (Yelloly and Henkel 1995, p. 9)

Facilitating an effective group offers immense satisfaction: experiencing people developing, growing, reaching fresh understandings, and learning how to support each other. Effective group work is like learning to drum collaboratively in rhythm:

> Rhythm, seamless, breathless, captivating. Ah ha! We do have rhythm. We can do it! Circle of faces, my friends.
> Rhythm of the heart, of the step, of the circulation of the blood. Change of the seasons. Night and day. Springtime and harvest. Marching, dancing, walking, skipping, running, jumping, talking, poetry. (Jenny Lockyer)

Creating a facilitated environment for a group to reflect and be critically reflexive enables them to communicate with each other in a way which would be difficult or impossible under other circumstances. When undertaken with a team who habitually works together, the process can be powerfully team-building. This is the subject of Chapter 10.

 Read to learn

Boyer, N.R., Maher, P.A. and Kirkman, S. (2006) Transformative learning in online settings: the use of self-direction, metacognition, and collaborative learning, *Journal of Transformative Education*, **4**(4), 335–61.

Hedberg, P.R. (2009) Learning through reflective classroom practice: applications to educate the reflective manager, *Journal of Management Education*, **33**(1), 10–36.

Reynolds, M. (1997) Learning styles: a critique, *Management Learning*, **28**(2), 115–33.

 Write to learn

Each chapter ends with *Write to learn*. For straightforward advice, sufficient for the exercises below, see *Write to learn* in Chapter 1, and see Chapter 6 for more advice. Each writing can be shared fruitfully with a group or confidential trusted other, if this seems appropriate once the writer has read and reflected on it first.

(Continued)

(Continued)

Exercise 9.1 Learning by observation

1. Do a *six-minute write* (see Chapter 6).
2. Think of a teacher, tutor, lecturer from any time in your life, whom you admire.
3. Describe them; include all characteristics negative and positive.
4. Write a narrative about an occasion of their teaching you remember well.
5. Return to your description of this teacher (3 above): replace their name with yours. Instead of 'Fred is ...', you now have 'I am ...'
6. Reread all you have written with care and reflexivity; change or add to anything if you want to, remembering to be positive about yourself.

Exercise 9.2 Silence

1. Do a *six-minute write* (see Chapter 6).
2. Think of a notable period of silence, or quiet in your life. It might be any length.
3. Write an account of that occasion and what you felt about the quality of silence.
4. Reread, reflecting what you would like to take out of this particular memory, and if there are any other silent or quiet times in your life.

Exercise 9.3 Personal learning goals

1. List your personal learning goals (useful with students at the beginning of a course).
2. Read and reflect, altering or adding as desired.

CHAPTER 10

REFLECTIVE PRACTICE AND TEAM DEVELOPMENT

Chapter 10 presents the powerful potential of *through-the-mirror* reflective practice for teams. Individual practitioners gain from the process, they also gain considerable team strength through effective communication. In-depth examples are given, explaining the process.

> Shape clay into a vessel;
> It is the space within that makes it useful. (Lao Tsu 1973, p. 11)

> Sunlight's a thing that needs a window
> before it enters a dark room.
> Windows don't happen. (Thomas 1986, p. 53)

Through-the-mirror writing is undertaken primarily for the self, and then for specific others, whether mentor or group. Such collaborative learning is deeply educative, facilitative of empathetic listening and communication, and can therefore be powerfully team-building. The writing and discussion processes facilitate an effective level of frankness and openness. A safe-enough environment can be created for elements of relationships and organisations to be faced and reconfigured. Barry et al. (1999) have persuasively written of their use of reflective writings in developing their team researching doctor-patient communication. Another example is *the patchwork text* reflective course assessment process which aids team development (Illes 2003). In this chapter I describe a course for senior social workers, and one for community health work. Informative descriptions of further team-developing reflective courses follow.

We get to know each other through the writings in a way we are never normally privileged to do. (Medical student)

Reflection in teams and groups I have come to term 'refractive practice'. Just as a stick refracts or appears to bend when placed in water, so a new member of a team refracts when placed in the medium of the team. Reflection is here conceived as a shared or distributed activity. (Bleakley 2002)

The growth of a team

Six officers-in-charge of this and the nearby old people's homes were waiting as I entered the long, narrow, huge-windowed room. Unlike me, they were used to the warm atmosphere, where old people move one shuffle at a time with the aid of a stick or frame, between tea table and television. They were all strangers to me; their area manager (my ex-Master's student) wanted a course *for them*, bringing these isolated professionals together into a collaborating supportive group.

My new colleagues later shared initial perplexity. They asked me, as so many others have: 'Writing is so difficult, why can't we just discuss these issues with each other?' One member commented in her final evaluation:

First day – not too keen. Did not know what to expect – wasn't going to be really clever – I am not an academic type person.

They were almost immediately plunged into the process. For six minutes we wrote whatever came into our heads in whatever jumbled order, without stopping. Since this writing was not to be shared, the morning's irritations, a shopping list, diatribes against an impossible colleague/family member, last night's unshareable nightmare were all possible subjects. Nobody ever has nothing in their head.

This *six minutes* put writing on the paper. It also allowed the busy business of everyday concerns to surface, be recorded and, hopefully, put on one side; or perhaps a flash of insight to be recorded. We immediately wrote a story about *a time when something vital was learned*, for a further 10–20 minutes. Once more: no stopping to think; thinking can block inspiration and flow. We would share all or part of this writing with each other, if appropriate.

Resting aching fingers, all six realised they could write; pens had scribbled frantically. Reading both pieces of writing privately with attention, to acquaint ourselves with the writing, and to look for previously unnoticed connections, was next.

Some boundaries

Before we read our pieces to each other we established initial ground rules. My suggestions were:

- We will be trying to tease out professional and possibly personal issues embedded within the stories, and draw out related, underlying themes that are of concern to the writer and the group.
- We will be doing this in a spirit of support and respect for each other.
- A thoughtful silence often arises after a piece has been read. As facilitator, I will not break it, as I could so easily do all the talking. The silence may be felt as supportive and reflective, or unnerving to the waiting writer. Someone must take responsibility for breaking it.
- While you are listening, be formulating provisional discussion queries/points. They might be questions, suggestions, or requests for further information.
- When you read you may feel hesitant, but the group will not perceive the imperfections of your writing as you do. They will be interested and involved.
- Everyone's thoughts are of value; yours *and* theirs must be heard.
- These pieces are fictions, although they may slide along a fiction–faction–reality continuum. The extent of this is not our business; fiction preserves confidentiality. Writers may wish to share more during or after the session.
- Confidentiality is essential; anything written or said in the group belongs to the group and cannot be spoken of outside without express permission.

We seven discussed fears and anxieties about sharing writing. A ground rule was careful timekeeping; everyone was to have their turn within the agreed period. No one should be under pressure to contribute to writing or discussion. I suggested I should not take up group time by bringing my own writing. Everyone wanted to be warm and involved, yet cautious and incurious; we laughed at ourselves – what a tightrope!

Everyone read out a snippet, a paragraph or all they had just written. The discussion was wide-ranging and rewarding, if careful, after our boundary-creating session. Group members were generous in the personal information they shared, much of which related to how and why they became involved in such demanding and potentially stressful work. Most felt immensely relieved afterwards: this course is about something I can do, and I *think* I might even be going to enjoy it. The unanimously experienced shadow, felt then and expressed later, was, *everyone but myself is a brilliant writer*.

Time was running out, a commodity in short supply for these officers; they decided to keep journals. Everyone was to write and bring a new piece in any form, next time. I suggested a topic this time, but subsequently all came from the group. I suggested *A Clean Sheet*, literal or metaphorical.

One writer felt extremely uncertain about her ability to write at home, but overcame her fears by setting her alarm for 15 minutes. The group had many discussions about staff relationships with residents, being concerned that there should be grace and loving care. One writer brought a wise yet humorous slant on all this, as her contributions always did.

More stories

All participants read their pieces: 'like opening windows on themselves for each other'. Headings for ensuing pieces included: 'dilemmas', 'leadership', 'changes', 'aspirations', 'perceptions', 'a conflict of loyalties' and 'a frustrating episode'.

There was always insufficient time for sharing their work and work-related issues. One participant thought fate had laid calamitous events to create writing topics. We decided it was probably always so, but the course made them aware, and able to deal with them.

Time was found to write about past, unsorted-out issues, such as clients' suicide. This led to a long discussion about dealing with death in a dignified and loving way. I was impressed, time and again, by thoughtful and caring professional attitudes.

The six gained confidence exponentially in their abilities, and felt happier writing regular reports, and so on. Rather than feeling the course writing should be clever or literary, they wrote as expression of things difficult or impossible to take elsewhere. Group trust led to supportive relationships radically altering their working experience, particularly those fresh to it, or taking on role changes. Each had been struggling with daily problems such as inspections, disciplinaries, all of which were now shared.

Writing and discussions confirmed that *through-the-mirror processes* enhance freedom and self-respect. Thinking of life as a story, and having the opportunity and courage to tell that story oneself, offers some measure of control.

Evaluation

Brief formative evaluations reviewing ground rules, format and content concluded each session. Once they arranged meetings beyond the course; that was their evaluation. One summative evaluation included:

> Coming each week has been a great source of strength and support to me.
> Sometimes I have come away feeling a more valued member of 'the team'.

There was no 'team' previously, only a handful of people in the same area doing much the same job. One fear was: 'I hope we don't lose it all!' They did not need me in order to continue. Feedback since has been that they still support each other through problems and challenges.

More team-building stories

Community health project team

This team invited me for two sessions to reflect upon busy, stressful work with disadvantaged communities. We met in their big, bright, animated room full of children's artwork. Derek Snaith, in his writing, focused upon feedback he received which gave him 'the realisation that I am doing something right within my work', and how that felt:

> She said that I was a *key worker* because I had helped start a social club for adults with learning difficulties in the area. What I had never realised in all my time here at Riverside was that my work was making a difference to people. I could tell from the passion in her voice that this initiative 'The Millennium Club' is something she and others have been looking for for years. And I still am shocked when positive feedback comes from those involved in helping to run the sessions and those who come along to enjoy it.
>
> This simple statement, and the subsequent realisation of the impact of my work has helped me in my mind to be more confident in my own abilities and my own views. I think I will be able to be myself more at work and be more assertive when it comes to dealing with people and groups who are there purely for self-interest or generally negative reasons.
>
> Because I now know that I have made a difference to people who are in need of supporters to do things for them and alongside them, it means I can stick my neck out and say more of what I think clearly, rather than a watered down mish-mash that is often not understood. (in Bolton 2003b, p. 19)

'We *never* normally *talk* to each other like this about what we *feel* and *think* about our work and the lives of the people with whom we work.' Many of the group shared feelings, hopes and anxieties, which surprised the others. They were amazed Derek needed feedback to assure him of the value of his work, and were able to reinforce it. One other staff member wrote about the way a negative encounter had knocked her confidence. Once more the group had not realised she was not as confident as she seemed, and were able to offer real support (adapted from Bolton 2003b).

Here is a description of an interdisciplinary team-building course:

Maria Garner: reflective practice in the workplace

As part of addressing poor performance, motivation and staff retention in the local unitary council for whom I worked, I undertook a postgraduate certificate course in business management. I found the reflective journal a safe place to question my actions and answer my own questions. I felt more in control and less stressed. I set out to evaluate workplace reflective practice for the course project.

I delivered three reflective writing sessions after work with 12 strangers of diverse professions. Discussion opened up added dimensions to the benefits of reflection. Participants felt safe to discuss their issues, and could share alternative views and possible future options. Even though participants worked in different areas they described common themes and situations. I tried to give group members experience of as many reflective practices as possible. Each session started with participants giving a single word to describe how they were feeling, followed by 5 minutes' free-fall writing. Both moved people to an internal focus, and brought them together.

Writing exercises connected past, present and future experiences. The helpfulness of turning reflective writing into poetry or story, and examples, were discussed to encourage people to express thoughts (W.H. Auden's *Funeral Blues*, Jo Cannon's *Performance* [Chapter 2]). No one had written poetry before but were pleased and amazed with the haiku they wrote and shared.

Evaluation confirmed the feelgood factor, lowering of stress levels, and the spreading of reflective writing to colleagues or family: 'It did more for me personally than anything I have tried before, uplifting'; 'Triggered much discussion back at work'; 'It felt like unloading'; 'It provided some answers'; 'I know why it happens now'.

This group was self-selected. The work could not be developed, however, as the council could perceive no organisational benefit. Staff performance and retention continues to fall and sickness levels rise. (Maria Garner)

Even a one-off session can positively affect later working relationships. A single session with an academic medical department led to excited, exciting writing and discussion. More than one reported to me years later how they could still sense the improved working relationship engendered that morning.

Angela Mohtashemi: management consultancy for team-building

An activity I have found very effective is writing group poems. I have done this with my own team. We started by listing on a flip chart all the words that came to mind when thinking about our team. Each individual then wrote a piece about how they felt as a member of the team, while I composed some linking lines. The group was moved by the commonality of themes and echoes of words and yet the distance between the different individual paths, in terms of both content and form. One participant's writing revealed his struggle to 'fit in' to the work environment while hanging on to his identity.

> Like the boat without a rudder,
> I move from highs and lows
> Kicked by the strength of the wind,
> Carried away by the endless immensity of the ocean
> I am learning to swim I told myself
> For when the boat stops I can jump and
> Make my own journey ... (Angela Mohtashemi)

Here is a description of a particular method used effectively in team-building:

Reflection and reflexivity using *through-the-mirror* methods have been seen to be powerfully team-building as well as professionally developing individuals. There are a huge range of methods used to facilitate reflection and reflexivity, engaged with in Chapter 11.

 Read to learn

Barry, C.A., Britten, N., Barber, N., Bradley, C. and Stevenson, F. (1999) Using reflexivity to optimise teamwork in qualitative research, *Qualitative Health Research*, **9**(1), 26–44.

Illes, K. (2003) The patchwork text and business education: rethinking the importance of personal reflection and co-operative cultures, *Innovations in Education and Teaching International*, **40**(2), 209–15.

York-Barr, J., Sommers, W.A., Ghere, G.S. and Montie, J. (2006) *Reflective Practice to Improve Schools*. Thousand Oaks, CA: Corwin Press.

Write to learn

Each chapter ends with *Write to learn*. For straightforward advice, sufficient for the exercises below, see *Write to learn* in Chapter 1, and see Chapter 6 for more advice. The exercises below can be written during a facilitated group, and read out thoughtfully to the group once each writer has read and reflected on it first, and if that feels OK to them. Each exercise invites personal reflection, which becomes shared, and team development on reading. Ample time needs to be allowed for group discussion following each exercise.

Exercise 10.1   Abstract to concrete

Do a *six-minute write* (see Chapter 6).

1. Write four concrete nouns (things, not abstract like love or surprise): anything, for example, bicycle, daffodil, horse, carrots.
2. Choose one, write a list of the qualities of this object.
3. Reread it, thinking of it as parallel with your work. Write what it tells you about your view of your work (see, for example, below).

(For example: 'My bicycle is my friend: versatile, adaptable, light and easy to carry, goes really well over bumpy ground as well as smooth, can be wheeled through one way streets, doesn't need a parking spot but can be chained safely to any railing, is waiting for me when I get back, has never had a puncture, means I meet all sorts of people who are really nice whereas in a car I'd be isolated, riding it I can see scenery and feel the air, I can ride along river or canal bank instead of always on roads, can dart around London traffic. The only problem are complex junctions, like in front of Buckingham Palace: to be avoided.' Reading this replacing *bicycle* with *my work*, adjusting a few other words as well, made me feel very positive about my work.)

Exercise 10.2   Asking questions

Do a *six-minute write* (see Chapter 6).

1. Discuss with your team group which of these questions might be useful as a heading for writing.

    (a) Why did you become a (your profession)?
    (b) What does your profession mean to you?
    (c) Describe your job as if to a child.
    (d) When someone says 'Oh that's just like a [your profession] … !', about you, what do they mean?

(e)   What do your patients/clients/students think of you?
(f)   Describe your ideal patient/client/student.
(g)   What are your professional ambitions?
(h)   What would you like to hear your boss say in your retiring do speech?

2. Each reread your writing with care, taking time to see if there are any correlations with the *six minutes* and anything you wish to add to or delete.

Exercise 10.3   Letter to Santa

Do a *six-minute write* (see Chapter 6).

1. Write a wish list letter to Santa, include dreams and hopes and realistic items.
2. Write Santa's reply.
3. Reread reflectively before sharing with your team group.

REFLECTIVE PRACTICE: OTHER METHODS

Chapter 11 describes how choice of reflective practice method for the self or students needs to be underpinned by clarity and consonance of principles, and the contexts and depth of learning required. Single and double loop learning is explained. Several different forms of reflective practice are described, all have values consistent with *through-the-mirror* reflective practice. E-learning, mentoring, and co-peer mentoring are described, and their value explained.

Reflective practice is a contested field. An acknowledged element of professional education in diverse contexts, it is approached in varied ways with different principles and desired outcomes. Essential to the success of reflection and reflexivity provision are: clarity and consistency of principles and appropriateness to context: 'There are no reflective activities which are guaranteed to lead to learning, and conversely there are no learning activities guaranteed to lead to reflection (Boud and Walker 1998, p. 193).

This chapter explains and exemplifies why consistency of principles throughout a course is vital. Mentoring, co-peer mentoring, portfolios, problem-based learning, action learning, and Socratic dialogue are described. *Through-the-mirror* writing could be a valuable element of any method which brings practitioners into critical relationship with themselves, leading to reflection and reflexivity.

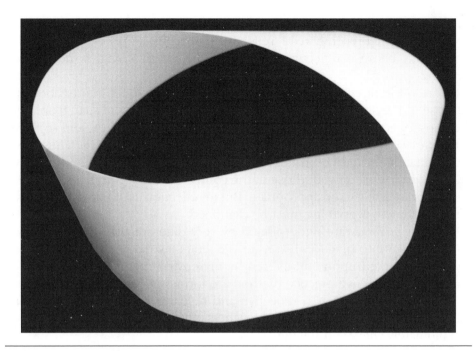

Figure 11.1   A Möbius strip

Depth of learning, contexts, principles

Reflective practice has been divided into *single loop* (reflection) and *double loop* (reflection and reflexivity) (see Brockbank and McGill 2004 for thorough explanation). Many approaches take practitioners round a *single loop* (for example, those that ask *What?*, *So What?*, *Now What?*, returning to *What?* again (Jasper 2008)), which is valuable. Practitioners finding the confidence and courage, however, to enter *double loop* critical worlds of reflexivity will gain qualitatively different perspectives and insight. This is a place where everything is 'as different as possible' (Carroll [1865] 1954, pp. 122–3) and yet the same. In *Reflective Practice* I use the metaphor of going *through* the mirror to gain this remarkable perspective, rather than merely reflecting on straightforward back-to-front mirrored images of self. The metaphor of *double loop* is rather like walking along a Möbius strip (Figure 11.1): you will travel inwards and outwards, exploring every plane. Walking a *single loop*, you will only explore one side.

Reflective practice, and even more reflexivity, leads to un-simple changes. It is inconvenient, messy, takes time, provokes students and practitioners to complain (at the very least) 'I have more questions than when I started'

(Hedberg 2009, p. 30). It needs skill, commitment, knowledge and experience from facilitators. I recently read 'reflective practice is simply ...' : I threw the paper away because reflective practice, to be worth doing, is not *simply* anything.

Before deciding what approach to use or offer students, clarity about its purpose in the specific context is essential. Elements of the search are, will the chosen method (a) create appropriate learning outcomes, and (b) have principles congruent with the rest of the course or practice. These two are intimately related because if the principles of the reflective and reflexive method are consistent with those of the course or practice, then the learning outcomes are likely to be appropriate. But in reflection and reflexivity nothing can be assumed, everything must be examined.

Different *methods* are underpinned by very different *principles*: *methods* put *principles* into practice. Just as my genetic makeup gives a blueprint for my being, worked upon and altered by my environment, so the principles underlying a reflective practice method are formative, yet inevitably adapted in use. Students faced with reflective and reflexive methods with different values and principles from the rest of their course will be baffled, defensive and ultimately angry and stalling.

For example, one *through-the-mirror* method is practitioners writing a confidential personal piece of intrinsic value within 30 minutes of starting a course, and with little other instruction than that. The principle is the participant taking full responsibility for their own learning and action (writing in this case).

I once ran a *through-the-mirror* session on a leadership course where students' outlook was underpinned by *learning styles* questionnaires (see Chapter 4). 'I can't do this, I now know I am a non-reflective personality', several said; and others demanded to be told what to do. These course members expected me, their facilitator, to take responsibility for their learning: their anger arose from bewilderment at this switch of principles. They expected, unsurprisingly, to be guided safely through activities appropriate to their *learning style*. It was a sticky beginning, and unfair on the students.

Principles and methods need therefore always to be consistent. Course designers need to know what they want their students to gain, be very clear about their purpose: just as learning objectives need to be clearly aligned with assessment criteria. At various points in *Reflective Practice* I have called such inconsistencies *muddles in the models* (see Chapter 3). Such muddles lead to confused, often angry students and un-cooperative, unreflective and certainly unreflexive attitudes. Practitioners and students can only be reflective, and particularly reflexive, if they know why they are doing it, respect themselves (know they are doing it for themselves rather than for the assessors, for example), trust the process they are using, and have confidence in facilitators, and their confidentiality.

Every discipline has its own context (such as values, attitudes, ways of learning and understanding). Cultural, political and social contexts also have important influence (Boud and Walker 1998). Certain methods (along with their underlying principles) will seem naturally appropriate to certain disciplines or professions. For example, law, medical, and business schools each have their own perspective. Reflexivity means taking nothing for granted; all assumptions are questioned. Even the choice of method, therefore, needs to be subjected to reflexive questioning.

Guidance through the swamp

Through-the-mirror methods accept that practice, reflection upon it, and particularly reflexivity, are messy, inconclusive, entail uncertainty, self-doubt and generally strong feelings. Reflexivity can lead previously focused practitioners to question their practice down to its fundamental principles. Donald Schon famously called it a *swamp*.

Many approaches to reflective practice attempt to support and guide practitioners not to get too *swamped*. These *single loop* unreflexive processes list cycles, frameworks, structures for assisted reflection, and stages to help practitioners and facilitators perceive how well they are doing. Van Manen reported Dewey's five steps (1995). Keith Morrison derived a four-stage process of reflective practice from Habermas (1996). Tripp lists items for the creation and analysis of *critical incidents* (Tripp 1995a, 1995b). Johns (1995) developed Barbara Carper's four ways of knowing: empirical, ethical, personal and aesthetic, and created a structured model for reflection (Johns 2000). Kolb created a much used learning cycle (1984); Gibb's cycle is ably described in nursing practice by Wilding (2008). Ramsey (2005) developed a narrative learning cycle. York-Barr et al. (2006) describe a four-step process for guiding reflection.

Different reflective practices

There are many ways of undertaking reflection and reflexivity; there are also many educational approaches with reflective elements. This section suggests some, and is by no means exhaustive. Internet searches yield sites giving ways of initiating and sustaining reflective practice (updated frequently, these only need *reflective practice*, or *reflexivity* in a search engine).

Practical descriptions of a range of approaches from an intensive literature review, are detailed in Kuit et al. (2001). Useful working methods in management education are outlined in Hedberg (2009), Cunliffe (2009) and Gray (2007).

Innovative creative methods for reflection are reported, such as using drama (Boggs et al. 2007), dance (Cancienne and Snowber 2003), video (Rosean et al. 2008), photography (Lemon 2007), letter writing (Yang and Bautista 2008), storytelling, reflexive conversations and metaphors, repertory grids and concept mapping (Gray 2007), and other creative approaches, the paper being written in the form of a play (Chambers et al. 2007). Cavallaro-Johnson (2004) uses cartoons. A fascinating experiment reported by Cook-Sather (2008) describes students becoming 'pedagogical consultants' (p. 473). They engage with teaching staff (faculty) in discussion offering feedback, 'both of which not only enrich the professors' capacity to reflect on their own practice, but also prompt students to reflect on theirs'. Lecturers gained invaluable insight about their teaching, and 'student consultants' felt they 'learned how to learn'.

Personal development plans and portfolios (PDP), used in many professional training courses, 'offer a framework for reflection' (Hinett 2002, p. 31). The UK Quality Assurance Agency defined PDPs as 'a structured and supported process undertaken by an individual to reflect upon their own learning, performance, and/or achievement and to plan for their personal, educational and career development' (2001, p. 1). Professional development plans and portfolios can be reflective and reflexive if students are facilitated towards critical attitudes and expected to write reflexively, drawing upon private writings for portfolios. Reflective writing portfolios (Deal 1998) (including such material as poems and 'free writes') for pre-service science teachers have been found to be very useful for 'encouraging positive attitudes towards science, developing an understanding of science concepts, providing embedded diagnostic information and creating "natural" opportunities for curriculum integration'. In addition, it 'seems to help students become aware of their own growth and beliefs regarding science' (Deal 1998, p. 244).

Problem-based learning presents medical and law students (among other professions) with 'real' problems. Students grapple with complex problems in groups or pairs, come to terms with them not having simple solutions, and learn to apply appropriate professional attitudes, skills and knowledge. The idea is they develop practical ethical values and principles, and group working skills. Virtual learning environments (VLEs) are often used to simulate situations (for example, Maharg and Paliwala 2002). *Through-the-mirror* methods could support these aims.

In *action research*, practitioners study their own social situation (for example, classroom) to increase practice effectiveness by improving the quality of action within it. Many go through four stages: plan, act, observe and reflect. Planning involves identifying the problem, formulating a hypothesis, identifying the theory in use and planning action. This is acted upon, observed, and data collected. All this is reflected upon: meanings, the relationship of espoused to practice theories and values, and how to develop practice. This process is reiterated, often with group support, attempting to bring theory and practice into greater congruence. Practitioners can use writing to gain critical reflective and reflexive abilities in critiquing practice, principles and ethical values.

Olwen Summerscales ran a course of reflective writing sessions with a multicultural group of inner-city social workers as action research (2006). The whole group were involved in the research in partnership, rather than being subjects (see Ladkin 2004). This element strengthened the learning from reflective writing. One participant concluded 'I can't believe this is me! I've flourished!', another how it helped diminish professional isolation. Summerscales proposes continuing the work to help the pace of change, working towards developing learning organisations (Senge 1992).

Action learning sets use Socratic non-analytic dialogue (Brockbank and McGill 2004; Dehler and Edmonds 2006; Saran and Neisser 2004; see also Angela Mohteshami in Chapter 1). Actions, thoughts and feelings are discussed as openly as possible. Socratic dialogue helps develop clarity, insight and therefore understanding of appropriate courses of action. *Paradigm shift*, *doubleloop learning* or *peak experience* (*epiphany*: see Joyce 1944) are key. Exposing experience to critical scrutiny in *action learning sets* can enable individuals to perceive and potentially alter previously taken-for-granted culturally framing *paradigms* or stories which culturally frame. They can then effect change. Writing can be used at various stages of this process: to inform and facilitate dialogue, reflect upon sessions, develop themes, ideas, inspirations, question assumptions and to create texts for discussion. Kuit et al. (2001) report a successful *action learning set* reflective journal group for academic staff. A fictional 'Socratic dialogue', written by researchers Turnbull and Mullins (2007) was based upon *The Screwtape Letters*, a religious tract by C.S. Lewis (1961a), in which Wormwood and Screwtape are apprentice and master in the art of wickedness. The authors adopted 'alternative persona' in reflexive writing dialogue to surface innate wisdom (see also Chapter 6).

E-learning

Experience of, and potential for online work is tremendous. I have run online postgraduate continuing professional development courses for medical practitioners, each compiling a portfolio of reflective writings, reflections upon the writings, responses from other participants and evidence of discussions with colleagues (such as team members), and research. Closed email communication enabled participants to write, comment, and make research suggestions. This mode of communication is particularly appropriate for busy, reasonably articulate professionals, especially those living in a remote region. A participant reflected: it 'enables you to *meet* colleagues you would probably never meet otherwise'.

E-communication requires careful facilitation. The lack of physical and voice clues puts weight on each word. Each utterance has to be weighed, checked for how it might be read. Care is needed, as people are vulnerable in *through-the-mirror* work. All participants need to be carefully inducted, to prevent rushed messages leading to misunderstandings and damage.

A phenomenological study of online reflection (Boyer et al. 2006) found facilitator roles vital in online reflection, which was transformatively effective leading to development in preconceived ideas, beliefs, habits and assumptions. Mori et al.'s study (2008) found electronic methods effective. Useful advice is given on organising and managing the process. No evidence is given, however, of students receiving education and support on how to write. The method might be greatly improved thereby. Blogs are used in legal reflection, see Higher Education Academy website (www.ukcle.ac.uk/directions/previous/issue12/blogs.html)

Julie Hughes uses virtual learning environments in teacher education for post-compulsory education:

> Virtual groups are built into tutor group activities with overwhelmingly positive responses: 'teaching and learning like a disco ball – multi-reflective' (student metaphor). Eportfolio allows for multiple asynchronous conversations. What changes is the role of the tutor: as e-mentor you are 'differently' available, and have a different role in the dialogue so it sort of deconstructs the idea of a personal tutor as once-a-semester contact.
>
> The standard, summatively assessed, paper-based 'teaching-practice port-folio' is it may be argued of little relevance to the new teacher. The e-portfolio's emphasis upon dialogue and reflexive patchwork writing (Winter 2003) offers the opportunity to explore the e-portfolio as a social practice and situated literacy (Street 1995). The patchwork e-portfolio offers unlimited peer and tutor 'talkback' (Lillis 2001) spaces as opposed to institutional summative feedback 'spaces for telling'. E-portfolio dialogue is not a one-off, its discoursal features are forward-looking and exploratory and it is concerned with the process-making nature of academic texts and literacies. (Julie Hughes)

Mentoring

The first mentor was a goddess. Telemachus, son of Odysseus and Penelope, is mentored by Pallas Athene in human form: "'For you, I have some good advice, if only you will accept it" … "Oh stranger," heedful Telemechas replied, "indeed I will. You've counselled me with so much kindness now, like a father a son. I won't forget a word'" (Homer 1996, pp. 86–7).

No mentor since then has been a god, although 'mentors are creations of our imagination, designed to fill a psychic space somewhere between lover and parent' (Daloz 1999, p. 18). Mentoring usually involves an experienced professional supporting a less experienced, ranging from formally organised, to the offer of a supportive hand.

Through-the-mirror writing could be an element at any stage of mentoring: to inform meetings, reflect upon them afterwards, or as email, letter or other e-communicative dialogue between meetings. 'Learning journals can be valuable between coach and client, developing and deepening the relationship, acting 'as a "window" into the client's feelings and experiences' (Gray 2007, p. 509). Mentor or coach can, for example, agree personal objectives with mentee, who then develops them in a learning journal discussed at sessions (Gray 2007). Mentoring or coaching using writing could be similar to group processes described in other chapters, with one participant and one facilitator.

Mentors help mentees step 'outside the box of his or her job and personal circumstances, so they can look in at it together. It is like standing in front of the mirror with someone else, who can help you see things about you that have become too familiar for you to notice' (Clutterbuck and Megginson 1999, p. 17). Mentors ask questions one does not, or cannot, ask oneself.

Mentors can act as role model, enabler, teacher, encourager, counsellor, befriender, facilitator, coach, confidante and supporter in 'unlearning' negative habits or attitudes (such as sense of lack of self-worth, or negative attitudes to diversity). These roles inevitably overlap, but research into helping-to-learn relationships shows that clarity of role expectations makes for greater effectiveness (Clutterbuck 1998). The pair need to be aware of whose interests are pursued: mentors or supervisors, also professional superiors, can be experienced by mentees as controlling, thus removing their authority. They need also to realise when a matter is beyond their relationship, and help required from elsewhere. Reverse mentoring is gaining in popularity: junior employee acts as mentor, senior employee as protégé (Garvey et al. 2009)

Mentoring deals with the whole person of the mentee: the professional base making this different from counselling. Mentors offer empathy and non-judgemental critique, helping reflection upon emotional, intellectual and behavioural content of issues. Mentors challenge: behaviour not people, assumptions not intellect, perceptions not judgement, values not value (Clutterbuck and Megginson 1999). Garvey et al. (2009) recommend not setting goals: 'mentors and their clients can engage in the busyness of goal setting at the expense of digging a bit deeper into difficult issues' (2009, p. 159).

Mentoring enables sharing of vital often confidential issues: uncertainties, hopes and fears, anxieties and angsts, shame or guilt, wants and aversions, the influence of intense emotions (positive or negative), tentative suggestions for action, lack of or partial understandings, questions of role, personal or career ladder issues, repeated errors or inadequacies, and stories of success, failure or conflict. 'Mentoring for me is about personal investment, and I wouldn't/ couldn't do it if I didn't give a bit of myself to all of them: equally I expect to see them investing in their students and each other' (Julie Hughes, post-compulsory education, Chapter 7). Everyone needs support, reassurance and challenge, even (or perhaps particularly) those at the very top:

> It's no disgrace for a man, even a wise man,
> to learn many things and not be too rigid.
> You've seen trees by a raging winter torrent,
> how many sway with the flood and salvage every twig,
> but not the stubborn – they're ripped out roots and all.
> Bend or break ...
> it's best to learn from those with good advice. (Sophocles 1982, pp. 95–6)

Co-peer mentoring

Reflection and reflexivity can be supported by co-mentoring pairs of peers with no problem of payment, control or god(dess) worship. Two professionals might agree to co-mentor, or pairs from a group work together independently between group meetings. They read and comment on each other's journals and discuss matters which might or might not be brought to the whole group, tentatively sharing issues with one trusted other. Some shared issues would otherwise not be aired, being inappropriate to the group. Confidential pairs can cover more ground than a group, so each participant receives intensive feedback, journal and portfolio. Prior paired work can enhance confidence in discussion (Carson and Fisher 2006; Brockbank and McGill 1998; Pereira 1999). Finnish teacher trainees are fruitfully paired with 'narrative friends' for portfolio development (Groom and Maunonen-Eskilinén 2006). This method is valuable, although sorting out boundaries and how to work together can take time.

> My art therapy students use artwork and writing for reflective practice in their own time, sharing experiences fortnightly with peers. Though many find the reflective work very useful ('when you have clients in your thoughts you need a private space'), initially many found the sharing burdensome. They felt they had to be careful about doubts, confusions etc. because of the difficulty of the transition from the safe private space of placement to the university, and because of assessment. Also many clinical institutions are beginning to claim students' material, even private process notes, as their property. Once they became more confident the peer-mentoring reflective practice was private and confidential, they used the process fully. (David McLaggan)

Co-peer mentoring supported my Master's students through course and portfolio challenges. Each pair created a working contract: many read and commented on learning journals and assignments in progress, and discussed professional and course issues. The student group also met without tutors: group co-peer mentoring. Co-peer mentoring effectively structures professional students quite properly learning from each other.

Elaine Trevitt and Carol Wood attended a co-mentoring set-up course. Although from different backgrounds within health, very different stages of career, and living 60 miles apart, they describe a successful relationship (see also Chapter 13):

 Chip and pin

Elaine Trevitt writes:

The plan was that we swap a bit of writing before meeting, so we have something to 'work on', though we don't always both do it. We meet at roughly three monthly intervals, bring ourselves up to date over a cup of coffee and lunch. Then discuss writing/work and any matters arising. Then to debrief and 'think forwards'. There is a gap between trains for me of about five hours, so this is our time. We had one (nearly) twenty-four hour meeting with a sleepover at mine with no particular plan or structure; I think we were sufficiently confident by then to trust it would work out to mutual advantage. Neither did we do any writing together though we might have done. We worked pretty well non-stop.

There are some similarities and some differences between us in work and outlook; we stress we have been neither *friend nor teacher* to each other, but peer-mentors. This has involved a building of trust that we shall each be given and give time and attention when and where it is needed. At the original peer-mentoring workshop Gillie asked us to think of 'binary pairings' as to consider how peer-partnerships might work (see Chapter 13). Mine was 'chip and pin': encoded within is access to wealth secretly hidden away. It may not be manifest, but when the connections are made, it comes spewing out from the hole in the wall (the writing). We are like chip and pin for each other.

We use emails and telephone, usually by prior arrangement to try and keep our contact 'businesslike', and keep our boundaries.

What has it done for me? It has been encouraging (courage making) and given me a sense of authenticity. And it has moved me on. As I write I realise more than I ever acknowledged before.

(Continued)

(Continued)

Carol Wood writes:

> It has left me standing on more solid ground in relation to my practice. We have worked on being truly congruent and fully present within work contexts through exploring and developing a strong sense of self as practitioner. A helpful vehicle has been metaphor (see Chapter 13). Peer-mentoring can work because we are peers respecting confidentially what each brings. Working in an increasingly time-pressured environment, I have valued immensely being given the space to 'stand back' and reflect in greater depth than I might otherwise, even when time constraints or sensitive material have made this difficult. From a safe practice perspective, it is essential for me to do this. It sits outside of any formal employment arrangement, allowing me to explore my 'stuff' without the potential filter of vested interests. This ensures I ask myself difficult questions I might otherwise shy away from. Finding out about our differences can bring new perspectives; there is also a lot of laughter within our sessions. (Elaine Trevitt and Carol Wood)

Carry Gorney, family therapist, and Joolz Mclay, art therapist, in an NHS child and family therapy team practised reflective writing together. This developed mutual understanding and teamwork:

> We are interested in language, images, metaphor, poetry and stories. Our relationship evolved in our shared office: showing each other snippets of our work, reported scraps of dialogue and listened to each other's descriptions of eyes, faces, clothes and movements. We told stories of the process of our work, of our anxieties, our successes and our feelings of helplessness. The writing developed from these stolen moments in our working day. We agreed to meet every couple of weeks and to develop and explore through writing. We met in the art room after work and began to create a safe space. We experienced this 'peer-supervision' as a confidential process, mirroring the therapeutic process.
>
> We agreed to write alone and meet together to read aloud. We listened to the words, the sentences and the spaces between words. We would reread each piece silently together and then put the paper aside. Conversations evolved around the children, the effect of the writing on each other and on our subsequent work. Then we wrote more.
>
> At first the writing we brought was stiff and professional, calmly and cognitively placing our practice within a context of intelligent observation. Then as we trusted each other more our writing began to flow from somewhere else. Sometimes it seemed to bypass our brains all together. It poured out of our hearts, our guts, our fingertips and our imaginations.

It moved in a circle of unexpressed, previously unidentified responses to the children we saw.

Joolz:
For me, the process has been one of untangling the professional from the personal and private self. By writing without constraint, without fear of judgement about clinical practice I have begun to rediscover and to nurture the inner voices of my private self. These voices have been strengthened through writing, through being heard, and through conversation. They have engaged me in dialogues with neglected and forgotten parts. They have drawn attention to things overlooked, ignored and misplaced. They have made me laugh and cry and feel I am not alone.

Words, by Carry [from the child client's perspective]
I tried to sit still; this woman was sat opposite me.
I couldn't understand what she was saying, too many words,
You see
Just a jumble of words.
They floated past.
I just sat there letting them come.

My Dad's words are different. They sort of hit me over the head,
A sharp pain running from my head to my heart, my Dad's words, when they
hit me.

Words happen to me. I don't understand them.
Sometimes I think if everyone talked slow, I'd get it.
I'd get what everyone goes on about.
It would all make sense.

School – the words are bad there. They come thick and fast,
Sometimes I put my head down on the desk 'cos it hurts.
It does my head in.
Sometimes I just run out of class, or even school, too many words jumping
at me,
Too many sounds they might catch me out. They might find out I don't know
jackshit, Nothing, nada in my brain.
Rotten like my Dad says, a bad un – I got those words all right.
Words are enemies
I'm an alien. (Carry) (Carry Gorney and Joolz Mclay)

This chapter touched upon the diversity of methods used for reflective practice across many disciplines, some of which can create supportive environments for *through-the-mirror* writing. Significant factors are: the principles of the course being consonant throughout, and the quality of the learning environment. The next section develops further understanding of the foundations of *through-the-mirror* reflection.

Read to learn

Dehler, G.E. and Edmonds, K.E. (2006) Using action research to connect practice to learning: a course project for working management students, *Journal of Management Education*, **30**(5), 636–69.

Garvey, R., Stokes, P. and Megginson, D. (2009) *Coaching and Mentoring: Theory and Practice.* London: Sage.

Gray, D.E. (2007) Facilitating management learning: developing critical reflection through reflective tools, *Management Learning*, **38**(5), 495–517.

Kuit, J.A., Reay, J. and Freeman, R. (2001) Experiences of reflective teaching, *Active Learning in Higher Education*, **2**(2), 128–42.

 Write to learn

Each chapter ends with *Write to learn*. For straightforward advice, sufficient for the exercises below, see *Write to learn* in Chapter 1, and see Chapter 6 for more advice. Each writing can be shared fruitfully with a group or confidential trusted other, if this seems appropriate once the writer has read and reflected on it first.

Exercise 11.1   Your heart-sink student, patient, client

Do a *six-minute write* (see Chapter 6).

1. Think of a client you find difficult.
2. Who do they remind you of?
3. What would you really like to say to them?
4. What do you wish you *had not* said to them?
5. How might you characterise why they irritate (for example, childish, bossy, demanding)?
6. Write an *unsent letter* to this person (which you'll *NEVER* send): say whatever you wish.
7. Write your student's reply to you (you'll *NEVER* show them this).
8. Write a final reflective piece about all this.
9. Reread, and reflect upon it.

Exercise 11.2   Your wise internal mentor or coach

Do a *six-minute write* (see Chapter 6).

1. Write a letter to your wise internal mentor/coach. This being observes what is going on all the time, supports, comforts, and can advise on difficulties and problems. It might be modelled on a real person, yet has a fictional name, rather than the name of a real person you know. Find out their name and write Dear ...
2. Write their reply.
3. Continue the correspondence.
4. You could do this by email. Write an email to your internal wise adviser (to your own e-address), save it to a special file on arrival in your inbox, and only write your reply after a predetermined time (for example, week).
5. Reread and reflect on your writing; any queries – write another letter or email to your internal mentor.

Exercise 11.3   Giving advice

1. Do a *six-minute write.*
2. A young person entering your profession has written to you asking your advice.
3. Write back to them, remembering what it was like when you started out, what kind of letter would you have liked to receive.
4. Write the young professional's reply.
5. Write a letter to yourself reminding yourself of the best advice anyone ever gave you.
6. Reread with attention and care, write more if that feels appropriate.

SECTION 3

REFLECTIVE WRITING: FOUNDATIONS

CHAPTER 12

THE POWER OF NARRATIVE

Chapter 12 is a closely argued, richly exemplified discussion of the role of narrative in personal and professional lives, and how this can be effectively harnessed for reflective practice. It describes how practitioner *through-the-mirror* writers need to take responsibility for their stories and their exploration, and the role of fact versus fiction in this work.

> Wherever we walk we put our feet on story. (Cicero)
>
> A man is always a teller of tales, he lives surrounded by his stories and the stories of others. (Sartre [1938] 1963, p. 61)
>
> I'm not sure I can tell the truth ... I can only tell what I know. (Cree hunter, in Clifford 1986, p. 8)

Why story or narrative writing rather than thinking, talking and discussing, or writing 'critical incidents' or 'events' or case notes? We relate to, remember, understand and readily form stories because they create humanly memorable and comprehensible structures such as narrative line (and then and then and then ...), causality (look – this happened because that happened), and plot (the fictive satisfaction of beginning, middle, and end). Narrative-making is the fundamental human sense-making system. We learn about our culture by story, from history books to the news or bedtime readings. Stories tell us how to see our place in society and its place around us, telling us what to expect of each other and ourselves, and enable us to communicate meanings, insights, perspectives and articulate complexities: 'Storytelling is therefore an important management skill' (Gray 2007, p. 499). Stories offer a way of making human sense of contemporary dehumanised, impersonal, highly regulated and unemotional organisations (Gabriel 1991, 1995).

Humans do not make rational logical decisions based on information input, instead they pattern match with either their own experience or collective experience expressed as stories (Klein 1999). Used wisely, narratives and stories have a powerful role in education and practice. Barthes maintained that 'Narrative is international, transhistorical, transcultural: it is simply there like life itself' (1987, p. 79); MacIntyre that 'we are all, in our actions and practices, storytelling animals, and storytelling plays a major role in educating us in the classic virtues' (1985, p. 8); and Lyotard 'narratives are the communal method by which knowledge is stored and exchanged' (1984, p. 23). Laurel Richardson, a pioneer of writing as a method of enquiry, said 'Writing stories and personal narratives have increasingly become the structures through which I make sense of my world, locating my particular biographical experiences in larger historical and sociological contexts' (Richardson and St. Pierre 2005, p. 966). And Attard (2008) systematically wrote narratives because he realised it was the best reflective tool to interpret his lived experience.

Stories are attentively listened to and remembered, such as Clough's powerful story about special educational needs (Clough 1996), and Landgrebe's about care of the dying (Landgrebe and Winter 1994). 'The deceptive power of [story] lies in the fact that single startling cases stick in the mind' (Macnaughton 1998, p. 202). Writing, exploring, and discussing our essential narratives is a route to taking responsibility and control of our lives, professional and personal. Paying critical attention to narrative enhances medical awareness of ethics, and deepens understanding (Engel et al. 2008).

The educative value of stories is great partly because they penetrate our understanding more deeply than our intellect, they engage our emotions. All learning involves emotion.

> Many hold their failures inside, allowing them to smoulder and decay; others step into self-destructive habits; others tell [and write] stories. (Borkan et al. 1999, p. 11)

Finding strategies to gain access to and articulate what we feel, know, think, believe and remember is a perennial problem of professional development. Who we are, what we stand for and why, are integrated with how we act. Our actions, deep-seated beliefs, ethics, ethical values, emotions, sense of professional identity, and the way we relate to our political, social and cultural world are all expressed in the stories we tell and write. Relating critically and feelingly to these stories, and those of our peers, society and culture, is a vitally educative process.

Human narrative-making can too readily be self-affirming, an attempt to create order and security out of a chaotic world: a critical relationship with everyday stories is essential. Our stories frequently do not explore sensitive issues, but express what we feel (or would like to feel) comfortable with. But for experiences to be developmental – professionally, socially, psychologically, culturally, spiritually – our world has to be made to appear strange. At the same time, the extraordinary has to be made to appear more ordinary before we can grapple with it:

> Narrative can be a way to domesticate human error and surprise … Story making is our medium for coming to terms with the surprises and oddities of the human condition and for coming to terms with our imperfect grasp of that condition. Stories render the unexpected less surprising, less uncanny: they domesticate unexpectedness, give it a sheen or ordinariness. 'That's odd that story, but it makes sense, doesn't it?' we say even when reading Mary Shelley's *Frankenstein*. (Jerome Bruner 2002, pp. 31, 90)

Reflecting upon and beginning to understand the role of narrative in our lives can develop practical wisdom from experience, and our ability to listen and perceive widely. And it can support practitioners in bringing a critical faculty to bear on the professional and political structures and assumptions which surround them. Narratives express and communicate the values, experience and wisdom of the narrator; they also develop and create values, as well as a sense of self-purpose.

Listeners and readers hear from their own point of view, qualitatively different from (sometimes even opposing) that of the teller. All stories are perspectival; none are objectively true; no story has only one meaning. They are essentially ambiguous and resist singular interpretation. Critically tussling with narrative at every level is not easy because it forces a questioning of taken for granteds, reassessment of previous certainties and assumptions, and recognition of contrasting (possibly opposing) points of view. Greater responsibility and authority can be enabled over role, relationships with professional organisation, culture and society (professional and personal), feelings, beliefs and ethical values.

Our storied nature

Information is retained in the human mind as narrative. We do not go to a particular section within a file within a drawer within a cabinet in our memories, we go to a particular place in a narrative: an association of events, faces, voices, place, foods, and sense of roughness or softness. Since the Enlightenment we have suffered under mechanical metaphors that bodies and minds are machines.

We are not. Our feeling, cognitive, physical, spiritual selves are intermixed; they condition and are conditioned by political and cultural contexts. All are experienced, understood and expressed as narrative. Narratives express the values of the narrator; they also develop and create values in the telling.

Narratives are central to human understandings, memory systems and communication, whether we know it or not. Lives are made sense of and ordered by the stories with which they are recounted: told and retold daily through actions, memories, thoughts, dreams, habits, beliefs, speech and behaviour patterns. We spend our lives storying and re-storying ourselves, and contributing to wider social stories around us: it is as natural to being a person as eating and breathing (Bruner 2002; Doyle and Carter 2003).

Strawson asserts that not everyone stories their lives (2004a, 2004b), that nothing positive will result from encouraging professionals to do so, that for example teaching medical students narrative competence is only another way of saying doctors should listen to their patients better. He misses the imperative need for educative strategies to enable such communication. Professionals need to listen both to themselves and to others: this can be developed by reflection, reflexivity and dialogue.

Educators know that understanding occurs when elements are expressed as stories (Allan et al. 2002; Clark 2002). This is a mature acceptance of how we are, rather than an assumption that only children need stories in order to understand (Gheradi and Turner 2002).

Daily constant interaction with other individuals, systems and organisations requires management, generally at a non-conscious level. Everyone shifts between a range of personae as they move in and out of days, and of each other's lives. Among other roles I am mother, wife, lover, sister, aunt, neighbour, colleague, professional and friend. In order to reduce anxiety, and ensure I relate more or less appropriately, I need to be aware of the history of each of these relationships and its meaning in terms of today's behaviour. I also perceive that I exist within a set of geographical places, within a time frame, as well as a political and cultural structure. My set of stories of myself has a chronological structure reaching back to farming forebears, a space structure locating me in Essex, Singapore, Cambridge, Derbyshire and London, and so on. To an extent all these tell me who I am, and how to relate to others, and to society.

If our lives were not constantly told and retold, storying each new experience, we would have no coherent notion of who we are, where we are going, what we believe, what we want, where we belong and how to be. Just as my skin holds my organs and body fluids in a form which is recognisably me (to myself as well as others), my psychosocial selfhood relies upon my grasp of my narratives of relationship, chronology and place.

We are embedded and enmeshed within the stories and story structures we have created, and which have been created around us: some we are aware of, some very much not. Family doctor Mark Purvis was unaware how deeply his life and work were affected by his brother's death when he was 9, until he wrote a reflective poem about it (Chapter 2).

These stories form a complex volatile system. Complex, because my apparently coherent life is constituted out of a range of interrelated plotlines, characters, and situations. Volatile, because it constantly changes with every individual action or event: mine and those around me.

My success as a person, or more correctly perhaps my happiness, rests on my ability to juggle this complexity, and my flexibility in response to the volatility and constant change created by my own behaviour, that of others, and of my social, political and professional surroundings. It is what a growing-up child learns, and a beginning professional in training and early years practice. It is also what an effective adult or professional continually undergoes.

Everyone naturally, to a lesser or greater extent, reflects, seeks support and advice, accordingly alters their behaviour, challenges others, and even drastically changes their life situation. Life changes such as a new job or house, marriage, birth, bereavement, illness or disability necessitate reformulations.

Constant repeating and refashioning of life stories is an essential part of living with their complexity and fluidity, but it can be uncritical. The stories told over coffee, or reflected upon in the car, are told in order to create a coherent and live-with-able structure. These reflections might ask: 'How could I have done it better?' or 'Do you think Mrs S thought it was OK?' The answers, whether in solitary reflection or in conversation, are unlikely to be challenging. Perceiving the taken-for-granted story structure for what it is, and seeking strategies for development, cannot be done in the car or over coffee. The car would certainly crash, and drinking colleagues become bewildered or even angry.

An extreme example is the sexually harassed secretary who complains to her friends, loses sleep and self-confidence, but continues to be unaware of how she tacitly invites sexual advances. Few colleagues have commitment and ability to support deep development. Similarly a professor and departmental head with a severe alcohol problem creates all sorts of explanations for the situation, none of which touches on the central problem, despite sincere efforts of his staff. No colleague, within the normal everyday departmental structure, knows how to challenge, or help him to see. The secretary or head of department becomes more and more enmeshed, more and more stuck.

These story structures, even while shifting and changing all the time, often seem inevitable, how things are, inviolable even: a set of taken for granteds. But each one of us is responsible for the creation of many of them and aspects of others, for connivance at, and even uncritical acceptance of, wider social narratives or 'norms'.

People vary a great deal in awareness of their story structure. Some, like Hamlet, struggle with it daily: questioning and reformulating their understanding of their own agency and control. Some, such as Celia in George Eliot's *Middlemarch*, live in blissful unawareness.

Some authorities have taken this further and postulated a non-storying type (Strawson 2004a, 2004b). But everyone else, at the very least, retells aspects of their day for re-creation, listening and re-storying collaboratively (*re-creation* is used advisedly here). They make further sense of their lives by relating to the social, political and spiritual narratives in which their lives are embedded: news or drama on television or radio, in newspapers, magazines and literature. Booker (2004) maintains that our stories 'emerge from some place in the human mind that functions autonomously, independent of any storyteller's conscious control' (p. 24).

Taking responsibility

Writing life stories enables writers to take responsibility for them. We learn by taking responsibility for re-storying ourselves. Education clarifies and develops personal stories, and the way they articulate with, impinge upon, and are impinged upon by societies' stories. Even rote learning is only effective if accommodated: 'I am the kind of person who knows times-tables.' Professional development aims to support in taking responsibility for integrating the learning from these accounts.

Reflective practitioners strive to recognise responsibility for their own life stories, the organisational, social and political structures in which they are enmeshed, and their actions within those structures. They can then create strategies for actions for which they take full responsibility. They also learn critically from the stories of others. Frank (1995, 2004) describes dynamic involvement with narrative or story as working *with* stories, rather than *about* them: 'what counts about any story is what those who hear it [and who tell or write it] choose to do with it' (2004, p. 209). Frank calls the *practical wisdom* this develops *phronesis*, from Aristotle: '*Phronesis* is the opposite of acting on the basis of scripts and protocols; those are for beginners, and continuing reliance on them can doom actors to remain beginners' (2004, p. 221).

Some practitioners or students come to professional learning with an assumption that tutors take responsibility. The slowness of reflective learning frustrates them, with its constant reflexive involvement. Surely the authorities should just tell them?

Well no. This is not rote learning of multiplication tables. When addressing the very stuff of our lives, only the protagonist – the main character – can tackle it from the inside, with the help of the outside perspectives of peers, and the expert support of tutors. In order to take responsibility for professional actions, and some of the actions of others, we need a clearer perception of how we build our world, and how others build it around us: its narrative and metaphoric structures and content. This perception will enable, necessitate even, development and even change.

Stories

We learn by storying and re-storying ourselves. We are brought up surrounded by stories: they flow through us and ratify us from birth, telling us who we are and where we belong, what is right and what is wrong. Many are traditional, whether or not they have been given contemporary dress. Tales where wicked stepmothers receive come-uppance explain that mothers can be horrid quite often, but good will ultimately conquer over evil (Bettelheim 1976). Lévi-Strauss (1978) tells us our myths offer us ways of classifying and ordering our society. We do not tell our mythic stories, they tell us. A language created each time they are told, they provide ways of dealing with the complexity of human relationships, and strange and often scary psychological worlds.

Small children are clear about story structure (Bruner 2002; Rowland 1984). A child requires any story to be told to the end. Their imaginative play is often continuous story, and first writings have a good grasp of structure. Ask a small child about their drawing or painting and they will tell its story, rather than describe the images. We too live our lives by telling stories about them. These stories are constructs. Life as it is lived is not structured like an *adventure*; adventures only happen in stories (Sartre [1938] 1963). And the story has to be communicated: told, or read. It cannot only be thought. A.A. Milne expressed this with perfect simplicity when his wise characters had this conversation:

> 'Is that the end of the story?' asked Christopher Robin.
> 'That's the end of that one. There are others … Don't you remember?' …
> 'I do remember,' he said, 'only Pooh doesn't very well, so that's why he likes having it told to him again. Because then it's a real story and not just a remembering.' (Milne [1928] 1958, p. 31)

Stories are the mode in which our culture is transmitted, from fairy stories to political history. Stories create the way we see our place in society, and the way we perceive it as moulded around us: telling us what to expect of each other and ourselves. They shape and make sense of our world by reiterating the social and political order. Soap opera, Verdi, strip cartoons and Shakespeare tell us what is good and what bad, what likely to succeed and what fail.

These meanings are usually implicit, as in Aesop's *Fables*. New Testament parables are perhaps the closest to didactic storytelling, with explicit meanings. Had Jesus and Aesop omitted the story, the lessons would not have been remembered for millennia. We remember to sow corn on good fertile ground rather than among stones; that it is more comfortable to assume the unattainable bunch of grapes is probably sour; and that killing your father and marrying your mother is not a good idea (Sophocles' *Oedipus*).

No story has only one meaning. A writer may perceive certain meanings clearly, and formulate specific questions. Different readers perceive other meanings, and pose different questions.

> The ambiguities of a fiction may be thought of as representing (in some sense) the ambiguities of the author's and the reader's personal awareness. The questions posed by the text are questions about the writer's and the reader's own experience and values. (Winter et al. 1999, p. 23)

Questions and theories arising from a single text may conflict: stories are essentially ambiguous. Discussion following readings can be fruitful because everyone has their own perspectival understanding. Many insights into a story's implicit meanings will be new to the writer and other listeners, and widen their view. 'A story by its very nature resists singular interpretation. Story captures nuance, indeterminacy and interconnectedness in ways that defy formalistic expression and expand the possibilities for interpretation and understanding' (Doyle and Carter 2003, p. 130).

Each reader views a story from their individual viewpoint, often refreshingly different from that of the writer. Perceptions of experience and selfhood are conceived, enmeshed within the frame of our social, political and psychological perspective: we cannot know ourselves and our experience independently.

Individual experience has been described in the reflective practice literature as raw and authentic (true); yet it is no more and no less than another story: a story which others will cap with their own, or their own view. The fundamental importance of narrative and story to medicine is well documented (Charon 2006; Engel et al. 2008) Narrative, particularly autobiographical, has been explored extensively in initial and in-service teacher training and research (Phillion 2002a, 2002b). Storytelling has been used by Reason (1988) as a research method, dealing with personal rather than professional development. Abbs (1974) and Lewis (1992) both use personal and autobiographical writing with trainee teachers.

Hargreaves (2004) is disturbed that where reflective accounts are assessed in nursing (and possibly other professional settings) only three story-forms are considered to be legitimate and given marks. In *valedictory* narratives the narrator recognises a crisis, responds appropriately and wins the day. *Condemnatory* narratives are the opposite: narrators lose the day. *Redemptive* narratives give a narrator exposing inappropriate values or practices, yet learning and redeeming themselves. Nurses who want to succeed write one of these, possibly fictionally, rather than engaging in honest and open reflection. The assessment of reflective practice is a potential barrier to the personal growth and integrity that programmes are trying to nurture. An alternative programme in teacher education (Clandinin et al. 1992) examined the potential for collaboration between students, schools and universities by making spaces for the stories of each to be shared. This proved a dynamic ground for understanding, assessing and reassessing experience. 'It is in restorying ourselves that it is possible to remake experience' (Clandinin and Connelly 1990, p. 31). Connolly and Clandinin's three-dimensional space of narrative enquiry looks at a dense weave of multi-perspectival, multi-chronological, and multi-located set of stories (Connolly and Clandinin 2000). Phillion and Connelly (2004) use this 3-dimensional space of narrative enquiry to help educate people to work in complex situations of diversity. Writing stories has been found to be a powerful tool in fostering teachers' professional growth (Huber et al. 2004).

Narrative exploration

The narratives and metaphors by which we structure our lives, the taken for granteds, are questioned and challenged: making the familiar strange, and the strange familiar. All our life stories can be questioned; many can be altered or struggled against. Life does not present us with inevitable chronological consequences of certain actions or events: we are free to choose how we act and influence others.

We have to take full responsibility, and can try out different characteristics for ourselves and colleagues; alternative ways of perceiving our environment; fresh angles from which to grasp our roles as protagonists of our life plots. This might entail the disappearance of a comfortable characterisation and plot development: the baddy might have previously unperceived good qualities, the good adviser might be lining his own nest, the impossible workplace might have a magically transformable space, the terrible blunder might have good consequences. And, of course, the opposite.

Bringing our everyday stories into question is an adventure. No one adventures securely in their backyard. Professionals need to face the uncertainty of not knowing what is round the corner, where they are going, how they will travel, when they will meet dragons or angels, and who their comrades are. They even have to trust why they are going. A student commented: 'What a relief it is to know that this uncertainty is essential; knowing that makes me feel less uncertain of being uncertain. Now uncertainty is my mantra.'

Certainty does not generate the flexibly enquiring attitude required by learning. An experienced practitioner learns all the time, and is open to being wrong. 'Certainty goes down as experiential knowledge goes up' (Phillion and Connelly 2004, p. 468). Some senior practitioners, in my experience, find this hard, being the most defended against reflective practice. Their defensive and self-protective reasoning is proof against uncertainty and doubt. Their sense of themselves in their role is too uncertain for them to lay it open to doubt and enquiry.

Practitioners engaged in *through-the-mirror* reflection explore experience, values and professional identities, and express aspects within certain personal and professional bounds which they expect to be respected. They are appropriately open to have understandings challenged, willing to have beliefs questioned, and courageous in discovering aspects underlying and affecting daily behaviour, of which they were hitherto unaware. They are open, willing and courageous *enough*: too much can be a recipe for disaster as can self-protective closedness.

An awareness of the complex interrelatedness of stories within practice facilitates an awareness of roles in relation to clients, students, colleagues and peers, and an effective working grasp of ethics and values, and can develop responsible empathetic attitudes. The acquisition of skills and experience in relating to, and handling, the everyday narratives of professional life develops this comprehension of complexity.

Writing about professional life can develop awareness of narrative structure (plot, characterisation, chronology, environment), sensitivity to perspective (from whose point of view is the story told?), and the function of metaphor, simile, metonymy, alliteration, assonance, and so on. Interpretive abilities can be developed: the narrator's role (omniscient? reliable?), the value of multiple perspectives (viewing the same situation from the point of view of doctor and patient, teacher and student), and inherent ethical and value structures depicted.

Reflexivity entails examining taken-for-granted roles and values in relation to individuals, organisations and systems, models and metaphors unwittingly lived and worked by. Here is a school head teacher reflecting upon his position:

 Jim Nind: personal narrative and well-being

I discovered reflective writing to try and make sense of my experience and my feeling of alienation, having been ousted from my first headship after struggling to establish a school I could really believe in. I started writing a serious reflective journal having got an angry spleen-venting account of events off my chest. It attempted to deal with the deeper issues surrounding the abiding sense of compromise I felt as the national curriculum took hold and I worked to re-establish myself.

My reflective meanderings channelled towards a Masters dissertation using Clandinin and Connelly's (1994) Personal Experience Method. I also began writing poetry with a self-counselling depth of intent last experienced in mid adolescence. A fluid way of working was offered by Ellis and Bochner's (2000) autoethnography through personal narrative, Richardson's (2000) writing as a method of enquiry and creative analytical practice (CAP), and her expanded notion of 'text' and the concept of 'intertext'.

The research process resembled the artistic process. My photo-essays, manipulated photo-images and allegorical stories offered fictionalised versions of myself facing dramas as a way of returning to past events, rehearsing current dilemmas and testing out possible futures. This writing became an exploration of loss and alienation and the reaffirmation and renewal of my being and self-respect. Neither introspective 'navel-gazing' nor 'cosy', my journey entailed reliving some of the trauma, and revealing buried aspects of myself and practice. Disinterring memories and undergoing mourning for a lost self, was essential for critical understanding.

I facilitated a degree module using writing. The starting point for course writing has often been the reflective voice of others, such as Sidney Poitier's (2000) cultural induction into racism, Bauby's (1998) account from within 'locked-in-syndrome', Joe Simpson's (1988) 'touching the void' and Frankl's (1985) 'search for meaning' grounded in the Jewish experience of life in a concentration camp. Each draws upon extreme circumstances most of us never encounter, but raises questions many of us recognise. A variety of poetic texts also offered kindred voices: echoing doubts and uncertainties, invoking and affirming common experiences, and pushing back the boundaries to perception. Mountain Dreamer's *Invitation* (Oriah 2000) was used to open dialogue about colleagues' deeply held hopes and desires. Telling the stories of our lives offers a realisation that we have been different people at different times and within different organisations, some discrepant (Goffman 1990). There are multiple possibilities for the people we might become (Mearns 1994; Maclure 2003).

Exploring narratives of the self and others enables a genuine listening: collaboratively challenging, questioning, adjusting and affirming of our possible selves and ways of practising. It gives us choice and agency. Therein lies the only approximation of authenticity we are likely to find. (Jim Nind)

Fact and fiction

Stories are not 'true'.

The stories we write are not reconstructions of chunks of *real life*. They cannot be. The *truth* in stories, as in ethnographic writing (Clifford 1986) can only ever be *partial*. No account, however carefully constructed, can ever be *true*. Told from the narrator's point of view, it contains the details they noticed and remembered, interwoven and shot through reflexively with their memories, dreams, prejudices, personal and cultural values, and so on (Denzin 1992); a different narrator, especially one from a different culture, would tell a different story.

Use of the imagination in such as this is not inventing out of nothing (Rolfe 2002). Writers draw upon memories of experiences which have touched them deeply: art is nearly always a working out of complex unresolved, unsorted-out areas of experience (Toibin 2009). These memories, by their very nature, do not present as straightforward accounts. They present as a muddle of half-remembered inconsistencies: unsatisfactorily *storied* experiences. Fiction offers a way of experimenting with storying experiences in different ways – less or more realistically, less or more close to the actual events.

> Through narrative, we construct, reconstruct, in some ways reinvent yesterday and tomorrow. Memory and imagination fuse in the process. Even when we create the possible worlds of fiction, we do not desert the familiar but subjunctivise* it into what might have been and what might be. The human mind, however cultivated its memory or refined its recording systems, can never fully and faithfully recapture the past, but neither can it escape from it. Memory and imagination supply and consume each other's wares. [*The subjunctive tense: 1. a set of forms of a verb which express states that do not exist. (www.tiscali.co.uk/reference/dictionaries), 2. wishes, commands, emotion, possibility, judgment, opinion, necessity, or statements contrary to fact at present (Wikipedia).] (Bruner 2002, p. 93)

Experiment found that the value of people writing about a fictional trauma is as effective therapeutically as if they had written about a memory (Pennebaker 2000).

Case studies, also, cannot be true, detached or impartial depictions, although they concern real people and events (Clark 2002). Necessarily perspectival, constructed edited texts, they can have only 'indirect or partial correspondence with reality ... despite their apparent verisimilitude' (Pattison et al. 1999a, p. 43). They include biases of inclusion and exclusion, prejudices and values, and are generally written by professionals, not service users.

'The telling and understanding of a really good story' is the best approach to 'the project of narrative [clinical] ethics' (Ellos 1998, p. 315; see also

Montgomery Hunter 1991). If this is the case, and if as Bleakley (2005) says, 'case studies are autistic' in their futile attempt to be true, detached and impartial, then fresh methods are needed, preferably from literature, the home of the story (Brody 2003; Charon and Montello 2002).

Even a video would only record what came within its field – no smell, taste, sense of touch, or sight and sound material outside its range. 'People talk about true stories. As if there could possibly be such things as true stories; events take place one way and we recount them the opposite way' (Sartre [1938] 1963, p. 62). The belief that any study can be objectively true, with a single 'teleological meaning' (Barthes 1977, p. 146), is itself a fiction. Everyone has selective perception:

Selective hearing syndrome: female

He: You are the most beautiful, fascinating, intelligent, witty, sexy, well balanced, creative woman I have ever met, even if you are a bit moody sometimes.
She: Me? Moody?

Selective hearing syndrome: male

She: You never take the children to the park, or read them a story; you never even cook an egg, and have never made the bed.
He: Bed? Now?

Reflective practitioners often need to examine a particular incident, exploring motives, feelings and thoughts, their actions and those of others, recording it as accurately and as widely as possible from their own memory, and possibly also consulting others' perceptions. And at times fictional ('subjunctivised' accounts to use Bruner's word above) scenarios are appropriate: what might have happened, what others might have thought, and so on. And on occasion genre gives the best exploration (as in fairy story, or romantic fiction: see Chapter 14). None can be *true*. Yet within some social work training there is an assumption that 'the aim of the narrative is to persuade the listener or reader [presumably the assessor] that the story is true and that the author is to be believed' (Knott and Scragg 2007, p. 28).

Stories might be what we live by. But life as lived lacks the comforting fictive form recognised from infancy, with a beginning, middle and end, clearly defined characters and sense of place. The function of the endless *stories* we tell and write is to give life a spurious, satisfying, recountable, and memorable sense of shape. 'Narrative seeks to redeem life and pain from chaos by creating sequence … In narrative form, one event seems to belong before and after others – not to happen randomly but to make sense exactly there' (Frank 2004, p. 213).

The identity, or *character*, of a person similarly is not static or fixed. 'We all talk about "me". How do we know that there is such a person as "me"?'

(Chuang Tsu 1974, p. 136). In life as lived, identities change and develop; telling and writing stories celebrates this, and enables dynamic understanding.

Stories are created in the recounting of life events. Sophocles, Aeschylus and Euripides depicted the great bloody events of their tragedies off-stage, recounted by such as a messenger. The murder of Agamemnon (Aeschylus 1999) is foretold graphically, immediately before it happens, by the prophetess Cassandra. Such episodes are told as stories – a story within the story of the play – for dramatic effect.

In life 'we always begin in the middle' (Lyotard 1992, p. 116), and 'we are always in the middle' (fourth-century BC philosopher Chuang Tsu). Here is the hero of *Nausea*, in the process of realising that those essential aspects of adventure – beginnings and endings – are only in stories, in the recounting of a life, rather than in life as lived:

> First of all beginnings would have had to be real beginnings. Real beginnings, appearing like a fanfare of trumpets, like the first notes of a jazz tune, abruptly cutting boredom short … Something begins in order to end: an adventure doesn't let itself be extended; it achieves significance only through its death …
>
> When you are living nothing happens. The settings change, people come in and go out, that's all. There are never any beginnings. Days are tacked onto days without rhyme or reason, it's an endless monotonous addition. (Sartre [1938] 1963, pp. 59, 61)

Trying to *live* our lives as *adventure* or *story* could only lead to depression or mental instability: 'I wanted the moments of my life to follow one another in an orderly fashion like those of a life remembered. You might as well try to catch time by the tail … You have to choose: to live or to recount' (Sartre [1938] 1963, pp. 63, 61). 'The past is beautiful because one never realises an emotion at the time. It expands later, and thus we don't have complete emotions about the present, only about the past' (Virginia Woolf, quoted in Holly 1989, p. 26).

Hélène Cixous asserts that only masculine stories have beginnings and endings. 'A feminine textual body is recognised by the fact that it is always endless, without ending … at a certain point the volume comes to an end but the writing continues and for the reader this means being thrust into the void.' And 'a feminine text starts on all sides at once, starts twenty times, thirty times over' (1995, p. 175).

Realising that accounts of practice do not need to stick to what happened in life as lived can offer confidence in the expression of experience, and widen the range of possible ways of reflection. Fiction can omit slow episodes or effectively combine events which took place at different times and with different people. Writing fictionally from deep professional experience can be more dramatic, leap over the boring bits, tackle issues head on; convey multiple viewpoints; sidestep problems of confidentiality, fear of exposure, and some of the inevitable anxiety which accompanies the exploration of painful events.

Writing about 'she' or 'he' rather than 'I' can be liberating. Fiction can feel safer to write – less personally revealing. Later rereading, sharing and discussing can offer a paced way of exploring areas which might otherwise seem too painful to address.

Fiction can be a vehicle for conveying the ambiguities, complexities and ironic relationships that inevitably exist between multiple viewpoints. It can offer an intelligible research summary of the huge body of data that qualitative research tends to provide. The creation of a fiction, with the awareness that it is a creation, can enable the writer to head straight for the heart of the matter (see also Rowland 1991; Rowland (Bolton) et al. 1990). 'Thinking up a plot and a range of characters in a certain context is analogous to formulating a theory of that context' (Winter 1988, p. 241).

Fictional characters and situations take on a life of their own. If writers try to discipline them to do what they want, the writing will be flat, lifeless and dull. Each character is an aspect of the author, and needs full expression via the creative process. This allows expression to the non-logical, non-rational parts of the writer's mind, allowing contact with previously unperceived internal voices.

Peter Clough's stories about education are an example of using narrative to challenge assumptions (2002). The text is hampered by dense explanatory prose: the stories could have carried the argument more powerfully within themselves. These narratives are perspectivally limited, all being from the point of view of fictional Peter Clough.

Critics have been dissatisfied with forms of research or reflection which make overt use of fiction. Just as few are satisfied with the copy of Michaelangelo's *David* in a Florentine piazza free of charge, with no queues: they need to see the very lump of marble from which Michaelangelo himself 'released' David. Stories, however, are not *objects* like *David*: they are constructions mediated through writers or narrators. There is no *real account* in literature, like the *real statue of David*: we need to lose an obsession with seeking objectivity, and enable authentic scientific experimentation and exploration.

Charon (2006) has reflected upon patients' charts as if novels. She says 'Literary critics who write about the novel provide useful frameworks for doctors who reflect on their practice' (2000a, p. 63). Helman's (2006) medical memoir, written like a novel gives invaluable insight.

There is a problem when reflective writings are discussed and assessed. Hargreaves (2004) maintains that nursing students are forced by the system to present reflections within a professionally acceptable frame or to fictionalise, while at the same time they have to sign to say that their work is a true, faithful reflection of their actual practice. She concludes: 'exploring the value of fictional narratives may reveal a powerful medium for the development and understanding of professional practice (2004, p. 199)', rather than requiring them to create absolutely accurate accounts of thoughts, feelings and actions.

Here is a narrative to explore social work experience, by Rosemary Willett:

 Evelyn

Only her father understood Evelyn. Only he knew that there were times when the noises and voices in her head made her angry and she wanted to lash out. There were times when she could not stand the people and bustle in the day centre. Then he took her to sit at the side of the canal while he fished, or to walk in the woods and look at the birds and animals.

Then, quite suddenly, he was gone. Admitted to hospital for a routine operation, he had a heart attack and Evelyn was alone. She had to live with people she did not know; there were too many of them and they did not realise that she needed her routine, her space, her time. And she missed her father's comforting presence desperately.

'Evelyn is violent, dangerous. Evelyn has challenging behaviour,' they said. So they locked her up; she was terrified. Later, she went to live with a family. Happier at first, the toddler's needs competed with her own and she wisely asked to move. She moved again after she threw a table; she had been accused of lying. Evelyn knew that she was not lying, only saying things as she saw them. 'Evelyn is a gypsy. Evelyn needs to move,' people said. 'Evelyn needs to learn anger management.'

The new place was smaller, quieter, more tolerant. When she is tense, she walks by the canal.

She looks after her bird. 'Roy is happy,' she says.

Rosemary's afterword

I came to this job after some years away from much contact with people with Learning Disabilities, and was immediately profoundly affected by their interesting, poignant and sometimes dramatic life stories which are not always reflected in Health or Social Services assessments or academic research. Working as a social worker in a multi-disciplinary team our major role is the assessment, co-ordination and review of services for our users and their carers. We become involved in people's lives offering clarification, support and some continuity, and possibly most important we give them our time.

To provide necessary services, maximise choices and maintain the quality of life which is everyone's right, it is clearly appropriate to evaluate a range of strengths, needs, skills and behaviours. However, it seems we categorise people in a way which overlooks or denies significant parts of the reality of their life experience, and their feelings about that experience.

Some of the language in these stories is deliberately stigmatising, because that is part of the reality. I hoped to give a different slant on why people are as they are: some explanation which may influence practice. Social workers can become institutionalised in thinking and action. We need to be moved by those we work with: a colleague was in tears on reading *Evelyn*, whom she knows well. It is personally fulfilling for me to *paint these pictures*. (Rosemary Willett)

Harnessing the power of story-writing in tackling the joyous but utterly messy and uncertain complexity of professional life can help us to hear the story without missing the plot. Narrative and metaphor are two powerful foundations of *through-the-mirror* writing (along with observation and description, see Chapters 1, 2, 5, 6 and 7). Chapter 13 gives a cogent and persuasive account of metaphor; what it is, how to use it, how it uses us, and why it is so powerful.

 Read to Learn

Clandinin, D.J. and Connelly, F.M. (1994) Personal experience methods, in N.K. Denzin and Y. Lincoln (eds), *Handbook of Qualitative Research*. London: Sage.
Gabriel, Y. (1995) The unmanaged organization: stories, fantasies and subjectivity, *Organization Studies*, **16**, 477–501.
Ramsey, C. (2005) Narrating development: professional practice emerging within stories, *Action Research*, **3**(3), 279–95.

 Write to Learn

Each chapter ends with *Write to learn*. For straightforward advice, sufficient for the exercises below, see *Write to learn* in Chapter 1, and see Chapter 6 for more advice. Each writing can be shared fruitfully with a group or confidential trusted other, if this seems appropriate once the writer has read and reflected on it first.

(Continued)

(Continued)

Exercise 12.1   Points of view

1. Do a *six-minute write*.
2. Write a narrative about an event which puzzles you, in as much detail as you can remember, call yourself 'I'.
3. Write about the same occasion, this time from the perspective of a significant other person who was there; this person will now call themselves 'I'.
4. Write about the same occasion, this time from the perspective of an omniscient narrator: in this version there is no 'I', you and the significant person become 'she' and/or 'he'.
5. Now write a final piece, reflecting on the significance of these three stories.
6. Reread to yourself with loving care, rewriting if you wish.

Exercise 12.2   Significant clothes

1. Do a *six-minute write*.
2. Describe a favourite set of work clothes in detail, including any features such as mends.
3. Describe buying (receiving or acquiring) these clothes, if relevant.
4. How do these clothes make you feel?
5. Describe your *least* favourite work clothing.
6. When do you wear these and why? Why do you dislike them?
7. Tell the story of an occasion when you wore them, in detail.
8. Read back to yourself with care. Add or alter or adapt.

Exercise 12.3   Stepping stones

1. Do a *six-minute write*.
2. Create a list of life (or work) *stepping stones*, giving the list a heading: the *aha moments* in my life; the writing in my life; trees; patients/clients/students/and so on; colleagues; places of work; whatever springs to mind.
3. Choose one from your list. Write a story ...
4. Read back to yourself with loving care, commenting and reflecting.

CHAPTER 13

THE POWER OF METAPHOR

Chapter 13 explains and illustrates the fundamental importance of metaphors in life and work, and how authority can be taken over them through reflection and reflexivity. Metaphor is explained in detail, and how to work with them for powerful insight and personal and professional development.

> Our ordinary conceptual system, in terms of which we both think and act, is fundamentally metaphorical in nature … human thought processes are largely metaphorical. (Lakoff and Johnson [1980] 2003, p. 6)

> Metaphor is the birth of meaning. (Hogler et al. 2008, p. 400)

Reflective practitioners look at life fully, perceiving right through the mirror rather then merely musing upon reflections. The world the other side of the mirror will seem different in strange and enlightening ways. Once the metaphorical nature of conceptual systems and communication is grasped, and fresh metaphors are tried over previously accepted ones, culture, society and work can never again be perceived in the same way. This chapter offers a route to grasping greater authority over, and responsibility for, our lives and work.

Metaphor is a frame through which we perceive, understand and feel, our conceptual system is 'fundamentally metaphorical' as Lakoff and Johnson say ([1980]2003, p. 6). A form of cultural interpretation, it is fundamental to communication, values, ethical beliefs and practices. Every utterance and every perception is imbued, or informed metaphorically (see Hogler et al. 2008, p. 400). Each metaphor, consciously used or created, gives authority, and extends and vivifies that which it describes. Metaphors used unwittingly restrict perception and understanding.

Metaphors are culturally powerful, forming understanding and attitudes, certain elements being foregrounded, others ignored. Take the image of the body as machine: it leads to assuming doctors can mend bodies with spare parts or oil, and physiology can be logged as in car owners' handbooks. The economy as marketplace? In the current economic climate I do not need to enumerate the problems this simplistic assumption has led to. A reflexive awareness and conscious use of metaphors and metaphorical systems therefore is vital to take authority. The way an issue is understood cannot be changed without changing the metaphors, or metaphorical systems, which express it. By paying attention to the metaphors we use, we can become critically aware of hitherto uncritically accepted and repeated world views. Conceptual frameworks constructive of values, understanding, and feelings and therefore actions can, to an extent, be chosen.

Responsibility for moral and social consequences of metaphors needs to be taken. 'Metaphors can kill' (Lakoff 1991). 'Evocative language can take on pernicious and evil power if wrong metaphors are chosen – we are liable to be captives of our own phrases and must be careful how we speak' (Osborn 1993, p. 306). George W. Bush responded to the attack on New York's Twin Towers with a '*Crusade* against Terror'. Metaphorically likening American forces to medieval Crusaders, was a clear declaration of war against Islam. The belief that hearing voices indicates incurable psychosis, like aliens arising from untameable and unknowable unconscious realms, might lead hearers to kill themselves or others. If these voices are perceived as part of the self, they can be talked to, reasoned with and controlled to some extent: a life project (Smith 2009; www.hearing-voices.org).

People are mostly unaware of professional, political and social metaphors and metaphorical systems they live and work with. When we struggle to conceptualise, grasp or explain an issue, the struggle is often a search for appropriate metaphors. I asked a group of medical undergraduates if one could give an example of metaphor. They looked blank and rather scared (I could see them thinking 'we're scientists . . .'). One responded, 'I can't think of any, my mind's a blank sheet', comically unaware she'd just used a brilliant metaphor: blank mind = blank sheet.

To enlighten groups about metaphor, I often initiate a discussion about prevalent metaphors in their profession. It only takes one participant to shout one out for the whole group to excitedly contribute, discovering a dominating force they can tackle. The ensuing task is to see if they can rewrite any habitual and unnoticed metaphors into new and dynamic ones. For example *hit the ground running* could become *take wings and fly*.

What is metaphor?

Metaphor, a major way of making sense of the world (along with narrative), is something otherwise unrelated or logically inconsistent standing in place of another: 'my work is the baby thrown out with the bathwater'. 'Giving the thing a name that belongs to something else' (Aristotle 1995, p. 105); Lakoff and Johnson describe it thus: 'the essence of metaphor is understanding and experiencing one kind of thing in terms of another' ([1980] 2003, p. 5). 'The use of metaphor implies ways of thinking and seeing that pervade how we understand the world' (Elkind 1998, p. 1715; Frankenberg 1986), *prescribe* even how it *ought* to be viewed and evaluated (Gray 2007).

Metaphor makes abstract concrete, a grasp of the ungraspable, make visible or audible that which is normally invisible or inaudible. Have you ever touched, heard, smelt or seen a feeling, emotion, or spiritual experience? Metaphors, whether written, painted or played, give vital everyday areas tangible form. The human mind thinks concretely: what *is* love, anxiety, guilt? Love is a beautiful, scented flower, anxiety a beast gnawing at your guts, guilt the heavy bird you should never have shot, strung inescapably around your neck (Coleridge [1798] 1969). For our purposes metaphor (my love *is* a red red rose) can be used the same way as simile ('My love is *like* a red red rose': Robert Burns [emphasis mine]). A simile is a metaphor with *like* or *as* creating the link.

Metaphoric images from the five elements are common in our culture: *my body was leaden, their heads were lumps of rock, our legs turned to water, he talked hot air, she breathed fire*. The body as container is another prevalent image: *I'm full to bursting with pride*. John Dewey used countless metaphors for the essence of being a teacher, including artist, lover, wise mother, navigator, gardener, servant, composer, physician, builder (Simpson et al. 2005).

Metaphors enable verbal painting, creation of symphonies, banquets, perfumes, silk, the use of all five senses to enable 'cognitive, affective and somatic ways of knowing' (Shafer 1995, p. 1331). C.S. Lewis (1961b) said some moments of bereavement could only be described in metaphor, true for many who turn instinctively to poetry to express intense emotion. A powerful image can be succinctly created. 'My throat is very sore' hardly compares with 'my throat is on fire'.

Our dominant cultural metaphors are static. Fluid and active elements are often expressed as *things*, commonly commodities. Nursing and teaching are relationship based. Yet teaching *plugs a knowledge or skills gap*, *a module*; nursing *delivers packages of care*. We have *human resource management*, rather than *personnel*, as if people were bricks. Everyone has a metaphorical way of understanding their lives (Brody 2003). Some with a half-empty glass and others half full, metaphorical expressions of native optimism or pessimism.

As a poetic device, metaphor is visible: poets and readers do not believe love *is* a rose. But scientists can believe theirs, and persuade the public for example the body is a machine (Pickering 1999). The metaphor becomes invisible.

> Metaphor is the rhetorical process by which discourse unleashes the power that certain fictions have to redescribe reality … The metaphorical *is* at once signifies both *is not* and *is like*. If this is really so we are allowed to speak of metaphorical truth. (Ricoeur 1978, p. 7)

'Metaphorical truth' is an essential aspect of our mental and physical understanding, the 'open sesame' to memories and understanding. 'Metaphor is the "aha!" process itself ' (Shafer 1995, p. 1332). And to psychiatrist Modell:

> Metaphor [is] the currency of mind, a fundamental and indispensable structure of human understanding. It is by means of metaphor that we generate new perceptions of the world; it is through metaphor that we organise and make sense out of experience … The locus of metaphor is now recognised to be in the mind and not in language … metaphors have their origin in the body. There is a privileged connection between affects and metaphor. As feelings are to some degree beyond our control, translating such feelings into metaphors provides us with some degree of organisation and control. Through the use of metaphor we are able to organise otherwise inchoate experiences, so it is not surprising that somatic experiences, such as affects, are transformed into metaphors … (1997, pp. 219–20)

Metaphor: some examples

Examining metaphorical structures is an essential reflexive process. Leslie Boydell describes the leadership programme she directs for the Institute of Public Health in Ireland as:

> a team of horses pulling a heavily laden wagon. The horses are of different sizes and colours and they are pulling at different speeds. One has the bit between its teeth and is going full tilt, another is taking it easy, a third wants to eat grass, while another is grumpy and nipping the others. But every so often we pull together and we fly. I am sitting on the wagon, inconspicuous, without a whip

or loud voice. I constantly keep my eyes on the road ahead to steer around any dangers. Other people come on board for a while and ride with me and use their greater strength to control the horses. (Leslie Boydell, in Denyer et al. 2003, p. 19)

Cecilia Forrestal, in describing the programme as an opened jigsaw box, depicts her learning graphically. Here's an extract: 'Well look at that! I thought that blue piece was definitely the sky. But no. It is water. And that piece of "cloud" is part of the "snow". Who would have guessed I could be so wrong? Now I can see the value of that sharp edge: you would have to have it to give shape to the whole picture' (in Denyer et al. 2003, p. 22). Jane Wilde, Institute Director, saw the programme as jewel-like stained-glass windows (in Denyer et al. 2003, p. 27), and:

> The stones in the river are dull and grey
> The sky low and gloomy lies on my shoulders
> And clouds are in my head
> A heron balances on a stone in the river
> We watched and waited for each other
> He held my gaze. Balanced
> Silent, still, surveying
> Later, gently with ease, he flew. (Jane Wilde in Denyer et al. 2003, p. 44)

Plato relied on metaphor to explain his theories. His exposition of the ethical responsibility of philosopher-educators is widely remembered and clearly understood through his graphic *cave* metaphor (1955).

Susan Sontag wrote a polemic (1991, p. 91) against metaphors in medicine and healthcare. Battlefield metaphors are commonly used for diseases like cancer, which 'doesn't knock before it enters … a ruthless secret invasion' (1991, p. 5).

Audrey Shafer argues that 'anaesthesia is much more complex than commonly used metaphors seem to suggest … new metaphors may need to be developed to help us completely understand how anaesthetics work' (1995, p. 1339). *Under* anaesthetic metaphor is unhelpfully simplistic, giving a negative sense, since *down* is normally metaphorically construed as bad, perhaps related to the image of devil and hell as underneath, and heaven above (*bottom of the heap, under the weather*).

> We ask [participants] to describe education as a pudding, then to write up their luxury version. Much of this activity is light-hearted, as we aim to keep a distance from personalistic accounts, heavy by definition, but nevertheless, startling, surreal images abound, aesthetically subverting the humdrum world of everyday practice. (Kemp 2001, p. 350)

This family medical practitioner (GP) used metaphor to help him to perceive how he might be experienced by a patient he is unable to help:

 Nigel Gibbons: portrait by a patient

If he was a dog he'd be an old greyhound, tense and stiff but droopy round the middle.

If he was a cat he'd be a Siamese small eyes, and coming over all superior, but lazy.

If he was a wild animal he'd be a weasel cunning and sly and always wriggling and slipping away from you.

If he was a bird he'd be a heron tall and staring at you with beady eyes, and then darting at you.

If he was an insect he'd be a busy bee bumbling about and blundering into things and no use at all.

If he was a fish he'd be a fat trout just sitting there, and then suddenly shooting off.

If he was a bit of furniture he'd be a tallboy all big and shiny and domineering, but just a lot of empty space up at the top and not much use down below. You keep putting things in but you can never get anything out when you want it.

If he was a car he'd be an Austin Cambridge years out of date, mediocre, middle of the road, too big, using up too much fuel, and you can't get the spares. If only he wasn't the way he is he'd be a proper doctor.

I was asked as an exercise to write a piece about a patient. I chose a familiar one. I found it quite a satisfying experience to share a distillation of my observations with others. It was a pleasure to be able to tell a story involving some of my observations, displaying anonymously some of what would otherwise have slipped into oblivion. It was written in a spirit of affectionate resignation about the impossibility of making any real medical progress in this case. Reflecting about my consultations in this detached and analytical way, and writing a parallel piece about the imagined observations of me by the patient, taught me that I should be acutely aware of the signs and signals that I give out when talking to people, just as much as I am aware of what I observe. (Gibbons 2003)

Reframing metaphors

Metaphors can express abstractions, memories, ideas, thoughts and feelings, and explore constructive contact with painful or difficult areas of experience and memory. Effective metaphors can appear to *come from nowhere*. Facilitators help images bubble up, presenting themselves on the page: an artistic process. It only seems like accident because we are used to the Cartesian 'I think, therefore I am': these metaphors do not arise through cognitive processes. Such powerful images occur once we have the courage to be 'absent-minded', or to pay attention to absent-mindedness (as Freud suggested about parapraxes). If reflective practitioners are encouraged to experiment *playfully* with words – *doodle* with metaphors, they can 'absent-mindedly' enter areas of experience, as well as Modell's (1997) and Harris's (2003) locked categories of memory. Metaphor can reveal because it sidles up sideways, giving non-traumatic images for traumatic events. Writers or artists might not understand their own metaphors initally (as dreams are frequently not understood); when they do, it is the indrawn breath of 'aha'. I've likened writing this third edition to knitting an intricate pattern with hundreds of needles and balls of wool of all colours: an interesting metaphor, as I can't knit. Metaphors can also enable contact with otherwise hidden memories:

> Cognitive metaphors form bridges between the past and the present; metaphor allows us to find the familiar in the unfamiliar. This means affective memories are enclosed as potential categories; we remember categories of experience evoked by metaphoric correspondence with current perceptual inputs. We can think of ourselves as owning a library of categorical memories of pleasurable and painful experiences, all of which at certain points in our life will be activated by means of metaphoric correspondence with current inputs.
> (Modell 1997, p. 221)

Traumatic memories lose connectedness with the rest of the memory, preventing living in the present and looking to the future. Metaphor is the only way to make contact with this material. A relatively safe way to make them accessible and communicable is writing poetry. Writing, as a powerful communicating force, can help to overcome the isolation the survivor experiences (Harris 2003).

Metaphor to develop reflexivity

There are many ways of encouraging professionals to become aware of habitual metaphors, and wield metaphor's perceptive power. Practitioners also create powerful new metaphors, like Boydell, Wilde and Forrestal above. Megginson and Whitaker ask management development participants to create metaphors for their career in a structured exercise (2003, pp. 34–6). Julie Hughes's education students, in a metaphor creating and exploration exercise, gave in-depth explanations why teaching was disco ball, river, road network, and mountaineering.

As a warm-up exercise, professionals write lists of binary pairs. They then play with them as metaphor, like assigning one of the pair to patient or student, and one to themselves. Charles Becker, a therapist, wrote this about himself and a female client:

silk & sand	I put the smooth on her rough
light & dark	she's in the light and I'm in the wings
Hansel & Gretel	I'm a boy and she's a girl and we're searching our way
mountains & streams	she flows round me and I stay fixed
horse & cart	she takes the lead and I follow on
grass & green	she's growing while I reflect her colour
sad & happy	I carry her tears as she learns to smile (Charles Becker)

Kate Milne, a family doctor, wrote about sunshine and showers:

My depressed patient and me. I am the sunshine. He is the showers. I try to brighten his life with pleasantries to help him pull through the storm. Maybe I am too light-hearted and I am minimising his sufferings. When the rain is fine the sun makes a rainbow. As the shower becomes heavy it clouds out the sun. Are my football stories irritating and patronising? He now chooses to see my colleague.

I found it useful putting my feelings down on paper as the situation put me in a dilemma. By sharing it with my group I was able to put the episode into perspective. It was interesting that the patient concerned is now causing my colleague some anxiety also. Maybe it is transference. (Kate Milne)

Carol Wood and Elaine Trevitt are practitioner peer-mentors (see Chapter 11); they played fruitfully with metaphor, even calling their joint educative process 'chip and pin' (see Chapter 11). Carol reports how metaphor enabled her constructively to perceive her *inner mentor*, whom she metaphorically personified as *Crow* (see Chapter 6 for dialogues with *inner wise self* and *internal supervisor*):

Over time, in exploration with Elaine, I realised *Crow* was, perhaps, a metaphor for my inner mentor. Realising *Crow* does not have to tread a tortuous winding road full of dark and dangerous pitfalls, but can rise above and fly, was something of an epiphany. Realising I did not always have to settle for compromise and a 'quiet life', that sometimes a discordant voice is vital to achieve best practice, I began to notice subtle changes in my practice and interpersonal relationships. Significantly, *Crow* enabled me to recognise and deal with suppressed anger at perceived injustice and the words that followed on led me to the place where I could comfortably assert that 'I AM' and could not be diminished by others and their tricky words. Elaine has found her own value in her own metaphors.

I believe that it is something within the power of metaphor that allows each of us to 'tune in' to the other easily. There is safety within metaphor because it can hold a myriad of layered meanings and their impact on our affect can be made explicit in our writing/dialogue or can remain implicit within the imagery. We do not presume to analyse and interpret each other's metaphor, or judge. We simply find ways to reflect what metaphors bring to our attention, giving their creator explorative opportunities. We are perhaps the looking glass for each other and each reflected metaphor takes us further 'through the looking glass'. (Carol Wood)

Playing with metaphors can help move practitioners and students from focusing upon everyday practical concerns, to a wider overview. They have been used in pre-service teacher training (Graham and Paterson 2010) to help students, among other issues, confront attitudes to diversity and disability in inclusive classroom settings. Students develop metaphors illuminating the role of *teacher*: gardener, tree in the rainforest, weather forecaster. For a further assignment they significantly developed their metaphors. Assessment carried 20 per cent of marks, students being required to: write educational life histories developing their metaphor; present a student-led seminar; and chart the development of the metaphor throughout the module. Lecturers worked alongside students, enhancing their understanding of metaphor. When metaphors were introduced in an initial lecture, students instantly understood and recognised the power of working with them.

Here is a teacher on another course: 'I thought that all teachers were the same, [but] when I heard what some of the other metaphors were, I thought, "this is so different from what I've been doing or what I've been experiencing", and I liked that' (Bullough 1991, p. 49).

Metaphor examination and creation informs organisational theory (Cunliffe 2008, Hogler et al. 2008).

In organizational studies, metaphors contribute to theory construction, help to structure beliefs and guide behaviour in organizations, express abstract ideas, convey vivid images that orient our perceptions and conceptualizations, transfer information, legitimate actions, set goals, and structure coherent systems. Because metaphors are enacted and surface through everyday language use, they can be used as tools to illuminate organizational practices, including capturing perceptions and reactions to ambiguity with organizational goals; norms, motives, and meaning in studying organizational culture; the nature of struggles between competing ideologies; and covert practices that mask power relationships by highlighting certain features while suppressing others. (Hogler et al. 2008, p. 396)

Metaphors are used in educational leadership (Pellicer 2008). Cherry and Spiegel's (2006) leadership students focused upon beliefs, values and ethics, using three themes: (1) touchstone, standard bearer; (2) advocate for a cause beyond oneself; (3) parent. School principalship training uses metaphor

(Linn et al. 2007), students responding to: 'The principalship is like … because …' (p. 163) with four 'themes: (a) protection and nurturing; (b) skill, adventure or problem solving; (c) challenge, risk and threat, (d) chance and luck. They generally depicted it as uncontrollable and unpredictable, yet each expressed determination and resolve to remain steadfast' (pp. 166, 168).

Practitioners often use metaphors unwittingly, as when Jo Turner wrote about rowing (About this book), and Jenny Lockyer drumming (Chapter 13). A doctor wrote a precise account of his drive to work: tricky roundabout, blind corner, frustrating traffic and so on. Such metaphors take writers by surprise. Here is a searching self-portrait:

 Jug by Sam Kyeremateng

A terracotta jug sits on a stone floor, in a dark space. The Jug ponders its existence in the world. It surveys the gloominess of its surroundings. Why am I here? Who am I? What am I? The unspoken questions are unanswered.

The Jug ponders itself. It was crafted with care. Someone had lovingly sculpted its form. Taking great care moulding its short spout and stout handle. Despite this the questions remain unanswered. It understood it was a jug. By its own admission it knew jugs could hold all manner of things. But it could not hold all things at once, and it could not decide what it should hold. It was not enough to be simply a jug, was it? It did not think it wished to be an empty vessel, and it did feel so very empty.

If it held water it could be used to sustain people or to hold beautiful things like flowers. If it held wine it could bring life to a party, solace to the lonely and joy to sad. If it held oil it could fuel a fire, or ease the workings of some great machine. If it held marbles it could be an ornament to be admired and adored. As the thoughts danced through its imagination the Jug realised that in the darkness of this room it could see no water or oil or wine or even stones let alone marbles and even if it could, it could not decide how to choose between them all. The Jug sat empty.

In the distance the sound of footfalls tapping the flagstones pierced the darkness. The Jug pondered a new thought. Perhaps someone would come and make the choice. Someone would find it and fill it up with something that would make it something worth being. Delighted by the prospect it sat thinking soon it would find the answer to all its questions. As the steps drew closer the Jug's excitement changed to anxiety. What if the person chose the wrong thing? Once filled with wine it could no longer hold water for fear of tainting the taste and vice versa. Would oily marbles have the same appeal? Panicked by the new dilemma the Jug remained frozen in the spotlight. The steps stopped. The Jug sensed the gaze of the unseen figure. After a moment the silence that had nurtured its thought became unbearable. The steps clacked back into life then faded.

The terracotta jug sat on a stone floor. In the silence it decided it was better just to be and not ask too many questions. To be an empty jug was enough for now.

Sam's afterword

I wrote this at a time of uncertainty: I'd like to think the sort of uncertainty that everyone experiences from time to time. Primarily it was about career paths. There was also, though, uncertainty about my place in society. As a black Scotsman (or Scotsman of African origin to be pc) I often wonder about my place in the world and what my attitudes should be. Being young, male and black all have their own associated dilemmas. Whilst I am undeniably Scottish, I have a deep love of my African roots. All this is further complicated by the media concept of *blackness* which is very different from that which has been passed to me by my parents. In my experience there are very few role models for the young, black Scotsman even in today's multicultural world. Even now the only one I can think of is the guy who was in *Porridge* with Ronnie Barker and I'm sure he doesn't count.

The story was never meant to be a self-portrait. I think I was just trying to capture certain emotions. It was certainly never meant to be published. Only now reading it again do I realise how embarrassingly personal (and at times sad) it is. Despite the blushes I am happy for it to be published as it surprises me by capturing my thoughts at a certain moment in time. I guess I hope that someone else might gain some comfort knowing that they are not the only ones to have similar thoughts of uncertainty. (Kyeremateng 2003, pp. 101–2)

Image and reflection

The reflection in Van Eyck's convex mirror in *The Arnolfini Portrait* (National Gallery, London) allows a view of the couple from both sides. Our night sky would be denuded without the power of reflection: the moon and the planets are only visible because they reflect the sun's light. 'The Lady of Shalott', cursed to live her life indirectly through mirror images, wove them into tapestry. When handsome Sir Lancelot appears in her glass she can stand it no longer: The mirror cracked from side to side / 'The curse is come upon me!' cried / The lady of Shalott (Tennyson [1886] 1932, p. 82). She dies because her curse was to perceive life only reflected.

Reflective practitioners need to look at life fully, and perceive right through the mirror rather then merely musing upon reflections. The route is a critical rendering and rerendering of life's narratives, and critical re-viewing of habitual metaphors.

 Read to learn

Bullough, R.V. (1991) Exploring personal teachers' metaphors in pre-service teacher education, *Journal of Teacher Education*, **42**(1), 43–52.

Cherry, D. and Spiegel, J. (2006) *Leadership, Myth and Metaphor*. Thousand Oaks, CA: Corwin Press (Sage).

Hogler, R., Gross, M.A., Hartman, J.L. and Cunliffe, A.L. (2008) Meaning in orga- nizational communication: why metaphor is the cake, not the icing, *Management Communication Quarterly*, **21**, 393–412.

 Write to learn

Each chapter ends with *Write to learn*. For straightforward advice, sufficient for the exercises below, see *Write to learn* in Chapter 1, and see Chapter 6 for more advice. Each writing can be shared fruitfully with a group or confidential trusted other, if this seems appropriate once the writer has read and reflected on it first.

Exercise 13.1   Empowering your work

1. Do a *six-minute write*.
2. Think of a picture, object of beauty (for example, a shell), or an element of nature (for example, a mountain, a tree) you particularly like.
3. Describe its qualities: those that make it inspiring, beautiful, restful …
4. Now replace the name of the thing with the name of your work (see, for example, below).
5. Reread to yourself with care, seeking any resonance between *six-minutes* and the longer write.

(For example, 1. This ancient Greek jug is graceful and elegant, yet also totally functional enabling it to contain liquid safely and pour effectively; it has a firm base and reasonably large capacity. 2. My work is graceful yet functional, with a large enough capacity and firm ethical and practical base. I can use it to carry wisdom to other people and pour it carefully, the amount they need.)

Exercise 13.2   Binary pairs (see example above)

1. Do a *six-minute write.*
2. List as many binary pairs as you can (for example, needle and thread, horse and cart, Adam and Eve, knife and fork).
3. Picture yourself and one other work person: client, colleague, whoever.
4. Write who is which from your pairs (for example, I am needle, my client thread); note which ones seem not obvious to assign.
5. Choose one, and write more (for example, I am a big fat shiny darning needle; she is a long length of dark grey wool darning a huge hole in the heel of this old sock).
6. Read back to yourself with care and imaginative involvement.

Exercise 13.3   If your work were a ...

1. Do a *six-minute write.*
2. Respond to each of these with a phrases for each:

   (a)   If my work were an animal what animal would it be?
   (b)   If my work were a piece of furniture what would it be?
   (c)   If it were a season or weather what would it be?
   (d)   A food?
   (e)   A drink?
   (f)   A flower?
   (g)   A form of transport?
   (h)   And so on.

3. Use the items of the list to create a description of a place, or very short story (for example, if you have a cat and a cup of cocoa on your list, a cat might lap from your cocoa while your back is turned ...).
4. Read back to yourself with imagination.

CHAPTER 14

WIDER AND DEEPER: OTHER WRITING FORMS

Chapter 14 gives an informed account of how the writing of genre including story, fantasy, folk tale, fable, myth, parody, writing for children and autobiographical reflective stories, as well as poetry, can elucidate and enlighten the reflective and reflexive processes. Illuminative examples are given.

> Important art … invites your attention to the previously over-looked and negligible, and shows that the unconsidered is deeply considerable. (Jonathan Miller 2009, p. 12)

> We should beware of what stories can do to the way we put the world together. (Antonia Byatt 2004, p. 4)

> Man is an animal suspended in webs of significance he himself has spun. (Geertz [1973] 1993, p. 5)

We have many selves and many potential voices, one clamouring for expression as fantasy, another wanting nurturing towards the tiny poetic form, haiku. There are a range of fictional forms (genres) such as fairy story, romantic fiction, detective, fantasy, fable, whodunit, social realism, sci-fi, comedy, Aga-saga, thriller. Writing these can enable the exploration of facets of the self and of experience. Genres tend to be formulaic with archetypal characters, place and type of plot. Writers are set free from having to depict realistic characters, chronology, events and environments. 'Writing "works" because it enables us to come to know ourselves through the multiple voices our experience takes, to describe our contexts and histories as they shape the many minds and selves who define us and others' (Holly 1989, p. 15). Writing in genre can help us perceive the 'webs of significance' (Geertz [1973] 1993, p. 5) we spin around ourselves. A grasp of genre and the way its form moulds content is vital for critical understanding; Antonia Byatt (2004, p. 4) warns that we need to understand the power of stories; this chapter shows how we need to understand the power of story form and genre as well. 'Realis[ing] the hospital chart is a genre with its own strict rules of composition, unlock[s] a powerful method of studying the text itself as well as the actions it tries to represent' (Charon 2006, p. 155). Mercedes Kemp asked students to write in genre, to '*create* self' (2001, p. 353).

This chapter provides exemplars of other forms of writing and explores how different prose genres and poetry can be useful in *through-the-mirror* writing. Different forms of writing can take writers by surprise, confronting them with issues forgotten, or previously assumed to be negligible. As Miller illuminates above, and 'I try ... to reintroduce people to the previously unconsidered. It's a passionate, almost religious belief of mine that it is in the negligible that the considerable is to be found' (Miller 2009, p. 12).

Story

Things come out because the story lets them out. (A reflective practice writer)

Unlike poetry, in which from the first word to the last you are placed in a world of extraordinary sensibility and delicacy or dynamism, a novel or a short story is a text in which it is impossible to be intense and creative all the time and to sustain vitality and dynamism in the language. When you tell a story, the moments of intensity must be supported by episodes that are purely informative, that give the reader essential information for understanding what is going on ... [It] is not possible in a novel, as in a poem, to use only intense, rich language. (Llosa 1991, p. 95)

We cannot intrude into another's thinking and feeling, and ethically would not want to. Fiction removes this practical and ethical barrier. Fictional characters have no privacy: they live and act and think and feel with no social cloaks between them and their readers. Writing fiction can be a way of finding out what might go on inside others or what might have happened to them in the past, influencing how they are in the present (see Bev Hargreaves, stories, Chapter 6). Fiction similarly gave Gully (2004) insight into his work with sexually abusive adults. Stories can be performed like plays (Alexander 2005; Holman Jones 2005).

People unwittingly live in genre, just as they think through metaphor. As soon as I suggest different genre to a group, several will set off instantly and unthinkingly towards *romance* or *detective* or *fairy story*: a particular genre will grab each (see the teacher's use of romantic story, Chapter 2). A nurse tried to write a *doctor–nurse romance*, swapping the roles to male nurse and woman doctor. She could not make it work: the genre relies on a power structure of habitual male dominance. We all laughed, but learned a great deal about medical-nursing relations, and the way they are seen by 'the public'.

 Amanda Howe: Strange love

A good-looking patient – that's a change. And smart – so why is he living round here? New patient card – always a frisson of expectation, so easy to impress on first acquaintance by a charming manner and efficient style.

He tells me he's in a hurry – 'got to get to London on business, just needs some antimalarials' as he's off to the Far East tonight. Exotic lifestyle then – and wonderful scent, Opium for Men? His shirt is white, bit creased, touchingly ruffled. Does he smoke? No. Keep fit? Yes. Drink? A smile – eye contact – 'now and again, how about you?'

He's flirting! But I don't mind. Married? No. Lives alone? Mostly. Will he be in Sheffield long? No, 'fraid not, just passing through.

I take a chance and suggest he might like a blood pressure check 'since he's obviously a busy man and probably doesn't get much chance to look after himself'. An excuse really. I see a masculine forearm, and some rather stylish leather braces, but not much flesh. Oh well – this is feeling rather unethical anyway.

He leaves, thanking me, shaking my hand – the firm dry grip of all romantic heroes. After he's gone, I notice the name on the computer. It reads Bond, J: patient I.D. number 11 – 007. (Amanda Howe)

Fantasy, folk tale, fable, myth

> Now that we have no eternal truth we realise that our life is entirely made up of stories … truth is made of stories. So we can rehabilitate myth … myths are the stories people live by, the stories that shape people's perception of life. (Don Cupitt 1991)

Fantasy is currently appropriate. Cultural, professional, political and familial forms all seem to be in flux. Organisations constantly upgrade, update, innovate, modernise, and no one expects to be long in a particular post. No longer can one be GP to the same families, village school teacher teaching children whose parents they also taught, or midwife remembering the mother's birth. Fantasy deals with people not knowing in what dimension they live, what kind of being they will meet, what kind of communication is appropriate. The values of the main characters remain reassuringly constant, as in *Star Trek* strong and moral, or obstructive and wicked; events either turn out very right or very wrong. Enjoying fantasy is part of our relentless attempt to create moral order in a chaotic world. Confronting elements in our everyday world by exploring fantastic ones has been called 'structured fabulation' (Gough 1998). Huxley's *Brave New World* ([1932] 1994), Orwell's *1984* ([1949] 1987), Shelley's *Frankenstein* ([1820] 1994), and Pullman's *His Dark Materials* (1995) are examples of fantasy which both create and critique our own world. A pre-service student teacher clarified his view of his chosen profession by writing a fairy story for his assessment (Berman et al. 2002).

Fairy, folk tales, fables and 'mythical thought always progress from the awareness of oppositions toward their resolution' (Lévi-Strauss 1963, p. 224); they consist of oppositions and contradictions which are mediated and resolved as the story progresses (Bradley Smith 2008). This makes such stories effective, if surprising, vehicles for reflective practice. They traditionally involve character archetypes such as the wicked witch, good godmother, hen-pecked ineffectual husband and father. Like ancient Greek plays, they help us to make sense of perplexing lives and fate. Just as people tend to tell their lives according to a particular genre, so they relate to particular archetypal characters. Are you, or a colleague, wily beautiful Scheherazade, Baba Yaga the witch, Anansi the tricksy spiderman, the boy who knew the king was wearing no clothes and was not afraid to say so, or perhaps 'Mudjekeewis, / ruler of the winds of heaven' (Longfellow 1960, p. 37)?

John Goodwin, higher education tutor for adult learners, uses fiction writing for reflection. His teaching team also undertakes reflective writing sessions to share professional issues. This was written in a half-hour *through-the-mirror* writing session, using folk tale to distance and yet focus the writing: especially useful when staffing had become a tense matter.

 John Goodwin: Pathway

She sat in a small dark room. Scared. Bored. Miserable. Alone. The wood man had left for his day's work in the forest bolting the door firmly behind him. Clunk went the bolt. Clack went the lock.

She waited for the hours to pass. Heavy long hours. Darkness began to fall in the forest. Birds made wing in the thickness. Clack went the lock. Clunk went the bolt. The door of the room was flung open wide. She peered out. No woodman.

'Hello,' she called. No voice answered.

'Anybody there?' she called again.

(Continued)

(Continued)

Still nobody answered. She got to her feet and went timidly to the door. Nothing but blackness. Her foot hesitated by the open door. Dare she step out? He had forbidden her to do so yet forward went her foot and touched pine needles on the cold earth. An owl shrieked.

Earth shrank. Pine needles vanished. There was no forest now only a clear path onward which she began to step slowly along. Cautiously. Nervously. Then there were others walking along the path each like herself stepping nervously and holding themselves back a little. At both sides of the path plans sprang up. Each was in gold writing on rolls of parchment. Each had a big red wax seal on it stamped with a crest of arms.

Then the plans began to speak. Excitedly. Enthusiastically. Happily. They sounded like her. Yet it was a strange and mysterious language. A language she'd never known in all her life. How she wanted the language to go on and on. Never stop. All the others along the path were speaking in the strange new language and now her lips moved too just like the rest.

The pathway was pulling her on. So on she moved. Quicker. Easier. All the others were moving too with the same ease and comfort. The pathway climbed skywards. It twisted and turned and the going was harder. Some fell off and were not seen again.

She had climbed long and hard and when now she looked back at the way she had come all she could see was a mirror. On the mirror was a bold and clear image of herself. Oh how she had changed. There was no way back now to the forest. The lock and bolt were broken beyond repair. (John Goodwin)

Parody

Parody helps us understand (or deride) an everyday matter. Students often write such as: 'Shall I compare thee to a heap of shit? … ', parodying Shakespeare's *Shall I compare thee to a summer's day?* (Sonnet 18). Like fantasy, parody often uses archetypes to which we all relate.

 Susanna Gladwin: Problem-solving

I did once and once only use a form of writing to help me resolve a problem: and it was amazingly effective – so rather surprising perhaps I've never used it since. It used the simple device of taking the A.A. Milne, *Winnie the Pooh* (1928)

format and style, and using his characters – Tigger and Eyeore and so on – as a sort of allegory to represent the various people and their relationships as I saw them in my own psychodrama. The extraordinary thing was, I started writing it in the vein of spleen and hurt and anger, a means of venting my spite against those who had hurt me. But as I went on, I found the very act of writing (and I suppose using that particular model) induced a feeling of generosity in me which spilled over not only in the little story (now lost!) but into the real-life relationships as well.

This actually did have a permanent effect on my working life, because it awoke me to an effect of creative writing I'd only intellectualised about before. I determined to introduce this form of writing into my English Literature students' experience, and from that small beginning a whole undergraduate degree course in writing has now sprung. (Susanna Gladwin)

Writing for children

Writing for or as a child can open up straightforward, lucid understandings and insight 'a child's wise incomprehension for defensiveness and disdain' (Rilke [1934] 1993, p. 46) (See also Chapter 2). Jonathan, a physician, speaks to his *writing self*, a child:

My head is full. Full of stories and poems. Some of them I've written and some of them I've listened to. And we've talked about writing stories and poems. I told my friends about the stories and poems that you've written. I wonder – would you write me some more? And will you read them to me?

And can I read my stories to you? Can we learn together about writing stories and poems? Can we? Can we? (Jonathan Knight)

 Mairi Wilson: Dear Sarah and Jenny

I know you have been puzzled about my job as a doctor for many years, especially because I always tell you, you say, when you tell me about your illnesses, that it will get better on its own. But that's the truth; people come to me all the time with things they perceive as illnesses which are not illnesses at all, or, if they are, will get better on their own. There is very little use of the skills and scientific

(Continued)

(Continued)

knowledge I struggled so hard to get into my brain and regurgitate at the right moment for the examiners. A lot of my work involves creating a pleasant space and place for people to come to when they feel they need help. What we do in there barely matters very often, but making the place welcoming and relaxing goes a long way to helping people feel better, and helping people feel better is the main part of my work.

Nowadays we put everything in terms of illness and disease, and pills or operations to 'cure' people, but they don't cure people really. For the main part, people and problems are much more complex and we really only ever scratch the surface.

I would like not to be embroiled in the machine that is the N.H.S. today. I would like the opportunity to be genuine and honest with people, without having to sell them something which, for the main part, I don't believe in – sometimes I feel like a dodgy car dealer, which is a bit of a funny thought, isn't it?! (Mairi Wilson)

Autobiographical reflective stories

A large proportion of reflective stories are based on direct experience. The term autobiography was invented at the start of the nineteenth century (Cox 1996). Such stories represent writers' viewpoints: a way of exploring and making sense of impressions, understandings and feelings. Memoirs from experienced practitioners can also be invaluable teaching material, as well as insightful reading (Helman 2006). Charon (2006) describes a personal illness narrative exercise: 'Affording students and residents (medical registrars) an opportunity to describe and share their illness experiences may counteract the traditional distancing of physicians' minds from their bodies and lead to more empathic and self-aware practice ... one means toward recognizing, acknowledging, and incorporating the physician's self-story into their clinical practice' (DasGupta and Charon 2004, pp. 351, 355), and 'offer unique subject positions from which to view and critique medicine' (DasGupta 2003, p. 242). Medical training tends to disembody doctors, separating them from patients: a Cartesian split of patients as bodies, doctors as minds (and women are bodies, men minds). Writing personal illness stories helps heal such splits, imaginatively enabling medical students to enter patients' worlds. Here is a senior midwife with long experience reflecting on a strange element of practice, and a psychotherapist reflecting on the influential role of reflective writing for his professional development:

 Mavis Kirkham: the wisdom of nausea

In recent years, I have cared for several women who have had long labours at home with successful outcomes. During these labours, I have inevitably become tired. After a long period with no apparent problems, I had to leave the room because of nausea. On some occasions I actually vomited. After a wash and a walk round the block to clear my head, I returned to the labouring woman. On each occasion she then started to push.

My first reaction to this was the traditional female response of blaming myself. I concluded that I am getting old, tired and possibly past coping well with long labours. I arranged better back-up against my own exhaustion and need to leave women at a crucial time.

Then I heard Susie Orbach give a lecture in which she described physical experiences of counter-transference in her practice as a therapist. This, and subsequent discussion with her, led me to realise that my nausea occurred at the same point in each labour.

My next labour my stomach somehow picked up that the woman was approaching second stage well before I could see or hear any signs. Because I learned this through my stomach, rather than my intellect, I had to leave the room, later returning with fresh energy that was picked up by the tired woman and her tired supporters.

This experience led me to ponder a midwife's ways of gaining knowledge, which are discounted because they do not appear in textbooks and are not congruent with measurable medical knowledge. A colleague told me how she is aware of changes in the smell of women as they progress in labour.

The rhetoric of reflective practice takes place within the accepted sphere of authoritative knowledge. Therefore it does not seem to have had much impact upon what we accept as knowledge or our recognition of patterns in our own experience. As women caring for others, we tend not to see our own feelings as important enough to reflect upon.

Reflecting on bodily knowledge has made me aware of the wisdom of my own perceptions and of the ways in which I can learn that are not intellectual. It has also made me aware that I am trained in ways of knowing that prevent me from acknowledging my own wisdom, which made me initially think I was old and inadequate rather than growing in awareness. (Adapted from Kirkham, 1999, p. 15)

Lane Gerber: we must hear each other's cry

For me the whole 'business' of my writing and the vignettes I use [as a psychotherapist with Southeast Asian refugees] is an attempt to find out what I am thinking/experiencing – which I don't know except as I begin to reflect and to 'talk' in written form about what is moving around inside me. It doesn't take full shape and meaning until I begin the writing process, which creates the meanings out of what has been inside me, unbirthed in thought or language.

I felt very strongly that I didn't want to separate my professional life from my personal life. So my writings about therapy have been about the interaction and wondering about who I am as I am in relationship with the other at the same time I am trying to understand their world.

I began writing letters to friends trying to find my way out of the career morass – really trying to find who I was. And 'writing', such as it was, enabled me to make a bit of sense out of what was inside me that I hadn't been able to do in any other way. Certainly not by talking. And it was the letters and then papers I wrote for grad school in which I found subject matter that counted for the course, but more importantly helped me express my despairs and longings and hopes. For me the writing was discovering something that felt real and true about me at a time when I felt on the verge of losing myself. (Gerber 1996)

Poetry

Maybe all poetry … is a revealing of something that the writer doesn't actually want to say, but desperately needs to communicate, to be delivered of. (Hughes 1995)

Every poem breaks a silence that had to be overcome. (Rich 1995, p. 84)

The inexplicable importance of poetry. (Cocteau [1930] 1968, p. 128)

Each poem is an experiment. The poem carries you beyond where you could have reasonably expected to go. The image I have is from the old cartoons: Donald Duck or Mickey Mouse coming hell for leather to the edge of a cliff, skidding to a stop but unable to halt, and shooting out over the edge. A good poem is the same, it goes that bit further and leaves you walking on air. (Heaney 2008, p. 3)

Some reflective practitioners use poetry for expression. Poetry's conciseness enables it to reach the parts that prose cannot, leaping straight to the heart of the matter. Poetry is an exploration of our deepest and most intimate experiences, thoughts, feelings, ideas and insights: distilled, pared to succinctness, and made music to the ear by lyricism. In order to make its point in as few words as possible, poetry relies on imaginative and insightful image, particularly metaphor and metonymy. For some, it is the only way to explore and express certain things, directly diving for the heart of the issue, with no messing around with sentence structure or grammatical sense: a way of saying exactly what you want to say, and finding out what you need to say (Abse 1998). Ted Hughes felt poetry is a vital form of expression:

> Maybe all poetry, insofar as it moves us and connects with us, is a revealing of something that the writer doesn't actually want to say, but desperately needs to communicate, to be delivered of. Perhaps it's the need to keep it hidden that makes it poetic – makes it poetry. The writer daren't actually put it into words, so it leaks out obliquely, smuggled through analogies [metaphors]. We think we're writing something to amuse, but we're actually saying something we desperately need to share. (Hughes 1995)

Poetry and metaphor can enable the exploration and expression of 'things we don't actually want to say', but 'desperately need to share', because meanings are released slowly and kindly. It can also be a graphic way of describing and explaining something, and gaining clarity for the writer (Perry and Cooper 2001).

Ted Hughes thought poetry should be an uncivilising force (Middlebrook 2003). Poetry strips away cloaking veneers, lays bare thoughts, ideas, feelings, values, dilemmas about identity, and so on, through image, metaphor and other poetic devices. These devices allow insight subtly, graciously and acceptably. Take another look at the poetry of Jo Cannon (Chapter 2), Mark Purvis (Chapter 2), Maggie Eisner (below) and Nigel Gibbons (Chapter 13). Each employs lightness, humour, gentleness, and image to communicate vital messages succinctly, subtly, yet surely.

Sir Philip Sydney was desperate to 'faine in verse my love to show', yet could not find a poem good enough: '"Foole," said my Muse to me, "look in thy heart and write"' (Sydney 1965, p. 165): he had to write it himself. The right words can be used in the right place, and only them; and these right words might be ones no prose writer could possibly put together.

Finding the right words and the right place is not always easy, but once found they offer expressive insight to reader, and clarity of understanding to writer. The poetic mind knows with a different wisdom from the cognitive: 'I like poetry because I can't make it do what I want it to do, it will only do what *it* wants. I didn't want to write that poem: I wanted to write a nice glowing poem about being a mother' (a medical course member).

Poetry often uses image, such as metaphor or simile, to express vital experiences in a few words. Strict form, such as sonnet or villanelle (controlled rhyme, rhythm, syllables or repetition), is often preferred for expression of deepest experiences. Such control seems to contain the otherwise uncontrollable unlimitedness of grief for a friend's death from AIDS (Doty 1996; Hamberger 1995), the work of a busy clinician (Campo 1997), or unrequited love (Shakespeare's sonnets). Yet 'Poetry should be ...

unobtrusive, a thing which enters into one's soul, and does not startle or amaze it with itself, but with its subject … if poetry comes not as naturally as the leaves of a tree it had better not come at all' (Keats 1818).

Poetry-writing, utterly absorbing and rewarding, offering immense surprises, tends to be self-affirming, as well as challenging and demanding. It draws upon deeply held memories, knowledge and values. Initial drafts can be intuitive, intensely absorbing, hypnagogic even, the hand writing without conscious direction: 'That willing suspension of disbelief for the moment, which constitutes poetic faith' (Coleridge [1817] 1992). Winnie-the-Pooh, who could express wisdom with supreme simplicity, said: '"It is the best way to write poetry, letting things come"' (Milne [1928] 1958, p. 268). Wordsworth took this a stage further: 'Poetry is the spontaneous overflow of powerful feelings; it takes its origin from emotion recollected in tranquility; the emotion is contemplated till by a species of reaction the tranquility gradually disappears' ([1802] 1992, p. 82).

Laurel Richardson (1992) 'breached sociological writing expectations by writing sociology as poetry. This breach has had unexpected consequences for my sense of Self'. Her carefully crafted poem was the expression of a research interview. She found it 'one way of decentering the unreflexive "self" … In writing the Other, we can (re)write the Self' (p. 136). Writing about another in poetry, particularly in the first person singular (I) is writing about the self as well as the other (see Chapter 6). Her research poetry-writing was a deeply reflexive experience.

 Angela Mohtashemi: poetry in management consultancy

I write myself to make sense of organisational life and couldn't imagine living without hearing my voice and practising being me. This poem explores the implied contradiction in Targeted Voluntary Severance: selecting people for redundancy with an apparent 'option' to go.

Targeted voluntary severance
We targeted them. Singled them out
Because they were old or simple
Didn't have the required milk
Dried up cash cows.
We asked them. It was voluntary.
When they wondered what would happen if …
We talked of subtle pressures. And no cash.
Best go now we said.
They were severed. We couldn't wait
To get them out. Gave them boxes
To collect their bits. Stains on the carpet

Affect morale.
And now they are gone.
Those who remain
Speak in whispers. (Angela Mohtashemi)

Sarah Gull, medical course supervisor, wields expressive haiku:

A Japanese lyric form of 17 syllables in lines of 5, 7 and 5 syllables (Drabble 2000), has a formal structure providing support in framing ideas. Could it be that the structure within a medical course: timetables, deadlines, examinations and so forth, are of neglected value in supporting students to think for themselves?

Educational
Objectives officially
Prescribed, dull the mind.

Could learning be an
Exploration of the world
Without set limits?

Yet ways of learning
Should enable the student
To adapt to Change. (Sarah Gull)

Janina Chowaniec explores similar themes in verse:

In research and in teaching
we are now supposed
to anticipate outcomes
that are easily measured.
The culture of audit
has fully espoused
the commodification
of academic endeavour.
These changes in climate
have led to confusion

fragmented identity
general distress,
for now we are living
the widespread illusion
that only such changes
will lead to progress ...

My years in full-time research were spent continually extending my knowledge and skills in adaptation to changes in the direction of science funding and prevailing paradigms ... But at its worst (and most intensive), it becomes a form of prostitution – of our subjects and ourselves, and is relentless, exhausting and futile. Now, the whole of HE is expected to commodify itself, driven by external pressures. (Chowaniec 2005, pp. 267, 269)

The following three examples of poetry are accompanied by explanations by their writers on how the poems came to be written and how useful they are to their writers.

 Poetry writing to help face fear

Working in the Spinal Unit how could I not be affected by the young men who were so suddenly traumatised by accident? How frightening the idea of the consequences of these terrible accidents: to me and mine? For months I wrote notes, typed up scribed poems, but I could not write from my own centre, I felt myself utterly gagged – helpless – paralysed ...

Then someone started talking about the way a paralysed body hears sound differently. I was intrigued and that night, after the notes I started to write. The poem came very quickly and received very little editing, for me, a mending, separating out. It held the awe and the anger that had dumbed me for months. And of course – it was about facing fear.

> ...
> What is a body when it discovers itself as a drum
> the world tuned to a new acoustic, centred in new space
> What is a body that echoes, resonates, re-locates –
> makes stereophonic initiation: a seedling sense pushing
> out from breakage and decay. Raw at first, in discord
> noise scrapes harsh, vibrates fire along the unknown tension
> of a timbrel-skin inside the self and sometimes dins
> tinnitus ringing through the lymph and blood as if
> all arbitrary sound came now with a collected purpose:
> to beat into the body, to strike *this this this* primal note –
> insistent, purposeful, stridently, determinedly alive
> What is the body beyond its sack and pieces, beyond its secret, aching
> diffusion, its inchoate random knowledge? (Rose Flint)

 Maggie Eisner's villanelle

On a muggy Saturday afternoon after a busy week at the Health Centre, I sat down with two hours to do my homework for the next day's meeting of the Reflective Writing Group. It's one of my very favourite things – I wonder why I always leave the writing till the last minute. I felt exhausted, uncreative and devoid of ideas. Six minutes *free writing*, recommended as a kind of warm-up, produced a long moan about how tired I was. Then I remembered reading how to write a *villanelle*:

> I'm spending too much time on work, I know,
> The pressure's putting lines upon my face.
> I'd like to sit and watch the flowers grow.
>
> Sometimes I feel the tears begin to flow:
> I'm leaden tired, I'm desperate for some space,
> I'm spending too much time on work. I know!
>
> Do they want blood? Why don't they bloody go?
> I'll crack if I continue at this pace.
> I need to sit and watch the flowers grow.
>
> Those piles of paperwork oppress me so,
> They never seem to shrink, it's a disgrace.
> I'm spending too much time on work, I know.
>
> If I could take my time and take it slow,
> If life could be a pleasure, not a race,
> Perhaps I'd sit and watch the flowers grow.
>
> If I got bored, there's places I could go,
> I'd stretch my limbs, write poetry, find grace.
> Must get to spend less time on work – although
> I might do more than just watch flowers grow.

When I'd finished it, I felt rejuvenated and alive. It's always good to express my feelings in writing, but I was surprised to feel so dramatically better. Possibly the villanelle, or the challenge of writing in a tight poetic form, had a specific chemical effect on my brain (maybe serotonin reuptake inhibition like Prozac, or dopamine release like cocaine). (Eisner 2000, p. 56)

Robert Hamberger: at the Centre (for Kettering MIND)

When we all went on holiday they put a photo in the paper. My husband was embarrassed. He said you with all those mental people. I said I'm not ashamed. I've had a breakdown and that's me. Like it or lump it. People think you should hide coming here.

(Continued)

(Continued)

> celebrate the woman
> scabbing her skin with a matchbox edge
> to make her husband listen
> celebrate the man
> who cracks jokes at the kettle
> on bad days

Anyone can get depressed. I can, you can. They want me to have injections. I'm all right without it. If you go in the sun you've got to cover your arms. Who needs that?

> they build their papier-mâché time
> carefully
> shred by shred
> so it won't unglue again

This isn't me. I had a job. I had a laugh. Look at my hands now. Mornings are worse. I take another tablet, go back to bed. I want to wake up and be like I was.

> at the centre
> you can tell your life
> to whoever sits beside you
> you can touch the shaking woman
> say I've been there
> and I know you will be well.

At the Centre was written towards the end of my first placement, when I was qualifying. I think writing it helped me to achieve two things simultaneously: to attempt to make sense of meeting a large, varied group of so-called 'mentally ill' people for the first time, and to – as some lines say – *celebrate the woman ... celebrate the man*. The dedication to Kettering MIND was also important, because I was bowled over by the positive, supportive work they do. I hope that reading the poem feels like meeting a group of new people collaring you, the reader. If it does, that mimics the experience that led to writing it.

A recognition I channelled into writing the poem was that the people I met felt a compelling need to tell their stories: this is my life, my perspective, my experience of the mental illness I'm currently going through. The busy Day Centre was full of voices – sometimes competing against each other and arguing, but usually sharing a joke, a laugh, and literally supporting each other by their presence. I suppose the poem attempts to give both voice and shape to those voices. The prose sections are simply transcriptions of statements made to me.

The last stanza concerns a creative writing workshop I held at the centre. Two seriously ill women attended regularly. We would all read out the work we'd produced at the end of each session. After Christine read hers, she was shaking and saying that she felt she would never get better. Gillian, who sat beside her, and whose mental illness was as serious and long-standing, calmly said what became the last lines of the poem.

This generous and supportive statement was not only moving, it seemed to sum up the ethos of MIND – of mentally ill people helping each other to attempt to become well again – so forcefully that it stayed with me. It reverberated and I couldn't let go of it. During the placement all these statements dropped into my ear and fizzed inside my head, showing me glimpses of other lives and perspectives, trying to tell me something I didn't know before. Writing them down towards the end of the placement got them out of my head and gave them shape. By setting them on paper, I could let them go. (Robert Hamberger)

Reflections in water

Linda, despite being partially sighted, drew my attention to a bridge over Durham's river, which her husband had described: I saw a powerful metaphor for reflective practice.

Bridges
Her hand on my arm
so I can be eyes for us both
on the stony path by the river,
she stops, look at the arch
of the old bridge and its reflection.
I can't see it, but can you?

The reflection wavers as a duck passes;
stone arch, and reflected arch together
make a perfect circle.

We've written together, shared pools
of deep thought, mirroring our lives
yet different: the one reflecting the other
touching, feeling, tasting, listening,
seeing beyond sight. (Gillie Bolton)

Completing the circle
A season ago we shared
A moment that captured our lives
Meeting, crossing and leaving;

The circle so perfect in stone and water
Would soon break
We parted on another bridge
Returning home, to live separate lives.
Even when the reflection is not visible, in shade or dark
The possibility of rejoining the circle is ever present
And vision is more than sight.
As our sharing of thoughts, ideas, experiences and feeling
Continues. (Linda Garbutt)

 Read to learn

Alexander, B.K. (2005) Performance ethnography: the reenacting and inciting of culture, in N.K. Denzin and Y.S. Lincoln (eds), *The Sage Handbook of Qualitative Research*. 3rd edn. Thousand Oaks, CA: Sage.

Gabriel, Y. (1991) On organisational stories and myths: why it is easier to slay a dragon than to kill a myth, *International Sociology*, **6**, 427–42.

Holman Jones, S. (2005) Making the personal political, in N.K. Denzin and Y.S. Lincoln (eds), *The Sage Handbook of Qualitative Research*. 3rd edn. Thousand Oaks, CA: Sage.

 Write to learn

Each chapter ends with *Write to learn*. For straightforward advice, sufficient for the exercises below, see *Write to learn* in Chapter 1, and see Chapter 6 for more advice. Each writing can be shared fruitfully with a group or confidential trusted other, if this seems appropriate once the writer has read and reflected on it first.

Exercise 14.1   Journalism

1. Do a *six-minute write* (see Chapter 6).
2. Write an article for *Journal of Shamanic Practice* explaining and describing your profession, its very heart or essence, and what it means to you.
3. Reread all you have written including the *six minutes*, add or alter as you wish.

Exercise 14.2   A senses poem

1. Do a *six-minute write* (see Chapter 6).
2. Write a line for each of these:

    (a)   something you saw which struck you yesterday
    (b)   a memory of a smell from a long time ago
    (c)   a sound from yesterday
    (d)   a taste for tomorrow
    (e)   a touch last week
    (f)   a feeling about the future.

3. Write more about one or more of these, to develop the poem.
4. Read and reflect.
5. If this is done in a group, they can be read to the whole group with no comment. If the group is very large, each person to read only one line. This can feel like a group poem.

Exercise 14.3   Who are you? What is your work?

1. Do a *six-minute write*.
2. Think of a well-known story you've loved and has been significant to you (Cinderella; Pride and Prejudice; Sherlock Holmes; Jeeves).
3. Rewrite it, setting it in your work.
4. What is different between the story and your work? What similar?
5. Who is 'you' in this story (Elizabeth Bennet/Mr Darcy or Charlotte Lucas/Mr Bennet?)
6. Are you this character consistently, or sometimes Cinderella and sometimes Buttons?
7. How do your colleagues fit into the other character roles?
8. Reread, reflecting on what insight this brings, what you feel about the ending, and any ways you might alter any of it.
9. Alternatively write a new story, set in your work, beginning *Once upon a time ...*

CHAPTER 15

REFLECTION ON REFLECTION

Chapter 15 concludes *Reflective Practice* with a firm promise that the *through-the-mirror* approach can enable critically reflexive development. Practitioners can be enabled to let go and rewrite assumptions, taken for granteds, ossified notions of themselves, and take greater responsibility for actions, thoughts and feelings, even ones of which they were previously unaware. Going *through-the-mirror*, rather than staring at the self reflected back to front in the glass, really can effect significant change and development.

> Courses like this might help you get out of the profession what you said you wanted from it in the beginning. (A practitioner, in Bradley Smith 2008, p. 462)

> Life never does more than imitate the book, and the book itself is only a tissue of signs, an imitation that is lost, infinitely deferred. (Barthes 1977, p. 147)

> 'Would you tell me, please, which way I ought to go from here?'
> 'That depends a good deal on where you want to get to,' said the Cheshire Cat.
> 'I don't much care where – ' said Alice.
> 'Then it doesn't matter which way you go,' said the Cat.
> 'So long as I get *somewhere*,' Alice added as an explanation.
> 'Oh, you're sure to do that,' said the Cat, 'if you only walk long enough.' (Carroll [1865] 1954, p. 54)

Reflective Practice began with the oxymoron of *certain uncertainty* which is at the heart of reflective practice. The only way to get anywhere in reflective practice is to do it, trusting the journey will be interesting and useful, having faith in and respect for yourself and your abilities to reflect as well as to practice, and generosity and positive regard for fellow travellers like clients and colleagues. Openness to not knowing when elements previously assumed to be true or essential are proved worthless, unnecessary or faulty is the only appropriate attitude: as Barthes (1977) pointed out, even the meaning of language slips about offering no safe hold in an unsafe world.

You will not know your destination, and never reach a definitive *somewhere* anyway, just as Alice got to the Mad Hatters' Tea Party – an illuminating experience – but had to move on again. She later met the Mock Turtle who helped her realise that the most productive journeys are undertaken without set purpose ('porpoise': Carroll [1865] 1954, p. 88) (see also Aristotle 1953). Writers might make surprising discoveries, quite possibly from insignificant, rather than critical, incidents.

Setting out into reflective practice with an open questioning mind, rather than previously determined goals, can lead to fresh dynamic territory, which at the same time is 'to arrive where we started/And to know the place for the first time' (Eliot [1936] 1974, p. 222). Reflective practice does not travel distances: it makes a great deal more sense of where we are. On the journey we come across what seem to be stumbling blocks. An oriental saying states: 'the boulder in your path *IS* your path'. *Through-the-mirror* methods turn stumbling blocks into stepping stones, albeit awkward slippery-seeming ones.

Returning to the place where you started everything seems 'as different as possible', although superficially the same, because you have gained such a width of perspective and knowledge of responsibility. This change has happened partly because the critical process has enabled you to find your own authoritative voice. You will know you have the power to change things, for example. Not massive things perhaps, but you now perhaps perceive you previously unwittingly acted to reinforce situations which silenced or ignored the voices of diverse people. Or you accepted that decisions could be value-neutral based on principles only of profitable efficiency, ignoring the human aspects of individuals because they are viewed as costs, effects and benefits (Cunliffe 2009b; MacIntyre 1985). You may be the leader of many, or of extremely few: whichever it is, you have learned that leadership is an ethical act (Pellicer 2008). Our work as practitioners puts moral requirements upon us. Or if you are a student, beginning on the adventure of your career, you will now know that although you might have perceived yourself as powerless, no one is powerless unless they *choose* to be. All your actions and utterances are your responsibility. Your life, your work are precious, you have the authority to use them ethically and wisely. Through reflective writing Susan Bradley Smith's Australian professional students (2008) found they rediscovered the profession they had hoped to enter at the beginning of their careers.

This enquiry needs a *thoughtfully unthinking* approach, similar to the way footballers are taught, or Eeyore begged Piglet: 'I think – ' began Piglet nervously. 'Don't,' said Eeyore' (Milne [1928] 1958, pp. 240–1). Reflective practice can be hindered by too much self-consciousness and self-awareness.

Letting go of hard and fast notions of myself, assumptions, taken for granteds, allows responsibility for a greater range of actions, thoughts and feelings, even those I was previously unaware of. We live in a culture where anything is considered to be somebody's fault: somebody has to pay; someone has the duty to sort me out: doctor, police officer, priest, therapist, counsellor, lawyer. Conniving in this means I do not take responsibility for myself. Who is my self anyway? I am no longer surrounded by a consistent nexus of family, neighbours, priest, the same boss and employees: these figures unreliably shift and change. I can change my body with plastic surgery or drugs, and invent different persona with bell-bottoms, mini-skirt, cheongsam or sari.

An outward consistent sense of self cannot be relied upon. Instead I invent myself anew all the time by telling and writing stories about myself: to make some kind of sense. And I locate and shift this growing self alongside others: through discussion and hearing their stories, and in the wider world through reading and discussing as many relevant texts as I can. '"I" doesn't exist, one constructs oneself' (Simone de Beauvoir, quoted in Guppy 2000). 'The unfinishedness of the human person [in] a permanent process of searching' (Freire 1998, p. 21). And 'The illiterate of the 21st century will not be those who cannot read and write, but those who cannot learn, unlearn, and relearn.' (Alvin Toffler, quoted Osterman and Kottkamp 2004, p. 51). Perhaps *me* is not a noun, but a verb, a process: *to me*, rather like the word *being*.

This can only be undertaken by the whole practitioner in a holistic aesthetic creative process, not flinching from the range of human experience, as Warner describes in this passage:

> The states of mind or feelings that art can excite have been helpfully distinguished in Sanscrit aesthetics, where they are called *rasas*, from a word meaning 'juice' or 'essence'. A fully achieved work of art should flow with all nine of them: their names might be transposed in English as wonder, joy, sexual pleasure, pity, anguish, anger, terror, disgust and laughter. (1998, p. 7)

Reflective practice does not offer solutions to final solutions, but enlightening provisional answers. If solutions are sought, and seemingly found, they will prove hollow, just as the *meaning of life* being *42* is meaningless (Adams [1984] 1995).

The Ekoi people of Nigeria (Gersie 1992), have a tradition of *story children* from long ago. Each story has to be told and heard for both *child* and hearers to be nourished and run free. Once heard and known, however, the wisdom in each story can never be unheard or unknown: therein lies its power. Listening to and telling such stories changes teller and listener irreversibly. Life changes us, pulling and pushing, as Adams points out here. Reflective practice can enable us to be authorities over our own lives, over 'the continual wrenching of experience':

> They were not the same eyes with which he had last looked out at this particular scene, and the brain which interpreted the images the eyes resolved was not the same brain. There had been no surgery involved, just the continual wrenching of experience. (Adams [1984] 1995, p. 493)

BIBLIOGRAPHY

Abbs, P. (1974) *Autobiography in Education*. London: Heinemann Educational.

Abell, S.K., Bryan, L.A. and Anderson, M. (1998) Investigating preservice elementary science teacher reflective thinking using integrated media case-based instruction in elementary science teacher preparation', *Science Teacher Education*, **82**(4): 491–510.

Abercrombie, M.L.J. (1993) *The Human Nature of Learning: Selections From the Work of M.L.J. Abercrombie*: J. Nias (ed.). Buckingham: Open University Press.

Abse, D. (1998) More than a green placebo, *The Lancet*, **351**, 362–4.

Adams, D. ([1984] 1995) So long and thanks for all the fish, in D. Adams, *A Hitch Hiker's Guide to the Galaxy: A Trilogy in Five Parts*. London: Heinemann.

Adams St. Pierre, E. (with Richardson, L.) (2005) Writing: a method of inquiry, in N. Denzin and Y. Lincoln (eds), *Handbook of Qualitative Research*. 3rd edn. London: Sage. pp. 923–47.

Aeschylus (1999) *The Oresteia*. Trans. T. Hughes. London: Faber & Faber.

Alighieri, Dante (1985) *Dante's Inferno*. Trans. T. Philips. New York: Thames & Hudson.

Alexander, B.K. (2005) Performance ethnography: the reenacting and inciting of culture, in N.K. Denzin, and Y.S. Lincoln (eds), *The Sage Handbook of Qualitative Research. 3rd edn.* Thousand Oaks, CA: Sage Publications.

Allan, J., Fairtlough, G. and Heinzen, B. (2002) *The Power of the Tale: Using Narratives for Organisational Success*. Chichester: Wiley & Sons.

Allende, I. (2000) The Guardian profile, interview by M. Jaggi. *Guardian*, 5 February, 6–7.

Anderson, C.M. and MacCurdy, M.M. (2000) *Writing and Healing: Toward an Informed Practice*. Urbana, IL: The National Council of Teachers of English.

Argyris, C. (1991) Teaching smart people how to learn, *Harvard Business Review*, **63**(3), 99–109.

Aristotle (1953) *The Nichomachean Ethics*. Trans. J.A.K. Thomson. Harmondsworth: Penguin.

Aristotle (1995) *Poetics*. S. Halliwell (ed.). 1457 b 6–9, p. 105. Cambridge, MA: Harvard University Press.

Atkins, K. and Murphy, K. (1994) Reflective practice, *Nursing Standard*, **8**(39), 49–56.

Attard, K. (2008) Uncertainty for the reflective practitioner: a blessing in disguise, *Reflective Practice*, **9**(3), 307–17.

Babcock, M.J. (2007) Learning logs in introductory literature courses, *Teaching in Higher Education*, **12**(4), 513–23.

Baernstein, A. and Fryer-Edwards, K. (2003) Promoting reflection on professionalism: a comparison trial of educational interventions for medical students, *Academic Medicine*, **78**(7), 742–7.

Barker, P. (1991) *Regeneration*. London: Penguin.

Barry, C.A., Britten, N., Barber, N., Bradley, C. and Stevenson, F. (1999) Using reflexivity to optimise teamwork in qualitative research, *Qualitative Health Research*, **9**(1), 26–44.

Barthes, R. (1977) *Image, Music, Text*. London: Fontana/Collins.

Barthes R. (1987) *Criticism and Truth*. Trans. and ed. K.P. Keuneman. Minneapoli, MN: University of Minnesota Press

Bauby, J.D. (1998) *The Diving Bell and the Butterfly*. London: Fourth Estate.

Bauer, L., Duffy, J., Fountain, E., Halling, S., Holzer, M., Jones, E., Leifer, M. and Rowe, J. (1992) Exploring self-forgiveness, *Journal of Religion and Health*, **31**(2), 149–59.

Belenky, M.F., Clinchy McVicar, B., Goldberg, N.R. and Tarule, J.M. (1997) *Women's Ways of Knowing: the Development of Self, Voice and Mind*. New York: Basic Books.

Bennett-Levy, J., Lee, N., Travers, K., Pohlman, S. and Hamernik, E. (2003) Cognitive therapy from the inside: enhancing therapist skills through practising what we preach, *Behavioural and Cognitive Psychotherapy*, **31**, 143–58.

Bennett-Levy, J., Turner, F., Beaty, T., Smith, M., Paterson, B. and Farmer, S. (2001) The value of self–practice of cognitive therapy techniques and selfreflection in the training of cognitive therapists, *Behavioural and Cognitive Psychotherapy*, **29**, 203–20.

Beowulf and Grendel (1973) Trans. M. Alexander. London: Penguin.

Best, D. (1996) On the experience of keeping a therapeutic journal while training. *Therapeutic Communities*, **17**(4), 293–301.

Bettelheim, B. (1976) *The Uses of Enchantment*. London: Penguin.

Beveridge, I. (1997) Teaching your students to think reflectively: the case for reflective journals. *Teaching in Higher Education*, **2**(1), 33–43.

Blake, W. (1958) *Songs of Innocence* (The Divine Image). A. Lincoln (ed.). Harmondsworth: Penguin.

Bleakley, A. (1999) From reflective practice to holistic reflexivity, *Studies in Higher Education*, **24**(3), 215–330.

Bleakley, A. (2000a) Adrift without a lifebelt: reflective self-assessment in a postmodern age, *Teaching in Higher Education*, **5**(4), 405–18.

Bleakley, A. (2000b) Writing with invisible ink: narrative, confessionalism and reflective practice, *Reflective Practice*, **1**(1), 11–24.

Bleakley, A. (2002) Pre-registration house officers and ward-based learning: a 'new apprenticeship' model, *Medical Education*, **36**(1), 9–15.

Bleakley, A. (2005) Stories as data, data as stories: making sense of narrative analysis in clinical education. *Medical Education*, **39**(5), 534–40.

Blodgett, H. (1991) *Capacious Holdall: An Anthology of Englishwomen's Diary Writings*. Richmond, VA: University Press of Virginia.

Bloom, B. et al. (eds) (1956) *Taxonomy of Educational Objectives: The Classification of Educational Goals: Handbook I: The Cognitive Domain*. New York: Longman.

Boggs, J.G., Mickel, A.E. and Holtorn, B.C. (2007) Experiential learning through interactive drama: an alternative to student role plays, *Journal of Management Education*, **31**(6), 832–58.

Bolton, G. (1994) Stories at work, fictional-critical writing as a means of professional development, *British Educational Research Journal*, **20**(1), 55–68.

Bolton, G. (1999a) *Writing Myself: The Therapeutic Potential of Creative Writing*. London: Jessica Kingsley.

Bolton, G. (1999c) Reflections through the looking glass: the story of a course of writing as a reflexive practitioner, *Teaching in Higher Education*, **4**(2), 193–212.

Bolton, G. (2003b) Riverside Community Health Project: experiences told by workers, in J. Kai and C. Drinkwater (eds), *Primary Care in Urban Disadvantaged Communities*. Oxford: Radcliffe Press.

Bolton, G. (2008) Boundaries of humanity: writing medical humanities, *Arts and Humanities in Higher Education*, **7**(2), 147–65.

Bolton, G. (2009) 'Writing Values: reflective writing for professional development', *The Lancet*, **373**, pp. 20–1.

Bolton, G., Howlett, S., Lago, C. and Wright, J. (2004) *Writing Cures: An Introductory Handbook of Writing in Counselling and Psychotherapy*. London: Brunner-Routledge.

Booker, C. (2004) *The Seven Basic Plots: Why We Tell Stories*. London: Continuum.

Borkan, J., Reis, S., Steinmetz, D. and Medalie, J. (1999) *Patients and Doctors: Life Changing Stories from Primary Care*. Madison, WI: University of Wisconsin Press.

Boud, D. (1998) Use and misuse of reflection and reflective practice, paper presented at seminar at Sheffield University, February.

Boud, D. (2001) Using journal writing to enhance reflective practice, in L.M. English and M.A. Gillen (eds), *Promoting Journal Writing in Adult Education*. San Francisco, CA: Jossey-Bass. pp. 9–18.

Boud, D. and Walker, D. (1998) Promoting reflection in professional courses: the challenge of context, *Studies in Higher Education*, **23**(2), 191–206.

Boud, D., Keogh, R. and Walker, D. (1985) *Reflection: Turning Experience into Learning*. London: Kogan Page.

Boyer, N.R., Maher, P.A. and Kirkman, S. (2006) Transformative learning in online settings: the use of self-direction, metacognition, and collaborative learning, *Journal of Transformative Education*, **4**(4), 335–61.

Bradley Smith, S. (2008) This sylvan game: creative writing and GP wellbeing, *Australian Family Physician*, **37**(6), 461–2.

Brimacombe, M. (1996) The emotional release of writing, *GP*, 13 December.

Brockbank, A. and McGill, I. (1998) *Facilitating Reflective Learning in Higher Education*. Buckingham: Open University Press.

Brockbank, A. and McGill, I. (2004) *The Action Learning Handbook*. London: Routledge Falmer.

Brody, H. (2003) *Stories of Sickness*. 2nd edn. Oxford: Oxford University Press.

Brookfield, S. (1990) *The Skilful Teacher: On Technique, Trust and Responsiveness in the Classroom*. San Francisco, CA: Jossey-Bass.

Brookfield, S.D. (1995) *Becoming a Critically Reflective Teacher*. San Franscisco, CA: Jossey-Bass.

Bruner, J. (2002) *Making Stories: Law, Literature, Life*. Cambridge, MA: Harvard University Press.

Bryan, C. and Clegg, K. (eds) (2006) *Innovative assessment in higher education*. Oxford: Routledge.

Bullough, R.V. (1991) Exploring personal teachers' metaphors in pre-service teacher education, *Journal of Teacher Education*, **42**(1), 43–52.

Bulman, C. and Schutz, S. (2008) *Reflective Practice in Nursing*. 4th edn. Oxford: Blackwell.

Bulpitt, H. and Martin, P.J. (2005) Learning about reflection from the student, *Active Learning in Higher Education*, **6**(3), 207–17.

Burney, F. (1898) *Evelina, or the History of a Young Lady's Entrance into the World*. London: George Bell & Sons.

Burns, T. and Sinfield, S. (2004) *Teaching, Learning and Study Skills: A Guide for Tutors*. London: Sage.

Byatt, A. (2004) Happy ever after, *The Guardian Review*, 3 January, pp. 4–6.

Cameron, J. (2002) *The Writers' Way: a Spiritual Path to Creativity*. New York: Penguin Putnam.

Campo, R. (1997) *The Desire to Heal: A Doctor's Education in Empathy, Identity, and Poetry*. New York: Norton.

Cancienne, M.B. and Snowber, C.N. (2003) Writing rhythm: movement as method, *Qualitative Inquiry*, **9**(2), 237–53.

Carr, W. (1995) *For Education: Towards Critical Education Enquiry*. Buckingham: Open University Press.

Carr, W. and Kemmis, S. (1986) *Becoming Critical: Education, Knowledge and Action Research*. Lewes: Falmer.

Carroll, L. ([1865] 1954) *Alice's Adventures in Wonderland*. London: Dent & Sons.

Carson, L. and Fisher, K. (2006) Raising the bar on criticality: students' critical reflection in an internship program, *Journal of Management Education*, **30**(5), 700–23

Carson, R. (1994) Teaching ethics in the context of the medical humanities, *Journal of Medical Ethics*, **20**, 235–8.

Cartwright, T. (2004) *Developing your Intuition: a Guide to Reflective Practice*. Greensboro, NC: Centre for Creative Leadership.

Casement, P. (1985) *On Learning from the Patient*. London, Tavistock

Casement, P. (1990) *Further Learning from the Patient*. London: Routledge.

Cavallaro-Johnson, G. (2004) Reconceptualising the visual in narrative inquiry into teaching, *Teaching and Teacher Education*, **20**, 423–34.

Chambers, P., Odeggard, E.E. and Rinaldi, E. (2007) Risk-taking and reflective learning, *Reflective Practice*, **8**(2), 163–76.

Charmaz, K. and Mitchell, R.G. (1997) The myth of silent authorship: self, substance and style in ethnographic writing, in R. Hertz (ed.), *Reflexivity and Voice*. London: Sage.

Charon, R. (2000a) Medicine, the novel and the passage of time, *Annals of Internal Medicine*, **132**(1), 63–8.

Charon, R. (2000b) Literature and medicine: origins and destinies, *Academic Medicine*, **75**, 23–7.

Charon, R. (2000c) Informed consent: the imperative and the therapeutic dividend of showing patients what we write about them, paper presented at the Narrative Matters: Personal Stories and the Making of Health Policy Conference, Airlie, Virginia, March.

Charon, R. (2004) Narrative and medicine, *New England Journal of Medicine*, **350**(9), 862–4.

Charon, R. (2006) *Narrative Medicine: Honouring the Stories of Sickness*. New York: Oxford University Press.

Charon, R. and Montello, M. (2002) *Stories Matter: The Role of Narrative in Medical Ethics*. New York: Routledge.

Cherry, D. and Spiegel, J. (2006) *Leadership, Myth and Metaphor*. Thousand Oaks, CA: Corwin Press (Sage).

Chirema, K.D. (2007) The use of reflective journals in the promotion of reflection and learning in post-registration nursing students, *Nurse Education Today*, **27**, 192–202.

Chowaniec, J. (2005) Exploring identity, *Teaching in Higher Education*, **10**(2), 265–70.

Chuang Tsu (1974) *Inner Chapters*. Trans. Gia-Fu Feng and J. English. London: Wildwood House.

Cixous, H. (1991) *Coming to Writing and other Essays*. D. Jenson (ed.). Cambridge, MA: Harvard University Press.

Cixous, H. (1995) Castration or decapitation? in S. Burke (ed.), *Authorship from Plato to the Postmodernists: A Reader*. Edinburgh: University of Edinburgh Press. pp. 162–77.

Clandinin, D.J. and Connelly, F.M. (1990) Narrative experience and the study of curriculum, *Cambridge Journal of Education*, **20**(3), 25–37.

Clandinin, D.J. and Connelly, F.M. (1994) Personal experience methods, in N.K. Denzin and Y. Lincoln (eds), *Handbook of Qualitative Research*. London: Sage.

Clandinin, D.J., Davies, A., Hogan, P. and Kennard, B. (1992) *Learning to Teach: Teaching to Learn: Stories of Collaboration in Teacher Education*. New York: Teachers College Press.

Clark, P.G. (2002) Values and voices in teaching gerontology and geriatrics: case studies as stories, *The Gerontologist*, **42**, 297–303.

Clark, R. and Ivanič, R. (1997) *The Politics of Writing*. London: Routledge.

Clark/Keefe, K. (2007) On a personal note: practical pedagogical activities to foster the development of 'reflective practitioners', *American Journal of Evaluation*, **28**(3), 334–47.

Clarke, A. (1998) Born of incidents but thematic in nature, *Canadian Journal of Education*, **23**(1), 47–62.

Clegg, S., Tan J. and Saeideh, S. (2002) Reflecting or acting? Reflective practice and continuing professional development in HE, *Reflective Practice*, **3**(1), 131–46.

Clifford, J. (1986) Introduction: partial truths, and on ethnographic allegory, in J. Clifford and G.E. Marcus (eds), *Writing Culture: The Poetics and Politics of Ethnography*. Berkeley, CA: University of California Press. pp. 1–26 and 98–121.

Clough, P. (1996) 'Again fathers and sons': the mutual construction of self, story and special educational needs. *Disability and Society*, **11**(1), 71–81.

Clough, P. (2002) *Narratives and Fictions in Educational Research*. Buckingham: Open University Press.

Clutterbuck, D. (1998) *Learning Alliances*. London: Institute of Personnel and Development.

Clutterbuck, D. and Megginson, D. (1999) *Mentoring Executives and Directors*. Oxford: Butterworth-Heinemann.

Cocteau, J. ([1930] 1968) *Opium: The Diary of a Cure*. London: Peter Owen.

Coleridge, S.T. ([1798] 1969) *Poetical Works* (The Rime of the Ancient Mariner) Oxford: Oxford University Press.

Coleridge, S.T. ([1834] 1978) *The Rime of the Ancient Mariner*. New York: Harper & Brothers.

Coleridge, S.T. ([1817] 1992) *Biographia Literaria*. London: Dent.

Connolly, D.M. and Clandinin, D.J. (2000) Teacher education: a question of teacher knowledge, in J. Freeman-Moir and A. Scott (eds), *Tomorrow's Teachers: International and Critical Perspectives on Teacher Education*. Christchurch, NZ: Canterbury University Press and Christchurch College of Education. pp. 89–105.

Cook-Sather (2008) 'What you get is looking in the mirror, only better': inviting students to reflect on college teaching, *Reflective Practice*, **9**(4), 473–83.

Cooper, A. and Lousada, J. (2005) *Borderline Welfare: Feeling and Fear of Feeling in Modern Welfare*. London: Karnac.

Copeland, W.D., Birmingham, C., La Cruz, E. and Lewin, B. (1993) The reflective practitioner in teaching: toward a research agenda, *Teaching and Teacher Education*, **9**(4), 347–59.

Cowan, J. and Westwood, J. (2006) Collaborative and reflective professional development: a pilot, *Active Learning in Higher Education*, **7**(1) 63–71.

Cox, A. (1996) Writing the self, in J. Singleton and M. Luckhurst (eds), *The Creative Writing Handbook*. London: Macmillan.

Crème, P. (2005) Should student learning journals be assessed? *Arts and Humanities in Higher Education*, **30**(3), 287–96.

Crème, P. (2008) Student learning journals as transitional writing: a space for academic play, *Arts and Humanities in Higher Education*, **7**(1), 49–64.

Crème, P. and Hunt, C. (2002) Creative participation in the essay writing process, *Arts and Humanities in Higher Education*, **1**(2), 145–66.

Cunliffe, A. (2008) *Organisational Theory*. London: Sage

Cunliffe, A.L. (2002) Reflexive dialogical practice in management learning, *Management Learning*, **33**(1), 35–61.

Cunliffe, A.L. (2004) On becoming a critically reflexive practitioner, *Journal of Management Education*, **28**(4), 407–26.

Cunliffe, A.L. (2009a) Reflexivity, learning and reflexive practice, in S. Armstrong and C. Fukami (eds), *Handbook in Management Learning, Education and Development*. London: Sage.

Cunliffe, A.L. (2009b) The philosopher leader: on relationism, ethics and reflexivity – a critical perspective to teaching leadership, *Management Learning*, **40**(1), 87–101.

Cupitt, D. (1991) Interviewed by Neville Glasgow, BBC Radio 4, 8 September.

Cutcliffe, J.R., Epling, M., Cassedy, P., McGregor, J., Plant, N. and Butterworth, T. (1998) Ethical dilemmas in clinical supervision, *British Journal of Nursing*, **7**(15), 920–3.

Daloz, L. (1999) *Guiding the Journey of Adult Learners*. 2nd edn. San Francisco, CA: Jossey-Bass.

DasGupta, S. (2003) Reading bodies, writing bodies: self-reflection and cultural criticism in a narrative medicine curriculum, *Literature and Medicine*, **22**(2), 241–56.

DasGupta, S. and Charon, R. (2004) Personal illness narratives: using reflective writing to teach empathy, *Academic Medicine*, **79**(4), 351–6.

Davidson, B. (1999) Writing as a tool of reflective practice, *Group analysis*, **32**(1), 109–24.

Davis, M. (2003) Barriers to reflective practice: the changing nature of higher education, *Active Learning in Higher Education*, **4**(3), 243–55.

Deal, D. (1998) Portfolios, learning logs, and eulogies: using expressive writing in a science method class, in E.G. Sturtevant, J.A. Dugan, P. Linder and W.M. Linek (eds), *Literacy and Community*. Commerce, TX: The College Reading Association.

Dean, H. (2004) The implication of the third way social policy for inequality, social care and citizenship, in J. Lewis and R. Surender (eds), *Welfare State Change: Towards a Third Way?* Oxford: Oxford University Press.

Dehler, G.E. and Edmonds, K.E. (2006) Using action research to connect practice to learning: a course project for working management students, *Journal of Management Education*, **30**(5) 636–69.

Denyer, S., Boydell, L., Wilde, J. and Herne, U. (2003) *Reflecting Leadership: Leadership for Building a Healthy Society*. Dublin and Belfast: Institute of Public Health in Ireland.

Denzin, N.K. (1992) The many faces of emotionality: reading *persona*, in C. Ellis and M.G. Flaherty (eds), *Investigating Subjectivity: Research on Lived Experience*. London: Sage, pp. 17–30.

Department of Education and Science (1978) *Primary Education in England*. London: HMSO.

Diski, J. (2005) Your dinner is the dog, *The Guardian Review*, 15 January, p. 31.

Dixon, D.M., Sweeney, K.G. and Periera, G. (1999) The physician healer: ancient magic or modern science? *British Journal of General Practice*, **49**, 309–12.

Doty, M. (1996) *Atlantis*. London: Jonathan Cape.

Doyle, W. (2004) Heard any good stories lately? A critique of the critics of narrative in educational research, *Teaching and Teacher Education*, **13**(1), 93–9.

Doyle, W. and Carter, K. (2003) Narrative and learning to teach: implications for teacher-education curriculum, *Journal of Curriculum Studies*, **35**(2), 129–37.

Dowrick, S. (2009) *Creative Journal Writing: The Art and Heart of Reflection*. New York: Penguin Group.

Drabble, M. (ed.) (2000) *The Oxford Companion to English Literature*. Oxford: Oxford University Press.

Drucquer, H. (2004) in, Bolton, G., Allan, H.S. and Drucquer, H., Black and blue writing for reflective practice, in G. Bolton, S. Howlett, C. Lago and J. Wright, *Writing Cures: An Introductory Handbook of Writing in Counselling and Psychotherapy*. London: Brunner-Routledge

Duffy, C.A. (1999) *The World's Wife* (Mrs Midas). London: Picador, Macmillan.

Durgahee, T. (1997) Reflective practice: nursing ethics through story telling, *Nursing Ethics*, **4**(2), 135–46.

Eagleton, T. (2008) Coruscating on thin ice, *London Review of Books*, 24 January, pp. 9–20.

Eagleton, T. (1983) *Literary Theory: An Introduction*. Oxford: Basil Blackwell.

Eastaugh, A. (1998a) The pursuit of self knowledge through a study of myself as a member of a group of co-tutoring facilitators, unpublished MA dissertation.

Economides, K. and O'Leary, M. (2007) The moral of the story: toward an understanding of ethics in organisations and legal practice, *Legal Ethics*, **10**(1), 5–25.

Einstein, A. ([1929] 2002) Interview with Sylvester Viereck 1929, Berlin. Quoted by K. Taylor (2002) When fact and fantasy collide, *Times Higher Educational Supplement*, 20/27 December, p. viii.

Einstein, A. (1973) *Ideas and Opinions*. London: Souvenir Press.

Eisner, M. (2000) A villanelle: writing in strict form, in G. Bolton (ed.), Opening the word hoard, *Journal of Medical Humanities*, **26**(1), 55–7.

Elbasch-Lewis, F. (2002) Writing as enquiry: storying the teaching of self in writing workshops, *Curriculum Enquiry*, **32**(4), 403–28.

Eliot, T.S. ([1936] 1974) *Collected Poems*. London: Faber & Faber.

Elkind, A. (1998) Using metaphor to read the organisation of the NHS, *Social Science Medicine*, **47**(11), 1715–27.

Ellis, C. and Bochner, A.P. (2000) Autoethnography, personal narrative, reflexivity: researcher as subject, in N. Denzin and Y. Lincoln (eds), *Handbook of Qualitative Research*. 2nd edn. London: Sage.

Ellos, W. J. (1998) Some narrative methologies for clinical ethics, *Cambridge Quarterly of Healthcare Ethics*, **7**, 315–22.

Engel, J.D., Pethel, L. and Zarconi, J. (2002) Hearing the patient's story, *Sacred Space*, **3**(1), 24–32.

Engel, J.D., Zarconi, J., Pethtel, L.L. and Missimi, S.A. (2008) *Narrative in Health Care: Healing Patients, Practitioners, Profession and Community*. Abingdon: Radcliffe.

English, L.M. and Gillen, M.A. (2001) *Promoting Journal Writing in Adult Education*. San Francisco, CA: Jossey-Bass.

Epstein, R.M. (1999) Mindful practice, *Journal of the American Medical Association*, **282**(9), 833–9.

Eraut, M. (1994) *Developing Professional Knowledge and Competence*. London: Falmer Press.

Etherington, K. (2004) *Becoming a Reflexive Researcher: Using Ourselves in Research*. London: Jessica Kingsley.

Evison, R. (2001) Helping individuals manage emotional responses, in R.L. Payne and C.L. Cooper (eds), *Emotions at Work: Theory, Research, and Applications in Management*. Chichester: Wiley & Sons. pp. 241–68.

Exley, H. (ed.) (1991) *A Writer's Notebook*, Watford: Exley.

Fanghanel, J. (2004) Capturing dissonance in university teacher education environments, *Studies in Higher Education*, **29**(5), 575–90.

Feltham, C. (2004) *Problems Are Us: Or Is It Just Me?* Felixstowe, Braiswick.

Fenwick, T. (2001) Responding to journals in a learning process, in L.M. English and M.A. Gillen (eds), *Promoting Journal Writing in Adult Education*. San Francisco, CA: Jossey-Bass. pp. 37–48.

Ferguson, H. (2005) Working with violence, the emotions and the psycho-social dynamics of child protection: reflections on the Victoria Climbié case, *Social Work Education*, **24**(7), 781–95.

Fins, J.J., Gentilesco, B.J., Carber, A., Lister, P., Acres, C.A., Payne, R. and Storey-Johnson, C. (2003) Reflective practice and palliative care education: a clerkship responds to the informal and hidden curricula, *Academic Medicine*, **78**(3), 307–12.

Flax, J. (1990) *Thinking Fragments*. Berkeley, CA: University of California Press.

Fook, J. (2002) *Social Work: Critical Theory and Practice*. London: Sage.

Fowler, J. and Chevannes, M. (1998) Evaluating the efficacy of reflective practice within the context of clinical supervision, *Journal of Advanced Nursing*, **27**, 379–82.

Fox, D. (1983) Personal theories of teaching, *Studies in Higher Education*, **8**(2), 151–63.

Frank, A. (1947) *The Diary of Anne Frank*. London: Macmillan Children's Books.

Frank, A. (1995) *The Wounded Storyteller: Body Illness and Ethics*. Chicago, IL: University of Chicago Press.

Frank, A. (2004) Asking the right question about pain: narrative and phronesis, *Literature and Medicine*, **23**(2), 209–25.

Frankenberg, R. (1986) Sickness as cultural performance: drama, trajectory, and pilgrimage root metaphors and the making social of disease, *International Journal of Health Services*, **16**(4), 603–27.

Frankl, V.E. (1985) *Man's Search for Meaning*. 5th edn. New York: Washington Square Press.

Freire, P. (1972) *Pedagogy of the Oppressed*. London: Penguin.

Freire, P. (1998) *Pedagogy of Freedom: Ethics, Democracy, and Civic Courage*. Lanham, MD: Rowman & Littlefield.

Freud, A. (1950) Foreword, in M. Milner (eds), *On Not Being Able to Paint*. London: Heinemann Educational.

Freud, S. (1995) Creative writers and day-dreaming, in S. Burke (ed.), *Authorship from Plato to the Postmodernists: A Reader*. Edinburgh: University of Edinburgh Press. pp. 54–62.

Gabriel, Y. (1991) On organisational stories and myths: why it is easier to slay a dragon than to kill a myth, *International Sociology*, **6**, 427–42.

Gabriel, Y. (1995) The unmanaged organization: stories, fantasies and subjectivity, *Organization Studies*, **16**, 477–501.

Garro, L.C. and Mattingley, C. (2000) in C. Mattingley and L.C. Garro (eds), *Narrative and Cultural Construction of Illness and Healing*. Berkeley, CA: University of California Press.

Garvey, R., Stokes, P. and Megginson, D. (2009) *Coaching and Mentoring: Theory and Practice*. London: Sage Publications.

Gee, S. (2002) *Thin Air*. London: Headline Review.

Geertz, C. ([1973] 1993) *The Interpretation of Culture*. London: HarperCollins.

Gerber, L. (1994) Psychotherapy with Southeast Asian refugees: implications for treatment of western patients, *American Journal of Psychotherapy*, **48**(2), 280–93.

Gerber, L. (1996) We must hear each other's cry: lessons from Pol Pot survivors, in C. Strozier and F. Flynn (eds), *Genocide, War, and Human Survival*. New York: Rowman & Littlefield. pp. 297–305.

Gersie, A. (1992) *Storymaking in Bereavement*. London: Jessica Kingsley.

Ghaye, T. (2007) Is reflective practice ethical? (The case of the reflective portfolio), *Reflective Practice*, **8**(2), 151–62.

Gherardi, S. and Turner, B. (2002) Real men don't collect soft data, in A.M. Huberman and M.B. Miles (eds), *The Qualitative Researcher's Companion*. London: Sage. pp. 81–101.

Gibbons, N. (2003) Portrait by a patient, in G. Bolton (ed.), Opening the word hoard, *Journal of Medical Humanities*, **29**(2), 97–103.

Gibran, K. ([1926] 1994) *The Prophet*. London: Bracken Books.

Glaister, L. (1999) *Sheer Blue Bliss*. London: Bloomsbury.

Glaze, J. (2002) Ph.D. study and the use of a reflective diary: a dialogue with self, *Reflective Practice*, **3**(2), 153–66.

Goethe, J.W. von (1998) Goethe's way of science; a phenomenology of nature, D. Seamon and A. Zajonc (eds). New York: SUNY Press. Review: wwwdatadiwan.de//SciMedNet//library// reviewsN69+N69Goethesci.htm (accessed 27 October 2004).

Goffman, E. (1990) *The Presentation of Self in Everyday Life*. Harmondsworth: Penguin.

Goldberg, N. (1991) *Wild Mind: Living the Writer's Life*. London: Rider.

Gomez, M.S., Burda Walker, A. and Page, M.L. (2000) Personal experience as a guide to teaching, *Teaching and Teacher Education*, **16**, 731–47.

Goodson, I. (1998) Storying the self, in W. Pinar (ed.), *Curriculum: Towards New Identities*. New York and London: Taylor & Francis. pp. 3–20.

Goodson, I. (2004) Representing teachers, *Teaching and Teacher Education*, **13**(1), 111–17.

Gough, N. (1998) Reflections and diffractions: functions of fiction in curriculum inquiry, in W. Pinar (ed.), *Curriculum: Towards New Identities*. New York and London: Taylor & Francis. pp. 91–129.

Gould, N. (2004) The learning organisation and reflective practice – the emergence of a concept, in N. Gould and M. Baldwin (eds), *Social Work, Critical Reflection and the Learning Organisation*. Aldershot: Ashgate.

Graham, E., Walton, H. and Ward, F. (2005) *Theological Reflection: Methods*. London: SCM.

Graham, L.J. and Paterson, D.L. (2010) Using metaphors with pre-service teachers enrolled in a core special education unit, *Teacher Education and Special Education*. In press.

Gray, D.E. (2007) Facilitating management learning: developing critical reflection through reflective tools, *Management Learning*, **38**(5), 495–517.

Greenwood, J. (1995) Treatment with dignity, *Nursing Times*, **91**(17), 65–6.

Groom, B. and Maunonen-Eskilinen, I. (2006) The use of portfolios to develop reflective practice in teacher training: a comparative and collaborative approach between two teacher training providers in the UK and Finland, *Teaching in Higher Education*, **11**(3), 291–300.

Grumet, M.R. (1981) Restitution and reconstruction of educational experience: an autobiographical method for curriculum theory, in M. Lawn and L. Barton (eds), *Rethinking Curriculum Studies: A Radical Approach*. London: Croom Helm. pp. 115–30.

Gully, T. (2004) Reflective writing as critical reflection in work with sexually abusive adolescents, *Reflective Practice*, **5**(3), 313–26.

Guppy, S. (2000) Feminist witness to the century, *Times Educational Supplement*, February, p. 27.

Hamberger, R. (1995) Acts of parting, *New Statesman*, 24 November, p. 49.

Hancock, P. (1998) Reflective practice: using a learning journal, *Nursing Standard*, **13**(17), 37–40.

Hargreaves, J. (1997) Using patients: exploring the ethical dimension of reflective practice in nurse education, *Journal of Advanced Nursing*, **25**, 223–8.

Hargreaves, J. (2004) So how do you feel about that? Assessing reflective practice, *Nurse Education Today*, **24**, 196–201.

Harris, J. (2003) *Signifying Pain: Constructing and Healing the Self through Writing*. New York: SUNY Press.

Harrison, R. (2004) Telling stories about learners and learning, in J. Satterthwaite et al. (eds), *The Disciplining of Education: New Languages of Power and Resistance*. Stoke-on-Trent: Trentham Books, pp. 169–80.

Hartley, L.P. (1953) *The Go Between*. London: Hamish Hamilton.

Hatem, D. and Ferrara, E. (2001) Becoming a doctor: fostering humane caregivers through creative writing, *Patient Education and Counselling*, **45**, 13–22.

Hatton, N. and Smith, D. (1995) Reflection in teacher education: towards definition and implementation, *Teacher and Teacher Education*, **11**(1), 33–49.

Heaney, S. (1980a) *Selected Prose 1968–1978*. London: Faber & Faber.

Heaney, S. (1980b) *Selected Poems*. 'Digging'. London: Faber & Faber. pp. 10–11.

Heaney, S. (2008) To set the darkness echoing (D. O'Driscoll interviewer), *Guardian Review*, 8 November, pp. 2–4.

Hedberg, P.R. (2009) Learning through reflective classroom practice: applications to educate the reflective manager, *Journal of Management Education*, **33**(1), 10–36.

Heel, D., Sparrow, J. and Ashford, R. (2006) Workplace interactions that facilitate or impede reflective practice, *Journal of Health Management*, **8**(1), 1–10.

Heifetz, R.A. and Linsky, M. (2002) *Leadership on the Line*. Boston, MA: Harvard Business School Press.

Heller, T. (1996) Doing being human: reflective practice in mental health work, in T. Heller et al. (eds.) *Mental Health Matters*. London: Macmillan.

Helman, C. (2006) *Surburban Shaman: Tales from Medicine's Front Line*. London: Hammersmith.

Hesse, H. ([1927] 1965) *Steppenwolf*. London: Penguin.

Hildebrand, J. (1995) Learning through supervision: a systemic approach, in M. Yelloly and M. Henkel (eds), *Teaching and Learning in Social Work: Towards Reflective Practice*. London: Jessica Kingsley.

Hinett, K. (2002) *Developing Reflective Practice in legal Education*. T. Varnava (ed.). Coventry: UK Centre for Legal Education, University of Warwick.

Hobbs, V. (2007) Faking it or hating it: can reflective practice be forced? *Reflective Practice*, **8** (3), 405–17.

Hogler, R., Gross, M.A., Hartman, J.L. and Cunliffe, A.L. (2008) Meaning in organizational communication: why metaphor is the cake, not the icing, *Management Communication Quarterly*, **21**, 393–412.

Holly, M.L. (1988) Reflective writing and the spirit of enquiry, *Cambridge Journal of Education*, **19**(1), 71–80.

Holly, M.L. (1989) *Writing to Grow: Keeping a Personal-Professional Journal*. Portsmouth, NH: Heinemann.

Holman Jones, S. (2005) Making the personal political, in N.K. Denzin and Y.S. Lincoln (eds). *The Sage Handbook of Qualitative Research*. 3rd edn. Thousand Oaks, CA: Sage Publications.

Homer (1996) *The Odyssey*. Trans. R. Fagles. London: Viking Penguin.

Hooks, B. (2003) *Teaching Community: A Pedagogy of Hope*. New York: Routledge.

Hoover, L.A. (1994) Reflective writing as a window on preservice teachers' thought processes, *Teacher and Teaching Education*, **10**(1), 83–93.

Horowitz, C.R., Suchman, A.L., Branch, W.T. and Frankel, R.M. (2003) What do doctors find meaningful about their work? *Annals of Internal Medicine*, **138**(9), 772–6.

Horsfall, D. (2008) Bearing witness: toward a pedagogical practice of love? *Reflective Practice*, **9**(1), 1–10.

Howard, J. (1997) The emotional diary: a framework for reflective practice, *Education for General Practice*, **8**, 288–91.

Huber, M., Huber, J., Clandinin, J. and Clandinin, D.J. (2004) Moments of tension: resistance as expressions of narrative coherence in stories, *Reflective Practice*, **5**(2), 182–98.

Hudson Jones, A. (1998) Narrative in medical ethics, in T. Greenhalgh and B. Hurwitz (eds), *Narrative Based Medicine: Dialogue and Discourse in Clinical Practice*. London: BMJ Books. pp. 217–24.

Hughes, L. and Pengelly, P. (1995) Who cares if the room is cold? Practicalities, projections, and the trainer's authority, in M. Yelloly and M. Henkel (eds), *Teaching and Learning in Social Work: Towards Reflective Practice*. London: Jessica Kingsley.

Hughes, T. (1967) *Poetry in the Making*. 'The Thought Fox'. London: Faber & Faber. pp. 19–20.

Hughes, T. (1982) Foreword, in S. Brownjohn, *What Rhymes with Secret?* London: Hodder & Stoughton.

Hughes, T. (1995) Interview, *Paris Review*, http://stinfwww.informatik.uni-leipzig.de/~beckmann/plath/thint.html (accessed 8 September 2004).

Hulatt, I. (1995) A sad reflection, *Nursing Standard*, **9**(20), 22–3.

Huxley, A.J. ([1932] 1994) *Brave New World*. London: Flamingo.

Hwu, Wen-Song (1998) Curriculum, transcendence and Zen/Taoism: critical ontology of the self, in W. Pinar (ed.), *Curriculum: Towards New Identities*. New York and London: Taylor & Francis. pp. 21–4.

Illes, K. (2003) The patchwork text and business education: rethinking the importance of personal reflection and co-operative cultures, *Innovations in Education and Teaching International*, **40**(2), 209–15.

Ixer, G. (1999) There's no such thing as reflection, *British Journal of Social Work*, **29**(4), 513–27.

Jasper, M. (2008) Using reflective journals or diaries, in C. Bulman and S. Schutz (eds), *Reflective Practice in Nursing*. 4th edn. Oxford: Blackwell.

Jasper, M.A. (2005) Using reflective writing within research, *Journal of Research in Nursing*, **10**(3), 247–60.

Johns, C. (1995) Framing learning through reflection within Carper's fundamental ways of knowing in nursing, *Journal of Advanced Nursing*, **22**, 222–34.

Johns, C. (2000) *Becoming a Reflective Practitioner: A Reflective and Holistic Approach to Clinical Nursing, Practice Development and Clinical Supervision*. Oxford: Blackwell Science.

Johns, C. (2004) *Being Mindful, Easing Suffering: Reflections on Palliative Care*. London: Jessica Kingsley.

Joyce, J. (1944) *Stephen Hero*. T. Spencer (ed.). New York: New Directions Press.

Joy-Matthews, J., Megginson, D. and Surtees, M. (2004) *Human Resource Development*. 2nd edn. London: Kogan Page.

Kathpalia, S.S. and Heah, C. (2008) Reflective writing: insights into what lies beneath, *RELC Journal*, **39**(3), 300–17.

Keats, J. (1818) Letter to John Taylor, 27 February.

Kember, D. et al. (1996) Encouraging critical reflection through small group discussion of journal writing, *Innovations in Education Training International*, **33**(4), 313–20.

Kemp, M. (2001) Fictioning identities: a course on narrative and fictional approaches to educational practice, *Reflective Practice*, **2**(3), 345–55.

Keys, C.W. (1999) Revitalising instruction in scientific genres: connecting knowledge production with writing to learn in science, *Science Education*, **83**, 115–30.

Kim, H.S. (1999) Critical reflective inquiry for knowledge development in nursing practice. *Journal of Advanced Nursing*, **29**(5), 1205–12.

Kipling, R. (1902) *Just So Stories*. London: Macmillan.

Kirkham, M. (1997) Reflection in midwifery: professional narcissism or seeing with women? *British Journal of Midwifery*, **5**(5), 259–62.

Kirkham, M. (1999) The wisdom of nausea, *Midwifery Today*, **52**, 15.

Klein, G. (1999) *Sources of Power: How People Make Decisions*. Cambridge, MA: MIT Press.

Knott, C. and Scragg, T. (2007) *Reflective Practice in Social Work*. Exeter: Learning Matters.

Kolb, D.A. (1984) *Experiential Learning*. London: Prentice Hall.

Kruse, S.D. (1997) Reflective activity in practice, *Journal of Research and Development in Education*, **31**(1), 46–60.

Kuit, J.A., Reay, J. and Freeman, R. (2001) Experiences of reflective teaching, *Active Learning in Higher Education*. **2**(2), 128–42.

Kyeremateng, S. (2003) Jug, in G. Bolton (ed.), Opening the word hoard, *Journal of Medical Humanities*, **29**(2), 97–103.

Ladkin, D. (2004) Action research, in C. Seale, G. Gobo, J.F. Gubrium and D. Silverman (eds), *Qualitative Research Practice*. London: Sage.

Lakoff, G. (1991) Metaphor and war: the metaphor system used to justify war in the gulf, *Viet Nam Generation Journal*, **3**(3) November, http://lists.village.virginia.edu/sixties/HTML_Texts/Scholarly/Lakoff_Gulf_Metap

Lakoff, G. and Johnson, M. ([1980] 2003) *Metaphors We Live By*. Chicago, IL: University of Chicago Press.

Laming, H. (2003) *The Victoria Climbié Enquiry*. London: Stationery Office. www.victoria-climbie-inquiry.org.uk/finreport/report/pdf

Landgrebe, B. and Winter, R. (1994) Reflective writing on practice: professional support for the dying? *Educational Action Research*, **2**(1), 83–94.

Lao Tsu (1973) *Tao Te Ching*. Trans. Gia Fu Feng and J. English). London: Wildwood House.

Le Grand, J. (2006) *Motivation, Agency and Public Policy: Of Knights and Knaves, Pawns and Queens*. Oxford: Oxford University Press.

Lemon, N. (2007) Take a photograph: teacher reflection through narrative, *Reflective Practice*, **8**(2), 177–91.

Levi, P. (1988) *The Wrench*. London: Abacus.

Lévi-Strauss, C. (1963) *Structural Anthropology*. New York: Basic Books.

Lévi-Strauss, C. (1966) *The Savage Mind*. London: Wiedenfeld.

Lévi-Strauss, C. (1978) *Myth and Meaning*. London: Routledge & Kegan Paul.

Lewis, C.S. (1961a) *The Screwtape Letters*. New York: Macmillan.

Lewis, C.S. (1961b) *A Grief Observed*. London: Faber & Faber.

Lewis, R. (1992) Autobiography and biography as legitimate educational tasks or pedagogic terrorism, paper presented to Teachers' Stories of Life and Work Conference, Chester.

Lillis, T.M. (2001) *Student Writing. Access, Regulation, Desire*. London: Routledge.

Linn, G.B., Sherman, R. and Gill, P.B. (2007) Making meaning of educational leadership: the principalship in metaphor, *NASSP Bulletin*, **91**(2), 161–71.

Llosa, M.V. (1991) *A Writer's Reality*. Syracuse, NY: Syracuse University Press.

Longfellow, H.W. (1960) *The Song of Hiawatha*. London: Dent.

Loughran, J. (2004) Review essay, *Teaching and Teacher Education*, **20**, 655–60.

Love, C. (1996) Using a diary to learn the patient's perspective, *Professional Nurse*, **11**(5), 286–8.

Lyotard, J.F. (1984) *The Postmodern Condition. A Report on Knowledge*. (Minneapolis, MN: University of Minnesota Press.

Lyotard, J.P. (1992) *The Postmodern Explained to Children*. London: Turnaround.

MacFarlane, B. and Gourlay, L. (2009) The reflection game and the penitent self, *Teaching in Higher Education* (in press).

MacIntyre, A. (1985) *After Virtue*. 2nd edn. London: Duckworth.

Maclure, M. (2003) *Discourse in Educational and Social Research*. Buckingham: Open University Press.

Macnaughton, J. (1998) Anecdote in clinical practice, in T. Greenhalgh and B. Hurwitz (eds), *Narrative Based Medicine: Dialogue and Discourse in Clinical Practice*. London: BMJ Books.

Maharg, P. and Paliwala, A. (2002) Negotiating the learning process with electronic resources, in R. Burridge, K. Hinett, A. Paliwala and T. Varnava (eds), *Effective Learning and Teaching in Law*. London: Routledge.

Manickavasagam, M. (2000) *The Sovereign Individual as a Legal Creation in Literature*. UCL Faculty of Laws: UCL Jurisprudence Review. pp. 1–16.

Marrow, C.E., MacAuley, D.M. and Crumbie, A. (1997) Promoting reflective practice through structured clinical supervision, *Journal of Nursing Management*, **5**, 77–82.

Marx, K. (1962) *Writings of the Young Marx on Philosophy and Society*, eds and trans. L.D. Easton and K.H. Gudat. New York: Anchor Books.

Mattingley, C. (2000) Emergent narratives, in C. Mattingley and L.C. Garro (eds), *Narrative and Cultural Construction of Illness and Healing*. Berkeley, CA: University of California Press. pp. 181–211.

McKenzie, J. (2003) The student as an active agent in a disciplinary structure: introducing the patchwork text in teaching sociology, *Innovations in Education and Teaching International*, **40**(2), 152–60.

McKenzie, J., Sheely, S. and Trigwell, K. (1998) An holistic approach to student evaluation of courses, *Assessment and Evaluation in Higher Education*, **23**(2), 153–63.

Mearns, D. (1994) Person centred counselling with configurations of self, *Counselling*, May, 125–30.

Meath Lang, B. (1996) Cultural and language diversity in the curriculum: towards reflective practice, in I. Parasnis (ed.), *Cultural and Language Diversity and the Deaf Experience*. Cambridge: Cambridge University Press, pp. 160–70.

Megginson, D. and Whitaker, V. (2003) *Continuing Professional Development*. London: Chartered Institute of Personnel and Development.

Mezirow, J. (1981) A critical theory of adult learning and education. *Adult Education*, **32**(1), 3–24.

Mezirow, J. (1991) *Transformative Dimensions of Adult Learning*. San Francisco, CA: Jossey-Bass.

Middlebrook, D. (2003) *Her Husband. Ted Hughes and Sylvia Plath: A Marriage*. London: Penguin.

Miles, M.B. and Huberman, A.M. (1994) *Qualitative Data Analysis: An Expanded Sourcebook*. London: Sage.

Miller, J. (2009) Interview by N. Wroe, *The Guardian Review*, 10 January, pp. 12–13.

Miller, S. (2005) What it's like being the 'holder of the space': a narrative on working with reflective practice in groups, *Reflective Practice*. **6**(3), 367–77.

Milne, A.A. ([1924] 1959) *The World of Christopher Robin (When We Were Very Young)*. London: Methuen.

Milne, A.A. ([1928] 1958) *The World of Pooh (The House at Pooh Corner)*. London: Methuen.

Modell, A.H (1997) Reflections on metaphor and affects, *Annals of Psychoanalysis*, **25**, 219–33.

Montgomery Hunter, K. (1991) *Doctors' Stories: The Narrative Structure of Medical Knowledge*. Princeton, NJ: Princeton University Press.

Montgomery, K., Chambers, T. and Reifler, D.R. (2003) Humanities education at Northwestern University Feinberg school of medicine, *Academic Medicine*, **78**(10), 958–62.

Moon, J.A. (1999a) *Learning Journals: A Handbook for Academics, Students and Professional Development*. London: Kogan Page.

Moon, J.A. (1999b) Reflect on the inner 'I' *Times Higher Education Supplement*, 15 October, pp. 34–5.

Moon, J.A. (2003) *Reflection in Learning and Professional Development*. London: Kogan Page.

Moon, J.A. (2004) *A Handbook of Reflective and Experiential Learning: Theory and Practice*. London: RoutledgeFalmer.

Mori, B., Batty, H.P. and Brooks, D. (2008) The feasibility of an electronic reflective practice exercise among physiotherapy students, *Medical Teacher,* **38**(8), e232–8.

Morrison, K. (1996) Developing reflective practice in higher degree students through a learning journal, *Studies in Higher Education*, **21**(3), 317–31.

Moustakas, C. (1990) *Heuristic Research Design, Methodology and Applications*. London: Sage.

Munno, A. (2006) A complaint which changed my practice, *British Medical Journal*, **332**, 1092.

Murray, D. (1982) *Learning by Teaching*. NJ: Boynton Cook.

Newton, R. (1996) Getting to grips with barriers to reflection, *SCUTREA Conference Papers*, pp. 142–5.

Nias, J. and Aspinwall, K. (1992) Paper presented to the Teachers' Stories of Life and Work Conference, Chester.

Noddings, N. (1992) *The Challenge to Care in Schools: An Alternative Approach to Education*. New York: Teachers College Press.

Orem, R.A. (2001) *Journal Writing in Adult ESL: Improving Practice through Reflective Writing. Promoting Journal Writing in Adult Education*. San Francisco,CA: Jossey-Bass. pp. 37–48.

Oriah, M.D. (2000) *The Invitation*. London: Thorsons.

Orwell, G. ([1949] 1987) *1984*. London: Penguin.

Osborn, J. (1993) AIDS – science, medicine, and metaphor (editorial), *Western Journal of Medicine*, **158**(3), 305–7.

Osterman, K.F. and Kottkamp, R.B. (2004) *Reflective Practice for Educators*. 2nd edn. Thousand Oaks, CA: Corwin Press (Sage).

Patenaude, J., Niyonsenga, T. and Fafard, D. (2003a) Changes in the components of moral reasoning during students' medical education: a pilot study, *Medical Education*, **37**, 822–29.

Patenaude, J., Nyonsenga, T. and Fafard, D. (2003b) Changes in students' moral development during medical school: a cohort study, *Journal de l'Association Médicale Canadienne (Canadian Medical Association Journal)*. **168**(7), 840–4.

Pattison, S., Dickenson, D., Parker, M. and Heller, T. (1999a) Do case studies mislead about the nature of reality? *Journal of Medical Ethics*, **25b**, 42–6.

Pattison, S., Manning, S. and Malby, B. (1999b) I want to tell you a story, *Health Services Journal*, 25 February, p. 6.

Paula, C. (2003) Bubbles in a pond: reflections in clinical practice, *Clinical Psychology*, **27** (July), 27–9.

Pavlovich, K., Collins, E. and Jones, G. (2009) Developing students' skills in reflective practice: design and assessment, *Journal of Management Education*, **33**, 37–58.

Pecheone, R.L., Pigg, M., Chung, R.R. and Souviney, R.J. (2005) Performance assessment and electronic portfolios: their effect on teacher learning and education, *The Clearing House*, **78**(4), 164–76.

Pellicer, L.O. (2008) *Caring Enough to Lead*. Thousand Oaks, CA: Corwin Press (Sage).

Pennebaker, J.W. (2000) Telling stories: the health benefits of narrative, *Literature and Medicine*, **19**(1), 3–18.

Pereira, M.A. (1999) My reflective practice as research, *Teaching in Higher Education*, **4**(3), 339–54.

Perry, C. and Cooper, M. (2001) Metaphors are good mirrors: reflecting on change for teacher education, *Reflective Practice*, **2**(1), 41–51.

Phillion, J. (2002a) Narrative multiculturalism, *Journal of Curriculum Studies*, **34**(3), 265–79.

Phillion, J. (2002b) Becoming a narrative inquirer in a multicultural landscape, *Journal of Curriculum Studies*, **34**(5), 535–56.

Phillion, J.A. and Connelly, F.M. (2004) Narrative, diversity, and teacher education, *Teaching and Teacher Education*, **20**, 457–71.

Phye, G.D. (ed.) (1997) *Handbook of Academic Learning*. San Diego, CA: Academic Press.

Picasso, P. (n.d.)www.cyber-nation.com/victory/quotations/authors/quotes_picasso_ pablo.html (accessed 14 February 2005).

Pickering, N. (1999) Metaphors and models in medicine, *Theoretical Medicine and Bioethics*, **20**, 361–75.

Pietroni, M. (1995) The nature and aims of professional education for social workers: a postmodern perspective, in M. Yelloly and M. Henkel (eds), *Learning and Teaching in Social Work: Towards Reflective Practice*. London: Jessica Kingsley.

Pinar, W.F. (1975) Currere: towards reconceptualisation, in W.F. Pinar (ed.), *Curriculum Theorising: the Reconceptualists*. Berkeley, CA: McCutchan. pp. 396–414.

Plato (1955) *The Republic*. Trans. D. Lee. London: Penguin.

Plato (1958) *The Protogoras and Meno*. Trans. W.K.C. Guthrie. London: Penguin.

Plato (2000) Apology of Socrates, in *Selected Dialogues of Plato* Trans. B. Jowett. New York: Random House.

Platzer, H., Snelling, J. and Blake, D. (1997) Promoting reflective practitioners in nursing: a review of theoretical models and research into the use of diaries and journals to facilitate reflection, *Teaching in Higher Education*, **2**(2), 103–21.

Plummer, K. (2001) *Documents of Life 2: An Invitation to Critical Humanism*. London: Sage.

Poitier, S. (2000) *The Measure of a Man: A Memoir*. London: Simon & Schuster.

Pollner, M. (1991) Left of ethnomethodology: the rise and decline of radical reflexivity, *American Sociological Review*, 56, 370–80.

Prigogine, I. (1999) Review of *Doubt and Certainty* by T. Rothman and G. Sudarshan, *Times Higher Education Supplement*, 24 September, p. 26.

Pullman, P. (1995) *His Dark Materials*. London: Scholastic.

Purdy, R. (1996) Writing refreshes my practice, *Medical Monitor*, 6 March.

Quality Assurance Agency (2001) *Guidelines for HE Progress Files*. Gloucester: QAA.

Rainer, T. (1978) *The New Diary: How to Use a Journal for Self-Guidance and Expanded Creativity*. London: Angus & Robertson.

Ramsey, C. (2005) Narrating development: Professional practice emerging within stories. *Action Research*, **3**(3), 279–95.

Reason, P. (ed.) (1988) *Human Enquiry in Action: Developments in New Paradigm Research*. London: Sage.

Redmond, B. (2006) *Reflection in Action*. Aldershot: Ashgate.

Regan, P. (2008) Reflective practice: how far, how deep? *Reflective Practice*, **9**(2), 219–29.

Reid, A. and O'Donohue, M. (2004) Revisiting enquiry-based teacher education in neo-liberal times, *Teaching and Teacher Education*, **20**, 559–70.

Reynolds, M. (1997) Learning styles: a critique, *Management Learning*, **28**(2), 115–33.

Rich, A. (1995) *What is Found There: Notebooks on Poetry and Politics*. London: Virago.

Richardson, L. (1992) The consequences of poetic representation: writing the other, rewriting the self, in C. Ellis and M.G. Flaherty (eds), *Investigating Subjectivity: Research on Lived Experience*. London: Sage. pp. 125–40.

Richardson, L. (2000) Writing: A method of inquiry, in N. Denzin and Y. Lincoln (eds), *Handbook of Qualitative Research*. 2nd edn. London: Sage. pp. 923–47.

Richardson, L. (2001) Getting personal: writing stories, *Qualitative Studies in Education*, **14**(1), 33–8.

Richardson, L. and Adams St. Pierre, E. (2005) Writing: a method of inquiry, in N.K. Denzin and Y.S. Lincoln (eds), *Handbook of Qualitative Research*. 3rd edn. London: Sage. pp. 958–78.

Ricoeur, P. (1978) *The Rule of Metaphor: Multi-disciplinary Studies in the Creation of Meaning of Language*. Trans. R. Czerny. London: Routledge & Kegan Paul.

Rigano, D. and Edwards, J. (1998) Incorporating reflection into work practice. *Management Learning*, **29**(4), 431–6.

Rilke, R.M. ([1934] 1993) *Letters to a Young Poet*. Trans. H. Norton. New York: W.W. Norton.

Robertson, P. (1999) Talk to King's Fund 'Arts in Hospital' forum, December.

Rockwell, J. (1974) *Fact in Fiction*. London: Routledge.

Rogers, C. (1969) *Freedom to Learn: a View of What Education Might Become*. Columbus, OH: Charles E. Merrill.

Rogers, J. (1991) *Mr Wroe's Virgins*. London: Faber & Faber.

Rolfe, G. (2002) A lie that helps us see the truth: research, truth and fiction in the helping professions, *Reflective Practice*, **3**(1), 89–102.

Rosean, C.L., Lundeberg, M., Cooper, M., Fritzen, A. and Terpstra, M. (2008) *Journal of Teacher Education*, **59**(4), 347–60.

Rowan, J. (1990) *Subpersonalities: The People Inside Us*. London: Routledge.

Rowe, J. and Halling, S. (1998) Psychology of forgiveness, in R.S. Valle (ed.), *Phenomenological Inquiry in Psychology: Existential and Transpersonal Dimensions*. New York: Plenum. pp. 227–46.

Rowe, J., Halling, S., Davies Leifer, M., Powers, D. and van Bronkhurst, J. (1989) The psychology of forgiving another: a dialogical research approach, in R.S. Valle and S. Halling (eds), *Existential-Phenomenological Perspectives in Psychology: Exploring the Breadth of Human Experience*. New York: Plenum.

Rowland (Bolton), G., Rowland, S. and Winter, R. (1990) Writing fiction as enquiry into professional practice, *Journal of Curriculum Studies*, **22**(3), 291–3.

Rowland, S. (1984) *The Enquiring Classroom*. Lewes: Falmer.

Rowland, S. (1991) The power of silence: an enquiry through fictional writing, *British Educational Research Journal*, **17**(2), 95–113.

Rowland, S. (1993) *The Enquiring Tutor,* Lewes: Falmer.

Rowland, S. (1999) The role of theory in a pedagogical model for lecturers in higher education, *Studies in Higher Education*, **24**(3), 303–14.

Rowland, S. (2000) *The Enquiring University Lecturer*. Buckingham: Society for Research into Higher Education and Open University Press.

Rowland, S. and Barton, L. (1994) Making things difficult: developing a research approach to teaching in higher education, *Studies in Higher Education*, **19**(3), 367–74.

Ruch, G. (2009) *Post-qualifying child care social work: developing reflective practice*. London: Sage.

Rust, C. (2002) The impact of assessment on student learning, *Active Learning in Higher Education*, **3**(2), 145–58.

Sacks, O. (1985) *The Man who Mistook his Wife for a Hat*. London: Picador, Macmillan.

Salvio, P. (1998) On using the literacy portfolio to prepare teachers for 'willful world travelling', in W.F. Pinar (ed.), *Curriculum: Towards New Identities*. New York and London: Taylor & Francis. pp. 41–75.

Saran, R. and Neisser, B. (2004) *Enquiring Minds: Socratic Dialogue in Education*. Stoke-on-Trent: Trentham Books.

Sartre, J.P. ([1938] 1963) *Nausea*. Harmondsworth: Penguin.

Sartre, J.P. ([1948] 1950) *What is Literature?* London: Methuen.

Schon, D.A. (1983) *The Reflective Practitioner: How Professionals Think in Action*. New York: Basic Books.

Schon, D.A. (1987) *Educating the Reflective Practitioner*. San Francisco, CA: Jossey-Bass.

Scott, T. (2005) Creating the subject of portfolios: reflective writing and the conveyance of institutional prerogatives, *Written Communication,* **22**(1), 3–35.

Scott-Hoy, K. (2002) The visitor: juggling life in the grip of the text, in A.P. Bochner and C. Ellis (eds), *Ethnographically Speaking: Autoethnography, Literature and Aesthetics*. New York: Altamira Press.

Senge, P. (1992) *The Fifth Discipline*. London: Century Business.

Shafer, A. (1995) Metaphor and anaesthesia, *Anesthesiology*, **83**(6), 1331–42.

Sharkey, J. (2004) Lives stories don't tell: exploring the untold in autobiographies, *Curriculum Enquiry*, **34**(4), 495–512.

Shelley, M. ([1820] 1994) *Frankenstein*. Ware: Wordsworth.

Shem, S. (2002) Fiction as resistance (medical writings: physician-writers reflections on their work), *Annals of Internal Medicine*, **137**(11), 934–7.

Shepherd, M. (2004) Reflections on developing a reflective journal as a management adviser, *Reflective Practice*, **5**(2), 199–208.

Shepherd, M. (2006) Using a learning journal to improve professional practice: a journey of personal and professional self-discovery, *Reflective Practice*, **7**(3), 333–48.

Shotter, J. and Cunliffe, A.L. (2002) Managers as practical authors: everyday conversations for action, in D. Holman and R. Thorpe (eds) *Management and Language: The Manager as Practical Author*. London: Sage. (pp. 15–37).

Simons, J. (1990) *Diaries and Journals of Literary Women from Fanny Burney to Virginia Woolf*. London: Macmillan.

Simpson, D.J., Jackson, M.J.B. and Aycock, J.C. (2005) *John Dewey and the Art of Teaching: Toward Reflective and Imaginative Practice*. Thousand Oaks, CA: Sage Publications.

Simpson, J. (1988) *Touching the Void*. London: Vintage.

Sinclair Penwarden, A. (2006) Listen up: we should not be made to disclose our personal feelings in reflection assignments, *Nursing Times*, **102**(37), 12.

Smith, D. (2009) I talk back to the voices in my head, *The Guardian Weekend*, 4 April, p. 10.

Smith, L. and Winter, R. (2003) Applied epistemology for community nurses: evaluating the impact of the patchwork text, *Innovations in Education and Teaching International*, **40**(2), 161–72.

Smith, P.A.C. (2001) Action learning and reflective practice in project environments that are related to leadership development, *Management Learning*, **32**(1), 31–48.

Smyth, T. (1996) Reinstating the personal in the professional: reflections on empathy and aesthetic experience, *Journal of Advanced Nursing*, **24**, 932–7.

Sontag, S. (1991) *Illness as Metaphor: AIDS and its Metaphors*. London: Penguin.

Sophocles (1982) *Antigone*. Trans. R. Fagles. New York: Penguin.

Stedmon, J., Mitchell, A., Johnstone, L. and Staite, S. (2003) Making reflective practice real: problems and solutions in the South West, *Clinical Psychology*, **27** (July), 30–3.

Stefano, G. (2004) George Stefano quoted by Ian Simple, The new pleasure seekers, *The Guardian Life*, 16 December, pp. 4–5.

Sterne, L. ([1760] 1980) *Tristram Shandy*. Vol. 2, ch. 11. London: W.W. Norton.

Stevenson, R.L. ([1886] 1984) *Dr Jekyll and Mr Hyde*. London: Penguin.

Stoker, B. ([1897] 1994) *Dracula*. London: Penguin.

Strawson, G. (2004a) Tales of the unexpected, *The Guardian Saturday Review*, 10 January, p. 19.

Strawson, G. (2004b) A fallacy of our age: not every life is a narrative, *Times Literary Supplement*, 15 October, pp. 13–15.

Street, B. (1995) *Social Literacies*. London: Longman.

Summerscales, O. (2006) Reflective practice and reflective writing, unpublished MA dissertation, University of Birmingham

Sutton L., Townend, M. and Wright, J. (2007) The experiences of reflective learning journals by cognitive behavioural psychotherapy students. *Reflective practice*, **8**(3), 387–404.

Svenberg, K., Wahlqvist, M. and Mattsson, B. (2007) A memorable consultation: writing reflective accounts articulates students' learning in general practice, *Scandinavian Journal of Primary Health Care*, **25**(2), 75–9.

Sydney, P. (1965) *The Poems of Sir Philip Sydney*. W.A. Ringler (ed.). London: Oxford University Press.

Tennyson, A. ([1886] 1932) 'The Lady of Shalott' in J. Wain (ed.), *The Oxford Library of English Poetry*. Oxford: Oxford University Press. pp. 79–83.

Thomas, R.S. (1986) *Selected Poems*. 'Poetry for Supper'. Tarset, Northumberland: Bloodaxe.

Thorpe, M. (2000) 'Encouraging students to reflect as part of the assignment process. Student responses and tutor feedback', *Active Learning in Higher Education*. **1**(1), 79–92.

Toibin, C. (2009) Literature, *Guardian*, 3 March, p. 11.

Trelfa, J. (2005) Faith in reflective practice, *Reflective Practice*, **6**(2), 205–12.

Tripp, D. (1995a) *Critical Incidents in Teaching*. London: Routledge.

Tripp, D. (1995b) SCOPE facilitator training *NPDP SCOPE Project Draft*. Perth, WA: Murdoch University.

Trotter, S. (1999) Journal writing to promote reflective practice in pre-service teachers, paper presented to the International Human Science Research Conference, Sheffield, July.

Truscott, D.M. and Walker, B.J. (1998) The influence of portfolio selection on reflective thinking, in E.G. Sturtevant, J.A. Dugan, P. Linder and W.M. Linek (eds), *Literacy and Community*. Commerce, TX: The College Reading Association.

Tsai Chi Chung (1994) *Zen Speaks*. Trans. B. Bruya, London: HarperCollins.

Turnbull, W. and Mullins, P. (2007) Socratic dialogue as personal reflection, *Reflective Practice,* **8**(1), 93–108.

Twining, W. (2006) *Rethinking Evidence.* New York: Cambridge University Press.

Tyler, S.A. (1986) Post–modern ethnography: from occult to occult document, in J. Clifford and G.E. Marcus (eds) *Writing Culture,* Berkeley, CA: University of California Press.

Usher, R. (1993) From process to practice: research reflexivity and writing in adult education, *Studies in Continuing Education,* **15**(2), 98–116.

Usher, R., Bryant, I. and Jones, R. (1997) *Adult Education and the Postmodern Challenge: Learning Beyond the Limits.* London: Routledge.

Van Manen, M. (1995) On the epistemology of reflective practice, *Teachers and Teaching: Theory and Practice,* **1**(1), 33–49.

Varner, D. and Peck, S. (2003). Learning from learning journals: the benefits and challenges of using learning journal assignments, *Journal of Management Education,* **27**(1), 52–77.

Verghese, A. (2001) The physician as storyteller, *Annals of Internal Medicine,* **135**(11), 1012–17.

Von Klitzing, W. (1999) Evaluation of reflective learning in a psychodynamic group of nurses caring for terminally ill patients, *Journal of Advanced Nursing,* **30**(5), 1213–21.

Ward, J.R. and McCotter, S.S. (2004) Reflection as a visible outcome for preservice teachers. *Teaching and Teacher Education,* **20**, 243–57.

Warner, M. (1998) *No Go the Bogeyman: Scaring, Lulling and Making Mock.* London: Chatto & Windus.

Watson, C. (2006) Encounters and directions in research: pages from a simulacrum journal, *Qualitative Inquiry,* **12**(5), 865–85.

Watson, C.E. (2003) Using stories to teach business ethics: developing character through examples of admirable actions, *Teaching Business Ethics,* **96**, 103–5.

Weedon, C. (1987) *Feminist Practice and Post-Structuralist Theory.* Oxford: Basil Blackwell.

Weick, K.E. (1995) *Sensemaking in Organisations.* Thousand Oaks, CA: Sage Publications.

Wilde, O. ([1891] 1949) *The Picture of Dorian Gray.* London: Penguin.

Wilding, P.M. (2008) Reflective practice: a learning tool for student nurses, *British Journal of Nursing.* **17**(11), 720–24.

Williams, A. (2002) 'Doing justice to human rights: the Human Rights Act and the UK law school, in R. Burridge, K. Hinett, A. Paliwala and T. Varnava (eds), *Effective Learning and Teaching in Law.* London: Routledge.

Williams, W.C. (1951) *Selected Poems.* London: Penguin.

Wilson, J.P. (2008) Reflecting-on-the-future: a chronological consideration of reflective practice, *Reflective Practice,* **9**(2), 177–84.

Winnicott, D.W. (1971) *Playing and Reality.* London: Tavistock Publications.

Winter, R. (1988) Fictional-critical writing, in J. Nias and S. Groundwater-Smith (eds), *The Enquiring Teacher.* London: Falmer. pp. 231–48.

Winter, R. (1991) Fictional-critical writing as a method for educational research, *British Educational Research Journal,* **17**(3), 251–62.

Winter, R. (2003) Contextualising the patchwork text: problems of coursework assignment in higher education, *Innovations in Education and Teaching International,* **40**(2), 112–22.

Winter, R., Buck, A. and Sobiechowska, P. (1999) *Professional Experience and the Investigative Imagination: The Art of Reflective Writing.* London: Routledge.

Wittgenstein, L. (1953) *Philosophical Investigations.* Oxford: Blackwell.

Woolf, V. ([1928] 1992) *Orlando.* Oxford: Oxford University Press.

Woolf, V. (1977, 1978, 1980) *The Diary of Virginia Woolf.* 3 vols. London: Hogarth Press.

Wordsworth, W. ([1802] 1992) Preface, in *The Lyrical Ballads.* Harlow: Longman, p. 82.

Wordsworth, W. ([1880] 2004) 'The Prelude', in Selected Poems. D. Walford Davies (ed.). London: Dent.

Wright, J.K. (2005) 'A discussion with myself on paper': counselling and psychotherapy masters student perceptions of keeping a learning log, Reflective Practice, 6(4), 507–21.

www.healthcarecommision.org

www.hearing-voices.org (accessed 27 April 2009)

www.nhsconfed.org/OurWork/latestnews/Pages/SummaryofLordLaming'sBabyPreport.aspx (accessed 6 May 2009)

www.ukcle.ac.uk/directions/previous/issue12/blogs.html (accessed 1 September 2009).

Yang, S. and Bautista, D.D. (2008) Reflection, arts, and self-inquiry: a letter to other for negotiating Korean English teacher identity, Reflective Practice, 9(3), 293–305.

Yeats, W. B. (1962) Selected Poetry. London: Macmillan.

Yelloly, M. and Henkel, M. (eds) (1995) Introduction, in Teaching and Learning in Social Work: Reflective Practice. London: Jessica Kingsley.

York-Barr, J., Sommers, W.A., Ghere, G.S. and Montie, J. (2006) Reflective Practice to Improve Schools. Thousand Oaks, CA: Corwin Press (Sage).

Zepke, N., Nugent, D. and Leach, L. (2003) Reflection to Transformation: A Self-help Book for Teachers. Wellington, NZ: Dunmore Press.

INDEX

Reynolds, M. 80, 175
Rich, A. 242
Richardson, L. 42, 96,
    141, 213, 244
Richardson, L. and St. Pierre, E.
    6, 96, 99, 130, 204
Ricoeur, P. 224
Rigano, D. and Edwards, J. 137
Rilke, R.M. vii, 7, 125, 142, 239
risk 17, 51, 62–67, 89, 141,
Robertson, P. 20
Rockewell 94
Rogers, C. 33, 43, 48, 49, 55, 56,
    57, 61, 162
Rogers, J. 97
roles: professional 29
romantic love story 27, 45, 215
Rosean, C.L. 190
Rowan, J. 142
Rowe, J. and Halling, S. 62
Rowland (Bolton), G.,
    Rowland, S. and
    Winter, R. 216
Rowland, S. and Barton, L. 130
Rowland, S. 12, 51–54, 61, 105,
    209, 216
Ruch, G. 37
Rust, C. 55, 149

Sacks, O. 20, 42
Salvio, P. 38
Sapochnic, C. 151–2
Saran, R. and Neisser, B. 191
Sartre, J.P. 28–29, 43, 87, 203,
    209, 215
Schon, D.A. 71, 189
Scott, T. 149
Scott-Hoy, K. 96
Senge, P. 5, 191
Shafer, A. 223, 224, 225
Shakespeare, W. 62, 95,
    161, 243
Sharkey, J. 7–8
Shaw, S.J. 119–121
Shelley, M. 97, 103, 209
Shem, S. 17, 97, 131
Shepherd, M. 128–130
silence 158, 168–170, 176, 179
Simons, J. 127
Simpson, D.J, Jackson, M.J.B.
    and Aycock, J.C. 223
Sinclair Penwarden, A.
    59, 142, 149
Smith, D. 222

Smith, P.A.C. 5
Smith, L. and Winter, R. 151
Smyth, J.M. 21, 105
Smyth, T. 41
Snaith, D. 181
Socrates 6, 28, 71, 157
Sontag, S. 225
Sophocles 33, 169, 194, 210, 215
Stedmon, J., Mitchell, A.
    Johnstone, L. and
    Staite, S. 136
Stefano, G. xviii
Sterne, L. 95
Stevenson, R.L. 73
Stoker, B. 97
Strawson G. 206, 208
Street, B. 192
stress 4, 5, 37, 41, 43,
    97–99, 181
Summerscales, O. 113, 191
super-ego 73
supervision 14, 61
supervisor (internal)
    88, 121, 228
suspension of disbelief 70, 90
Sutton, L., Townend, M, and
    Wright, J. 61, 128, 132, 137,
    142, 146, 149
Svenberg, K., Wahlqvist, M. and
    Mattsson, B. 86, 99, 152
Sydney, Sir Philip 243

tacit knowledge 15, 16
teacher education 6, 9
teams, teamwork
    xvii, 86, 177–184
Tennyson, A. 231
therapeutic groups/writing 61
therapy see counselling
Thomas, R.S. 177
Thorpe, M. 155, 161
Tipper, J. 108
Toffler, A. 254
Toibin, C. 214
Tolstoy, L. 89
transference (and counter-) 170
transitional space 131
Trelfa, J. 5, 157
Trevitt, E. 195, 228–229
Tripp, D. 79, 189
Trotter, S. 126, 142
Tsai Chi Chung 10
Turnbull, W. and Mullins, P.
    87, 88, 121, 191

Turner, J. xviii, 230
Twining, W. 34
Tyler, S. A. 87

UK Conference of Postgraduate
    Education Advisers
    in General Practice
    (UKCEA) 35
uncertainty (certainty) xx, 7, 19,
    32, 33, 63, 70–71, 79, 129,
    189, 252–253
unconditional positive regard
    33, 37, 48, 50, 61, 161, 162
Usher, R. 51, 53, 57, 71, 98–99

values xvii, xx, xxi, 12, 13, 29, 34,
    36, 7, 58–59, 130–131, 158
    espoused xix, 4, 138, 190
    in practice xix, 4, 190
van Manen, M. 189
Varner, D., Peck, S. 137,
    143, 147
Veidt, C. 73
Verghese, A. 15, 95, 97
voice (writers) 90–91
von Klitzing, W. 97
vulnerability 36, 35–6, 60, 61,
    115, 174

Ward, J.R. and
    McCotter, S.S. 150
Warner, M. 254
Watson, C. 34, 71, 82, 96, 130
Weedon, C. 88
Weick, K.E. 9
Wilde, J. 225
Wilde, O. 73
Wilding, P.M. 189
Willett, R. 218–219
Williams, A. 4
Williams, Ann 77
Williams, W.C. 92
Wilson, J.P. 15
Wilson, M. 239–240
Winnicott, D.W. 131
Winter, R. 3, 28, 89, 95, 105, 141,
    151, 192, 210, 217
Winter, R., Buck, A. and
    Sobiechowska, P. xv-xvi, 49
Wittgenstein, L. xiv
Wood, C. 195, 228–229
Woolf, V. 95, 108, 127, 216
Wordsworth, W. 25, 43,
    45, 91, 244